D0775595

comparing notes

comparing notes

how we make

sense of music

ADAM OCKELFORD

PEGASUS BOOKS
NEW YORK LONDON

COMPARING NOTES

Pegasus Books Ltd
148 West 37th Street, 13th Floor
New York, NY 10018

Copyright © 2018 by Adam Ockelford

First Pegasus Books hardcover edition May 2018

ISBN: 978-1-68177-744-3

10 9 8 7 6 5 4 3 2 1

Printed in the United States of America
Distributed by W. W. Norton & Company, Inc.

Contents

Acknowledgements   viii

Prelude **Insights from the Blind**   1

1. How Does Music Work?   10
Heinrich Schenker: The Radical Conservative   11
Positivism and Postmodern Approaches   19
Music Analysis Using Linguistic Models   25
Explaining Music in its Own Terms: Arnold Schoenberg   35
Degrees of Repetition   38
Intervals and Transposition   44
Coda   49

2. The Zygonic Conjecture   52
Derek   55
Building a New Theory of How Music Works   61
Connections between Connections   72
Frameworks of Pitch   81
Rhythm and Metre   96
Timbre, Loudness and Location   108
Coda   113

3. How We Construct Musical Meaning   121
Structure in Music and Syntax in Language   122
Responding to Sound   123
Structure and Content in Music   124
Meaning in Language   128
Meaning in Music: The Art of Simplicity in Sound   132

Complexity and the Problem of 'Greatness'   146
Other Forms of Musical Meaning   158
Defining Music   165
What *isn't* Music?   168
Coda   177

4. **We Are All Musical**   180
From Music Theory to Developmental Psychology   183
The *Sounds of Intent* Project   191
Musicality in Blind Children and Those on the Autism Spectrum   205
Exceptional Musical Ability: Savants   216
Coda   227

5. **Composing, Performing and Listening**   230
The Challenge of Understanding Composers' Work   231
Defining Originality in Music   245
What Constitutes a Piece of Music?   264
Understanding the Listening Experience   275
The Problem of 'Atonal' Music   287
Coda   295

Postlude -**Notes Compared**   302

Further Reading   322
List of Figures   327
Index   333

For Sir Paul Ennals

ACKNOWLEDGEMENTS

Thanks to my agent, Andrew Lownie; Andrew Franklin, Louisa Dunnigan, Joe Staines, Valentina Zanca and Penny Daniel at Profile Books; my friends and colleagues, Desmond Sergeant, David Hargreaves, Graham Welch, Evangelos Himonides and Ian Cross; students, Angela Voyajolu, Michael Thorpe, Hayley Trower, Evangeline Cheng, Adam Reece and Annamaria Mazzeschi; photographer Robert Maidment-Evans for permission to use the image of Derek Paravicini and me in Figure 18; Rosie Chomet for drawing the images used in Figures 19–22; the Wesleyan University Press for permission to cite the opening of Christopher Small's book *Musicking: The Meanings of Performing and Listening* on p. 230; and most importantly, my forbearing family, Sue, Felicity, Eloise and Tom.

Insights from the Blind

HOW DOES MUSIC WORK? How does it make sense and what does it mean?

Seeking answers to these seemingly innocuous questions has pre-occupied me for the last three-and-a-half decades. The genesis of my search can be traced back to the time when I first began working as a volunteer at Linden Lodge, a residential special school in London, in the late 1970s. All the pupils were blind or partially sighted and an increasing number of those recently enrolled, I was informed, had a range of learning difficulties too (many of whom today would be described as being on the autism spectrum). Little wonder, then, before my first visit to Linden Lodge, that I was warned not to be surprised if the youngsters I encountered had delayed or aberrant language, and were unable to initiate or sustain a conversation, sometimes repeating words or phrases over and over again with no apparent meaning (exhibiting so-called 'echolalia'). Don't assume that they will understand what you say, I was advised, and expect some to show more of an interest in the sensory qualities of everyday objects than their function: tapping bowls and drinking glasses to make them ring, for example, and repeatedly pressing the same button on 'speak and spell' games, rather than trying to produce words.

Given accounts like these, my assumption before visiting the school had been that the main challenge in working with the pupils would be in reaching down to their modest levels of musical accomplishment from the rarefied heights of my life as a student at the Royal Academy of Music. I had recently performed Bach's celebrated Italian Concerto on the harpsichord and taken the lead role in Mozart's elegant Oboe Quartet, K. 370; I was in the midst of analysing Beethoven's esoteric late Piano Sonata, Op. 110; and I was getting to grips with composing in the terse style of the first movement of Bartók's 4th String Quartet. In the previous year I had won prizes for keyboard harmony, music theory, and for my contribution to a performance of an oboe trio by the recherché French Baroque composer, Joseph Bodin de Boismortier.

Confident in my knowledge and abilities, honed through countless hours of study and practice, I imagined that I would be able to engage the children in some relatively unsophisticated musical activities (maybe joining in with well-known songs, playing hand-held percussion instruments and the like). Then after a couple of years or so, I would tactfully move on, freeing up my evenings once more to pursue a career doing 'proper' work as a professional musician.

But I was wrong. On both counts.

* * *

On my first evening at Linden Lodge, I was shown round by Paul Ennals, later to be knighted for services to children as Chief Executive of the National Children's Bureau, but more significantly then the mobility officer at the school, whose job was to teach the pupils how to move around safely using a white cane. Paul also happened to be a competent amateur musician and my landlady's son, and it was through this connection that he had cajoled me into coming along to meet these 'amazing kids' with a gentle insistence that eventually eroded my increasingly tenuous excuses to be elsewhere. So, here I was, politely hiding my scepticism as he pushed open a door onto a rather dingy, narrow corridor that the fading autumnal light was barely able to penetrate. (I remember thinking that lighting probably wasn't a priority at the school.)

In the gloom I managed to make out three or four doors on the left. From the first there emanated the strains of what sounded like early twentieth-century piano music. Was it late Frank Bridge, I wondered? Or maybe even Scriabin. The series of complex chords high up on the keyboard continued. Whoever was playing them was doing so with great finesse. Paul had said that there were one or two good musicians on the staff at Linden Lodge, but even so I hadn't been expecting this level of sophistication.

There was a click as Paul opened the door, and the playing stopped abruptly. It was even darker in the practice room than in the corridor. Very odd, I thought. Without saying anything, Paul flicked on the light switch.

I was astonished to see not an adult, but the diminutive figure of a boy on the piano stool. He couldn't have been more than 10 or 11 years old. He didn't turn round to greet us, nor did he say anything. I was immediately struck by the fact that his eyes appeared to be roving randomly without fixing on anything. I knew that I would always remember this, my first encounter with a blind child. Curiously, he was shaking with what appeared to be silent laughter or excitement, or maybe both.

Paul's voice reached out to him, as though putting a reassuring hand on his shoulder.

'Hi Anthony, it's Paul. And here's Adam.'

The boy didn't respond, but stood up and shuffled tentatively towards the window, and ended up, somewhat disconcertingly, facing away from us. He gave me the sense that by vacating the stool one of us was expected to take his place.

I wanted to say something, but, suddenly overcome with embarrassment, found myself bereft of speech. Paul must have sensed my discomfort and (as he always did) effortlessly picked up the thread of our conversation.

'I told Anthony you're keen on twentieth-century composers,' he said, managing to speak for the pair of us – and to us both – at the same time.

'Right.'

It suddenly dawned on me that Anthony must have been waiting for my arrival, and that the Bridge-cum-Scriabin was intended as a welcome to Linden Lodge. He still didn't say anything, but the shaking of his upper body grew more intense. I felt a prickling sense of expectation, but was tongue-tied once more.

Again, Paul came to the rescue: 'And I said you might play something for him.'

I hastily considered what would make an appropriate offering based on what Anthony had played for me. The idiosyncratic opening of Liszt's Piano Sonata in B minor came to mind. I sat down and, after a moment to gather my thoughts, set off with the quiet, *staccato*, open-octave Gs. Then came the contrast of the brooding, tonally ambiguous descending scale, which broke off, disconcertingly, leaving the expected bottom note hanging, unheard, in the air.

A moment's silence.

Out of the corner of my eye, I noticed that Anthony was now standing motionless, apparently listening with rapt attention. I took this as a positive sign and, feeling a newfound engagement with the music myself, I closed my eyes and focused on the sound of the next notes: two further hesitant Gs in octaves, sotto voce. Then another lugubrious scalar descent, this time with additional chromatic twists that deepened the sense of foreboding. Again, the melody halted prematurely, with the anticipated lowest note remaining unplayed, charging the silence that followed.

A moment's repose, and then my hands started to move in readiness for the last two detached strokes of the slow introduction. But I was interrupted by a jolt on my left arm and, looking round, I was surprised to see that Anthony had unobtrusively made his way back towards the piano stool. Having found me he didn't stop: the nudge turned into a shove, and it became evident that he wanted me to stand up so that he could take over. I obliged.

'There you go,' I said, trying to sound cheery. In reality I was a little disappointed; maybe the Liszt hadn't gone down so well after all.

But I was wrong. And what happened next was to change for ever the way I thought about music.

I watched, intrigued, as Anthony's hands deftly felt over the keys,

Figure 1 *The opening bars of Liszt's Sonata in B Minor.*

using the asymmetrical pattern of black notes as points of reference, and came to rest on the opening Gs of the Liszt sonata. A moment's pause and then the two tones sounded, hushed and terse, exactly as I had played them. Just like a recording. It was uncanny. The first descending scale followed flawlessly; sombre and introspective. Then the reprise of the Gs and the second scale, quirky chromatic inflections reproduced perfectly, the final discontinuity impeccably timed. Anthony had captured both the notes and the mood of the music precisely. He stopped at exactly the same point that I had, and remained completely still, as though waiting for more.

I was transfixed. How was it possible for a boy who was blind and (I assumed from his lack of verbal communication) had learning difficulties to play this sophisticated music after hearing it only once? Anthony couldn't have seen what I had done and yet he had just reproduced the introduction to the sonata, naturally, fluently, without prompting. It wasn't merely the fact that the notes were correct: he seemed to have an effortless, mature understanding of the music, with an intuitive feel for the unfolding emotional narrative.

Figure 2 *Anthony playing* Summertime *at a concert for a Wandsworth Primary School in the early 1980s to my bewhiskered accompaniment, while members of the Linden Lodge singing group (led by their teacher, Kevin Deegan, off to the right) listen intently.*

But above all, and although I couldn't (yet) bring myself to tell Paul, I knew that, in spite of my advanced musical training and thousands of hours of practice, I would have struggled to do what Anthony had just achieved, apparently with little or no effort at all.

* * *

In the days and weeks that followed, I tried to rationalise what I had seen and heard. I asked Paul to fill me in on Anthony's background. If I were to work with him purposefully, I felt I had to have some knowledge (if not understanding) of the extensive musical journey that he must already have made in the first decade or so of his life.

Largely through the tireless efforts of his mother, and the enthusiasm of the music teacher at his previous school, Rushton Hall in Northamptonshire, Anthony had had tuition on a range of instruments from an early age, including the piano, the drums, the recorder, the saxophone, the clarinet – whatever came to hand, it seemed. Given the option, as a small child, he would spend all his waking hours engaged in making music in one form or another. Paul was of the view that while he was unusually talented among the children at Linden Lodge, his ability to learn music quickly, to play by ear and to improvise – alone and with others – was by no means unique. Like them, Anthony's knowledge of music theory was elementary, and he was unable to use the Braille version of music notation to read or write what he could play. As far as he was concerned, music functioned like a natural language, that for him was more powerful, more persuasive, more authentic than words. No one had taught him to understand how that language worked; mere exposure to music had been enough. And, Paul assumed, experimenting with instruments for countless hours, encouraged by the adults around him, who, having no comparable experience to draw on, could only follow their instincts, had proved sufficient for Anthony to learn to use music as a form of expressive communication.

I was fascinated by Paul's account of how Anthony had come to engage with music so effectively, though in my mind it raised more questions than it answered. How could it be that a young boy who was blind and had learning difficulties had developed more advanced musical skills than many of the students at the Royal Academy of Music?

As someone who had been taught to perform, improvise and compose through years of structured tuition, I had assumed that this was the only way that musical skills could be acquired, passed on painstakingly from one generation of musicians to the next. But evidently not. So what did Anthony's example say about the way that people develop the capacity to engage with music?

Clearly, for this person at least, music made sense without any verbal explanation. Therefore, I reasoned, it must be possible to come to understand the rules governing the way music works just by listening; they must be self-evident. That is, without prompting and without recourse to any other information, the brain (or, at least, Anthony's brain) was able to fathom how music functions, and through that understanding attribute meaning to abstract patterns of sound. What an incredible thought! It implied that a series of notes, each of which in itself apparently signified nothing, could somehow evoke thoughts and feelings beyond their perceptual qualities as sounds. How could this be?

* * *

Seeking answers to these questions has intrigued thinkers across the ages, from Socrates to Schopenhauer: why is it that abstract patterns of sound that don't mean anything in a literal sense actually mean so very much to us as human beings? Indeed, in Western societies, we are bombarded with music for around half our waking moments.[1] In shops, during advertisements on the radio, television or online, in the dentist's waiting room or as the plane taxis prior to take-off – music is there to influence the way we think, feel and behave. Why? Because, as every filmmaker knows, music is unique in its power for stirring the emotions, without listeners even needing to be aware of its presence. And, as music therapists' work with dementia patients and autistic children has shown, music has the capacity to plumb the depths of the mind and tap into memories (happy, sad, profound or everyday) that words alone are not able to touch. The sheer beauty of music can make grown men and women weep. Some even think that music brings them closer to their God. There is music for every occasion: from adolescent rites of passage to wedding celebrations, from relieving the tedium of manual work to emboldening soldiers to fight. There is music to help people get high, chill out and make love. There is even music for the departed and music to be buried to.

In the chapters that follow, I set out a fresh way of tackling the question of how music works. This draws on a number of sources: the ideas of twentieth-century Western musicologists and composers, whose opinions still drive much academic thinking about music today; Edmund Husserl's phenomenological approach to the perception of sound, which focuses on personal experience;[2] and some recent discoveries in the field of music psychology – an interdisciplinary area of enquiry that has forged its own identity in the last three or four decades to become a major focus of research, particularly in relation to neuroscience.

But there is also a wholly new ingredient in the mix: the insights that

I have gleaned over the years from working with children on the autism spectrum. Anthony was the first, but there have been hundreds of others since my initial visit to Linden Lodge School in 1979. I soon realised that for some of these youngsters – particularly those who have learning difficulties, for whom verbal language is likely to be problematic – music can offer a unique window onto thoughts and feelings that would otherwise be hidden from view. It was only later that I came to appreciate that, beyond this, autism affords us an alternative and powerful way of understanding how so-called 'neurotypical' people create, process and respond to music. This is possible because the human tribe exists on continua of interests, abilities, propensities and traits, and, by observing people who function at the extremes of our species' natural neurodiversity, we can better understand the ordinary, everyday, musical experiences that are characteristic of us all. But, most importantly, it's my belief that, through the prism of the overtly remarkable, we can discover the uncelebrated exceptionality in each of us. We are all musical by design, and most of our musical abilities, which exceed the capacity of even the most advanced computers, are acquired without conscious thought or effort when we are still in the early years.

I

How Does Music Work?

BY WAY OF INTRODUCTION to his seminal book, *Emotion and Meaning in Music*, published in 1956,[1] the American musicologist Leonard Meyer revisits the classic philosophical positions taken up in music aesthetics, providing an analysis that will help us to chart a course through the work of some of the main twentieth-century thinkers on Western music. Meyer characterises the main arguments as existing on two continua. First, he describes the view that musical meaning originates from the stuff of music itself (organised sound), a stance that he terms 'absolutist', and contrasts it with the 'referentialist' position, whose proponents believe that the sense of music is borrowed from its external context. Second, Meyer distinguishes between 'formalist' and 'expressionist' types of musical understanding. A 'formalist' approach is characterised by a conceptual grasp of how the sounds that constitute a piece are organised, and is acquired through conscious reflection – what Daniel Kahneman[2] would today call 'slow brain' responses: for example, knowing that the first movement of Beethoven's 5th Symphony is in 'sonata form'. 'Expressionist' musical understanding comprises listeners' 'fast brain' emotional reactions, which arise unthinkingly, intuitively: for instance, sensing that the same Beethoven movement sounds 'powerful yet agitated'. According to Meyer, the internal or external, and fast or slow listening styles, are likely to operate in conjunction, so a listener who hears music dispassionately, purely as a series of structured sounds, would be classed as an 'absolute formalist', for example, while we would expect a 'referential expression-ist' to respond affectively to a piece according to an external association forged at some point in the past. Meyer's own theory of musical meaning, derived from expectations set up and frustrated solely through patterns of sound, tends towards an 'absolute expressionist' position. Here, referential meaning, derived from the world beyond music, is regarded as subordi-nate, while an emphasis on an emotional response leans more towards an intuitive (rather than a structural) way of listening.

Given Meyer's taxonomy, we should not be surprised that the range of perspectives adopted by music theorists is very wide: from those who sought to identify external forces at work in the organisation of music, such as Heinrich Schenker (who looked to God for music's divine inspir-ation, and found it in the Austro-German tradition of composition) and Susan McClary (whose postmodern sociological perspective led her notoriously to hear the male sex act in Beethoven's 9th Symphony), to 'absolutists' such as the Austrian composer and theorist Arnold Schoen-berg (who contended that it is *repetition* that brings coherence and intel-ligibility to compositions). Other 'absolutists' appropriated ideas from disciplines beyond music, exemplified in Leonard Bernstein's *The Unan-swered Question* and *A Generative Theory of Tonal Music* by Fred Lerdahl and Ray Jackendoff, which both derive their rationale from Chomskyan linguistics. Viewing these apparently contradictory lines of thinking as a whole, it might seem that, in academic circles, at least, there has been no consensus as to how music works (surely a strange state of affairs given that it is a means of communication that we all appear able to grasp). Yet there are hidden similarities in the various explanations of music that have been advanced, and we begin by identifying these parallels.

Heinrich Schenker: The Radical Conservative

Heinrich Schenker – whose writing is invariably earnest and at times self-consciously esoteric – was arguably the most important Western music theorist of the last one hundred years. Working in *fin-de-siècle* Vienna, he singlehandedly changed the way that we make sense of European classical music of the eighteenth and nineteenth centuries. The culmination of Schenker's life's work was his magnum opus *Der Freie Satz* ('*Free Composition*') of 1935, which opens with the time-honoured assertion that music reflects the divine order: 'All that is organic, every relatedness belongs to God ∴ even when man creates the work.'[3] Schenker's line of argument tends to be obscured by the mists of his fervent musical chauvinism: he takes every opportunity to proclaim the superiority of Austro-German classical music, and his analyses focus exclusively on works penned by composers such as Bach, Haydn, Mozart, Beethoven and Brahms. But beneath this nettle of bigotry lies the remarkable conjecture that the works of this period are all ultimately elaborations of the 'chord of nature', so-called because it is present in the harmonics that are inherent in many natural (and therefore, in Schenker's view, divinely determined) sounds.

It is possible to hear what Schenker meant by silently pressing down a combination of five keys – two Cs, an E and two Gs – on the piano, and have a second person play a low C loudly and release it straight away (see Figure 3). The sounds of the depressed keys will remain, ringing in the air. This is Schenker's 'chord of nature'.

The effect is due to the fact that piano strings do not just oscillate at one rate, but as a composite of many different frequencies *at the same time*, which, as Pythagoras observed, exist in simple mathematical relationships to one another. Usually these fuse in the ear to give the impression of tone-colour or 'timbre'. However, as the experiment illustrated in Figure 3 shows, they can be made easier to hear by freeing appropriate strings to vibrate, enabling them to pick up on the frequencies present in the original sound. The lowest five of these form Schenker's 'chord of nature', which musicians refer to rather more prosaically as a 'major' harmony. This single unit of musical thought features pervasively in almost all Western styles. However, for Schenker, there was more to the function of the 'chord of nature' than this: for him, it lay at the structural heart of every classical masterpiece.

Schenker sought to demonstrate his theory through a complex system of analysis that takes the form of richly annotated graphs, in which staves

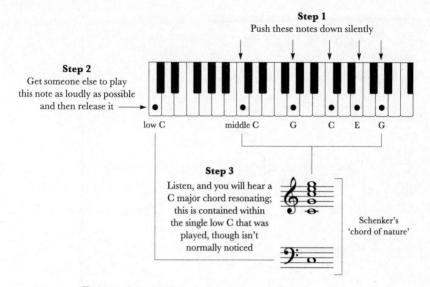

Step 1
Push these notes down silently

Step 2
Get someone else to play this note as loudly as possible and then release it

low C   middle C   G   C   E   G

Step 3
Listen, and you will hear a C major chord resonating; this is contained within the single low C that was played, though isn't normally noticed

Schenker's 'chord of nature'

Figure 3 *Schenker's 'chord of nature', generally known as the 'harmonic series', can be reproduced on the piano.*

are overlaid with long curved lines and beams connecting unorthodox musical symbols and caret-topped numerals indicating the degrees of the scale.[4] These engaging figures seek to show how the 'surface' of the music – the individual notes and chords, several of which usually pass by every second – can be regarded as ornamenting a simpler, slower-moving melodic line and harmonic sequence, which are conceptually more structural and metaphorically exist further towards the musical 'background' (which is where Schenker believed the 'chord of nature' to exist in its most elemental form).

Some sense of what Schenker meant – in reverse – can be gleaned by listening to the way that composers have traditionally formulated sets of variations, particularly those from the Baroque and Classical periods of Western music, which often adhere faithfully to the structure of the theme, while the number of notes and the rapidity with which they pass by tend to increase incrementally. A well-known example is Handel's Air and Variations from his 5th Suite for Harpsichord, known as *The Harmonious Blacksmith*. Here, the opening of the theme is based on nothing more than two, alternating major chords, which become elaborated with

Figure 4 *Fragment of Schenker's analysis of Bach's chorale* Ich Bin's, Ich Sollte Büssen.[5]

increasing numbers of notes. The underlying structure remains easy to hear, though, as the ear is guided good-naturedly through ever more flamboyant figuration.

As Schenker's thinking evolved, he sought to delve ever further into the constitution of music using the principle of recursion: once his first

Figure 5 *The opening bars from the Air and Variations of Handel's* Harmonious Blacksmith.

analytical pass had stripped away the top layer of detail, leaving structural features that were just below the musical surface, he realised (in theory,

The '**fundamental structure**' exists as an outgrowth
of the **harmonic series**

Figure 6 *Schenker's 'fundamental structure' transforms
the harmonic series, extending it in time.*[6]

at least) that he could repeat the process, whereby some of the events
that had been regarded as load-bearing at one level could be conceived
as ornamental on the next, and so on, as the increasingly sparse lines
of music in Figure 4 show. Through these means, Schenker concluded
that all great pieces of music (judged from his own view of musical distinction) were elaborations of the same deep structure. This comprised a
descending pattern of three notes, harmonised by two different chords
– a template that he called the *Ursatz* (or 'fundamental structure'). In the
final analysis, even this was considered to stem from a single chord, based
on harmonics 1–6 of 'natural' sound (see Figure 3 above).

So, in answer to the question 'How does music make sense?', Schenker would doubtless have replied 'Through prolongation of the chord of
nature', meaning that the same, 'home' harmony – in musical terminology,
the 'tonic triad' – governs entire pieces, even though it does not physically
sound the whole time.

* * *

Does Schenker's theory stand up to scrutiny? His assertion – 'formalist'
in Meyer's terms – that chords based on the harmonic series metaphorically lie beneath and support the musical surface intuitively feels right.
Handel's *Harmonious Blacksmith* makes sense because the ear can readily

hear the same pattern of chords that underpins each variation. But to what depths does the harmonic hierarchy extend? There is no evidence, either in the form of scores or written testimony, that Western classical composers had any notion of the Ursatz. Admittedly, the movements of pieces created in what has been called the 'common practice' period in the West almost invariably begin and end in the same key (the chords marked 'I' in the Ursatz in Figure 6), and those in major mode usually make an early move to the 'dominant' (founded on the fifth note of the scale, corresponding to the second Ursatz harmony). But this is a far cry from saying that composers had a deeper, inaudible structure in mind – even subconsciously – as they worked. The perception of modulations (changes of key) that occur can perfectly well be explained by an internalised, imaginary framework of pitches and intervals, which we all appear to possess and which functions more or less 'in the moment'. It is rather like going for a walk, and knowing how to get home again. Pedestrians don't need to have their house constantly in view: they can work out where they are from the layout of the roads along which they have journeyed.

But they can only do that when they're in familiar territory, and don't stray too far from base or stay away for too long. Similarly, it seems to be the case that the vast majority of listeners, who do not have advanced musical training or 'absolute pitch' (known as 'AP' – a long-term memory for individual notes), and who cannot read a score (which functions rather like a musical road map), don't hear long-term tonal relationships at all. For most listeners, the auditory journey offered by a piece of music is rather like being a tourist in a taxi: he or she may experience a series of momentary impressions[7] – turns that are made to the left or right, buildings whose idiosyncratic architectural features catch the attention – but without having any broader sense of a direction of travel. Certainly this was the view of leading British musicologist Nicholas Cook who, in the 1980s, very much against the fashion of the time,[8] criticised Schenkerian analysis as being far removed from the way that people normally hear music. He pursued this claim in the pages of the journal *Music Perception*, describing an experiment in which he manipulated pieces by Beethoven, Liszt, Mendelssohn, Chopin and Brahms, having them end in the 'wrong' key – thereby destroying the symmetry of the Ursatz, in that the third harmony of the fundamental structure was no longer the same as the first. So the pieces could not be considered prolongations of the 'chord of nature'. However, as Cook predicted, most listeners were oblivious to the change. Schenker's retort would no doubt have been that 'great' music can only truly be appreciated by an artistic elite, and, indeed, *Der Freie Satz* contains savage onslaughts on 'the masses', whose shallow lives apparently render them incapable of hearing the deeper order in music.

> The masses, however, lack the soul of genius. They are not aware of background, they have no feeling for the future. Their lives are merely an eternally disordered foreground, a continuous present without connection, unwinding chaotically in empty, animal fashion. It is always the [bourgeois] individual who creates and transmits connection and coherence.[9]

That is to say, in Schenker's view, musical structure, and, in particular, the notion of levels in a harmonic hierarchy, *reflect* social strata.

While Schenker's polemic is far-fetched and repellent to modern ears, it would be a mistake to allow his jarring prejudices to drown out the more modest claims of his theory – in particular the notion that harmonies can exert an influence in passages of music beyond their immediate presence. This is shown, for example, in Figure 4, in which the lowest stave indicates that a single harmony (of A flat major) is heard as the controlling influence of the entire first line of the chorale, even though it physically sounds in only four of its 11 chords. To use an analogy: one can imagine harmonies like this acting rather like the warp threads in a tapestry, lying hidden from view, but providing the necessary substructure on which the ornamental weft is woven, and so forming an essential (though, for most people, probably unrecognised) component of the finished work. However, just as the warp threads give no sense of a tapestry's individuality, which is dictated by the distinct colours and patterns of the weft, neither do the underlying or implied harmonic sequences of a piece of music define its identity. That is the role of motifs and themes – snatches of melody that are audible in the foreground while, by implication, articulating the background structure. Since it is such melodic detail that initially attracts the ear, and that subsequently resides in memory like a tag to call to mind or identify a given work, so it follows that a comprehensive theory of how music works must be able to account, among other things, for the immediacy of the musical surface.

This is not part of the Schenkerian proposition, however. Musical order is held to emanate from a higher authority: God. Given this absolutist standpoint, Schenker evidently felt no compulsion to explain *why*, for example, a particular motif or theme arises from a given harmonic prolongation or progression in preference to any other. However, what he *does* demonstrate is how essentially the same harmonic structure can be realised in many different ways – just as, in language, a single grammatical form can support the generation of myriad sentences. Nonetheless, in the same way that coherent syntax in language is no guarantee of meaning (let alone literary merit), neither does a cogent harmonic structure ensure lucid (much less beautiful) music.

Positivism and Postmodern Approaches

An explicit connection between music and society surfaced again half a century after Schenker's death, though in a very different epistemological context: the postmodernist tide of thinking that swept through the arts and humanities in the latter part of the 1900s. Musicologists were relatively late on the postmodern scene, led by figures such as Christopher Ballantine, Professor of Music at the University of Natal. His book, *Music and its Social Meanings*, published in 1984, set out to tackle the problem that he perceived to exist in musicology of 'the artificial insulation of musical understanding from the realm of social meanings.'[10] In contrast, his own view, ostensibly similar to that adopted by Schenker, though actually reflecting a very different perspective, was that 'social structures crystallize in musical structures ... in various ways and with varying degrees of critical awareness, the musical microcosm replicates the social macrocosm.'[11]

If this sounds inordinately referentialist (to use Meyer's terminology), we must remember that Ballantine was reacting against the excessively absolutist, mathematically-inspired music analyses that filled so many journal pages at the time he was writing. This approach had been inspired by thinking such as that of the American musician-cum-mathematician

Milton Babbitt, who, in 1958, had penned the infamous 'Who cares if you listen?' article in *High Fidelity*,[12] in which he argued that so-called 'serious' music should be by specialists, for specialists. Inevitably, music analysis had to be no less exclusive. Here, Yale-based music theorist Allen Forte was among those leading the way, establishing 'set theory' in the musicological lexicon, and showing how groups of pitches can be regarded as equivalent if one can be changed into another through certain systematic transformations.[13] The problem with Forte's fiercely logical system is that it bears little relation to what listeners are actually capable of hearing; it seeks to impose an external means of understanding musical structure that is purely conceptual, rather than being perceptually based.

This speaks to a wider problem with positivist music analysis, such as that by Babbitt and Forte: it is undertaken in what may be called the 'rationalist' or Cartesian tradition, whose criterion of truth exists in the intellectual rather than the sensory domain. The issue is this: due to the highly constrained nature of the universe of possible musical sounds in the Western tonal system, repetition and regularity are inevitable *after any four notes*; the fifth will always result in duplication of some kind. And just because repetition exists does not mean that it is relevant to the musical experience; indeed, virtually all of it is inaudible. In other words, the search for extrinsic forces of musical organisation that take objective similarity between sets of notes or their transformations as evidence – that is driven by anything other than by perception – is like panning for fool's gold: alluring and deceptively easy, but ultimately of only pyritic value.

The problem with these positivist approaches that reduce music to tables of figures and Venn-like diagrams is that while they notionally provide answers to questions of the 'What?' variety that pertain to musical structure, they cannot say *why* a composer chose a particular group of notes, nor what they would be likely to mean to listeners as a form of musical communication. It is these very issues that Ballantine seeks to address when he writes about music's 'social meanings'.

Consider, for example, his account of sonata form, which, he contends, sprang from the same impulse as the French Revolution: a way of musical thinking that 'generates contradictions between ... opposing

Figure 7 *The opening theme of Beethoven's* Eroica *Symphony.*

tonalities, themes, rhythmic characters' – a musical embodiment of the Hegelian dialectic.[14] Does this assertion ring true in European classical music of the late eighteenth and early nineteenth centuries, though? Take, for example, a piece whose composition we know to have been inspired by the ideals of revolutionary France: Beethoven's 3rd Symphony, the *Eroica*. The first movement opens with two short E flat major chords for full orchestra, *forte*, followed by a quiet, sweeping theme in the 'cellos, using notes from the harmonies that have just been heard. Then comes an unexpected swoop down to a low C sharp, resolving felicitously onto a D, harmonised initially as G minor and then as a seventh chord of B flat major, and so back home to E flat. So simple. So sophisticated. So achingly beautiful.

But is a knowledge of the French Revolution required for the music to be comprehensible? Is being aware of the circumstances of Beethoven's life *necessary* to grasp what occurs musically? No. The moment-to-moment logic of Beethoven's music, and its broader narrative, are self-evident (and self-sufficient). The first part of the theme makes sense since it emerges from pitches heard in the previous chords. The unexpected C sharp makes sense as a chromatic inflection of the D that follows. The D makes sense since it leads the ear back to an E flat.

Can Ballantine's assertion that social structures crystallise in musical structures add anything to this explanation? It is difficult to see what, since the organisation of society and the disposition of music are entirely different things, operating in discrete modalities. Accordingly, it doesn't seem possible for there to be a *causal* relationship between them. What does appear to be entirely reasonable, though, is to assert that Beethoven was cognitively and emotionally affected by his life circumstances, that such effects must have had an impact on the way he thought and felt, and that his compositions inevitably reflected his thinking and feelings. Therefore, through this chain of consequences, it seems safe to say that the society in which Beethoven lived, and his position within it, must have influenced the nature of the music that he created. But that is very far from saying that one was the cause of the other.

In fact, even identifying what elements or features of a work can reasonably be attributed to societal influence is fraught with difficulty, in the absence of a composer's declaration to that effect. (And even then, one could question the extent to which such information could be relevant to the musical experience of listeners who may be many generations removed.) Aside from the postmodern dogma that knowledge, being socially constructed, is whatever an individual wants it to be, how can such connections logically be made, conclusions rationally drawn?

Let us put one of Ballantine's claims to the test: that Beethoven's transformation of themes stemmed from the post-Revolutionary belief that humans could change by dint of their own efforts.[15] The thinking here appears to run as follows:

1. People can develop.
2. Musical ideas can develop.
3. Since both people and musical ideas can develop, and (1) precedes (2), then (2) must result from (1).

But surely this is nothing more than a sophisticated version of the *post hoc ergo propter hoc* fallacy, whereby, in general terms, if A has the property x_i, B has the (identical or similar) property x_{ii}, and B occurs after A, then A must have caused B. Naturally, this need not be true. One may as well assert that as Beethoven had four of something (limbs), and the *Eroica* has four of something else (movements), and since Beethoven had arms and legs before he composed the symphony, then its overall structure must be derived from his anatomical makeup.

Of course, a postmodernist could rebut this argument saying that, 'If I hear that connection, then, by definition, it is valid.' For sure, it may have a certain validity *for that individual*. But Ballantine's assertion that thematic transformation in Beethoven arises from the post-Revolutionary ideology that humans are in charge of their own destiny, and can therefore change, is not prefaced by phrases such as 'in my opinion ...' or 'there is a chance that ...' Through this means, purely interpretive statements can surreptitiously acquire the status of 'fact'.

In fairness to Ballantine, he is far from being unique in using an academic sleight of hand to make his opinions appear more valid than the evidence warrants. In fact, much the same can be said of many other musicologists, including Schenker, whose analyses are based on a wholly imaginary 'Ursatz'. Even traditional approaches to music analysis suffer from the same problem, whereby beliefs come to masquerade as facts. Take, for example, the six volumes of essays written in the first half of the twentieth century by the British musicologist Donald Tovey, whose modus operandi was to elide accounts of musical features with their effect upon him as an expert listener, in a manner typical of programme notes. The result is a series of elegant, often idiosyncratic and occasionally insightful musings. For instance, in relation to the last movement of Brahms' 4th Symphony, he writes: 'The theme, stated, with trombones, in harmonies too remarkable to be intended to bear repetition, descends angrily with rolling drums and pizzicato chords into the depths of the orchestra ...'[16] Prising this poetic elision apart suggests that there is a connection between certain orchestral effects (a percussive rumble and plucked strings) and a particular emotion (anger), whereby the former is considered to be the source of the latter. But this is purely Tovey's opinion, which is ultimately descriptive (an affirmation of belief) rather than ana-lytical (an explanation of *how* or *why* things occur in the way they do).

Like Tovey, Ballantine expresses views that today seem quite mild, given what was to come in the years shortly after *Music and its Social Meanings* was published – when adherents of a new postmodern sub-discipline that became known as the 'new musicology' got to work. This moved beyond the desire to situate the study of music in cultural contexts to embrace other streams of relativist thought (which take meaning to be a mutable, human construct), including feminism, gender studies,[17] queer theory,[18] and, somewhat later, disability studies.[19] In Ballantine's book, the omission of caveats, which would have discouraged readers from drawing general conclusions from his personal perspectives, is harmless enough. But in the writings of an iconoclast such as music theorist Susan McClary, the elision of qualifying phrases is at best provocative and at worst reckless.

For example, in the January 1987 issue of *Minnesota Composers Forum Newsletter*, she wrote of Beethoven's 9th Symphony: 'The point of recapit-ulation in the first movement ... is one of the most horrifying moments in music, as the carefully prepared cadence is frustrated, damming up energy which finally explodes in the throttling murderous rage of a rapist incapa-ble of attaining release.' The ending of the piece is said to be a celebration of the kind of sexual desire that culminates in violent ejaculation, which McClary concludes 'has very little to do with lovemaking; it represents something closer to masturbation – at best.'

Thinking back to the erroneous *post hoc ergo propter hoc* form of argu-ment, one can understand how the first part of McClary's fallacious phallic fantasy came about, since there is conceivably an analogous relationship between musical and sexual climaxes, and deferring a peak in music may in some way be like delaying orgasm. The rationale behind the 'rage of the rapist' and the reference to autoeroticism are, by any standards, extraordi-nary, though, and, indeed, these metaphors were omitted in a subsequent version of McClary's seminal article that was reproduced four years later in her book, *Feminine Endings*.[20] One might as well argue (with tongue firmly in cheek) that the theme from Mozart's Variations for Piano, K. 265, known to English-speaking listeners as *Twinkle, Twinkle, Little*

Star, expresses male sexual inadequacy: the modestly paced, unchanging binary metre indicative of insipid pelvic thrusts, incapable of arousing excitement; the constrained rise in pitch in bars 2 and 3 suggestive of diffident, even feeble tumescence; and the slowly declining contour of the melody, reiterated on four occasions, emblematic of the repeated experience of pitiful impotence. Such an account of *Twinkle, Twinkle* is hardly persuasive, however; evidently, musicogenic sexual fantasies require a special kind of venereal imagination that isn't as easy to arouse as McClary's fluid prose makes it seem.

Postmodernism in the extreme form peddled by McClary and her apologists is nothing more than a form of pseudophilosophy, whose meaning can be constructed (in a postmodern way) as intellectual pink slime: lacking any nutritional value (in the sense of being able to feed the mind) and capable of metamorphosing into any shape that a given context requires, having no structural spine of its own.[21] And while it is poles apart from the pseudorationalism of Schenker, or the positivism of Babbitt and Forte, all these approaches share the same flaw, in that none has regard for how the *majority* of people hear music *most* of the time. Similarly, while each line of thought sheds some light on the issue of how music works, neither provides a cogent account of how music is comprehensible or what it communicates. Other, 'absolutist', musicologists who emerged in the 1970s sought to address this issue by turning to linguistics and semiotics as fresh sources of guidance and ideas.

Music Analysis Using Linguistic Models

The first and most publicly renowned of these ventures was set out by the musical polymath Leonard Bernstein in his book *The Unanswered Question*, based on six interdisciplinary lectures originally delivered at Harvard University in 1973. Here, Bernstein seeks to explain how musical structure functions using linguistic concepts and terminology, inspired by the work of Noam Chomsky, who assisted in the preparation of the talks. Chomsky's notion of 'transformational generative grammars', which prevailed at the time, was particularly important: this was the idea that the same 'deep' structures (comprising relationships between the *functions* of words) could give rise to many different utterances.

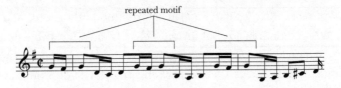

Figure 8 *The opening melody of Bach's* Brandenburg
Concerto No. 3 *uses a musical form of anaphora.*

Bernstein was especially interested in forms of structure found in
poetry and rhetoric that are underpinned by *repetition*, since he discerned
parallels between these and the relationships that exist between motifs
in music. Consider, for instance, 'anaphora', the restatement of a word or
words at the beginning of successive phrases:

> **And do you now** put on your best attire?
> **And do you now** cull out a holiday?
> **And do you now** strew flowers in his way
> That comes in triumph over Pompey's blood? Be gone!
>
> from a speech by Marullus, Act I, Scene I, *Julius Caesar* by William Shakespeare

Bernstein contends that the same structural technique is used in
music, an assertion that he illustrates with passages from Beethoven's 2nd
Symphony and Mahler's 5th. Another example opens the first movement
of Bach's *Brandenburg Concerto No. 3*. Here, the repetition of a simple
three-note motif heard functioning as anaphora at the beginning of the
piece drives Bach's melodic inspiration for a further 135 bars in a *tour de
force* of creative economy and imagination.

The overt form of repetition that anaphora offers, plain to hear at
the beginning of successive phrases, is a commonplace syntactical feature
of music – a marked contrast to its status in verbal language, where it is
relatively rare and invariably fulfils a special function, emphasising and
intensifying what is being conveyed. Given the lack of semantic meaning
of musical motifs, such unmissable reiteration assists the ear as it strives
to make sense of abstract narratives in sound – particularly on a first
hearing, when memorability is key.

Other forms of rhetorical construction that are shared by language
and music are unusual in both media, although, from the examples that

Schubert: *Unfinished* Symphony (first movement, second theme)

Benny Andersson and Björn Ulvaeus: *Super Trouper* (chorus)

To-night the Su-per Trou-per lights are gon-na find me, shin-ing like the sun, ___

smil-ing, hav-ing fun, ___ feel-ing like a num-ber one.

Figure 9 *Examples of chiasmus in music.*

Bernstein gives, it could be that their rarity enhances their impact when they do occur. One such is 'chiasmus', the symmetrical A B : B A form, famously used by John F. Kennedy in his inaugural presidential address: 'Ask not what your country can do for you; ask what you can do for your country.' Bernstein's musical illustration, the lyrical second subject from the first movement of Schubert's *Unfinished* Symphony, is particularly beautiful, and is contrasted here with a more contemporary example from a section of the chorus in *Super Trouper*, by Benny Andersson and Björn Ulvaeus.

Why should chiasmus occur only infrequently in music? Surely its repetition – indeed, twofold duplication – must assist musical under-standing and memory? Unlike the linguistic examples, which, through reversing the order of words or phrases, invert their relationship with one another, thereby changing their meaning and giving the narrative as a whole sufficient forward momentum to propel it through its lexical symmetry, in music it seems that the absence of semantic content could result in the A B : B A form lacking a sense of purpose, as it sets off in a particular direction then immediately backtracks, ending where it started. The plausibility of this conjecture is supported by the fact that both the Schubert and Andersson/Ulvaeus extracts have small changes in the second half of the chiasmus that appear to mitigate against any feeling of stasis: in the melody from the *Unfinished* Symphony, the second 'B' segment has additional quavers, imparting an increased sense of movement, and, in *Super Trouper*, 'A' on its second appearance is moved down a tone to end on the tonic (home) key, affording a feeling of closure at the end of the phrase.

Beyond specific examples such as these, Bernstein is of the view that *all* relationships between motifs in music are like linguistic transformations in Chomsky's original sense, since they can be understood as surface instantiations of a deeper structure. But the crucial thing for Bernstein is that, in music, transformations of motifs can be recognised as such because some of their elements are repeated. The issue of *how* repetition enables music to make sense, and how it combines with difference to convey meaning, is left hanging, though; as far as Bernstein was concerned, 'transformations *are* the meaning of music'.[22]

* * *

If Bernstein's text is warmly inspirational though somewhat lacking in scholarly rigour, then the opposite is true of the work of Belgian linguist-cum-musicologist Nicolas Ruwet and Jean-Jacques Nattiez, Professor of Musicology at the University of Montreal. Both sought to introduce concepts from semiotics – the science of how signs convey meaning – into the field of music theory. Their semiotic readings of pieces[23] work on the assumption that a stream of music can be broken down into discrete units, and that the systematic ways in which these are related to one another over time constitute a form of syntax, comparable to that found in language.

This begs two questions: how are the units of music identified? and how can syntax work in the absence of semantics? In language, words cannot function syntactically unless they are either understood themselves or their grammatical function is clear from the context of adjacent words that *do* mean something, through a psycholinguistic process known as 'syntactic bootstrapping'.[24] For example, a six-year-old child may hear her parents talking about whether 'a cerise top would go with her blue bottoms'. Without knowing what 'cerise' meant, she would intuitively know from its position in the sentence that the word described a quality of her top, and even, by analogy with 'blue', may realise that it was a colour. However, in Ruwet's approach, syntax and segmentation amount to the same thing, emerging from a common analytical process: the identification of repetition. (Segmentation is an additional necessary step in music since, unlike language, it doesn't come 'pre-segmented' in the form of words.) That is to say, it is repetition that enables the analytical units of music to be identified, and it is repetition that defines their syntax (the functional relationships that may exist between them). Making reference to the French ethnomusicologist Gilbert Rouget, Ruwet puts it thus: 'it is on repetition – or absence of repetition – that our segmentation is based. When one sequence of notes appears two or more times, with or without variation, it is considered a unit.'[25] Units are given labels (typically letters), and the syntactical structure of a passage of music is represented as a chain – for example, A + B + A + C + A, which means that three appearances of a unit tagged as 'A' are intercalated with units 'B' and 'C'.

But 'A' is only identified as such because it occurs more than once; it is defined retrospectively through being repeated. Therefore, Ruwet has had to take up a position where segmentation is required to determine syntax, but at the same time, syntax is necessary to specify the boundaries of musical segmentation – resulting either in senseless circularity or appealing parsimony, according to one's point of view. Consider, for example, the first three lines of the British national anthem, *God Save the Queen*.

The opening sentence is set to two distinct motifs, one each for 'God save our' and 'gracious Queen!'. The words 'Long live our' re-use the pattern of three notes found at the beginning of the melody, but sung a little higher. These two segments are regarded as analogous (an association that is shown by their vertical alignment on the page in Figure 10). But in what sense would a listener hear them as 'equivalent'? Clearly, they are related through similarity, but in terms of this form of semiotic analysis, the same connection would exist whether the segment was repeated exactly (at the same pitch) or transposed to sound higher or lower to any degree. Yet the musical effects would be very different.

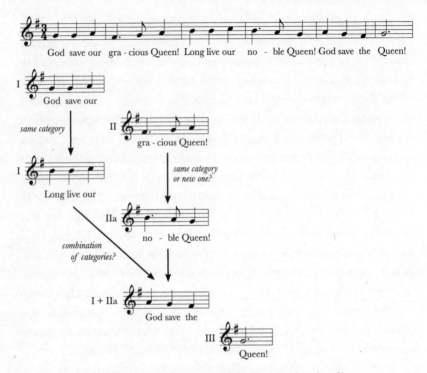

Figure 10 *The opening of the British national anthem.*[26]

The words 'noble Queen!' use the same rhythm as 'gracious Queen!' in the first line, but the melodic contour – the 'shape' the three pitches make by ascending or descending – is inverted: instead of going up, the tune comes down. So there are both similarities and differences for the analyst to contend with. British musicologists Jonathan Dunsby and Arnold Whitall reflect this ambiguity in two possible readings, the first of which regards the motif as distinct, while the second implies that it is similar enough to belong to the same category (see Segment IIa in Figure 10). Yet surely the essence of the relationship between the two is that it embodies sameness and difference at the same time? One can characterise Ruwet's brand of semiotic analysis as black or white – either motifs are related or they aren't – even though the essence of most music is its innumerable shades of grey: *partial* relationships and ambiguities that permit a range of interpretations.

The problem of determining the lineage of segments becomes even more acute in the third line of the anthem: 'God save the …' Here a descending pattern of three notes of equal duration is used that seems to borrow material both from the contour of the preceding segment 'noble Queen!', and the rhythm of the opening 'God save our …' So there is no single ancestral line – the type of cloning demanded by Ruwet's system. Rather, in appropriating and combining musical 'DNA' from two sources, the process of arriving at the fifth segment of the melody is more akin to the fusion of gametes in sexual reproduction (a genetic simile in the Dawkins' tradition rather than a carnal allusion *à la* McClary).

This is not the only difficulty with Ruwet's style of semiotic analysis. Consider what it has to say about the first three lines of *God Save the Queen*. While it highlights the high degree of repetition that is present, it loses sight of some of the characteristics that make the melody what it is. In particular, it is the matter of *differences* that is problematic. While the units appearing in any one column may be the same in terms of internal structure, they fulfil distinct musical functions in relation to one another. So, the process of segmentation captures some dimensions of the music, but by no means all. Moreover, there is no attempt to explain *why* a composer should have selected certain units rather than others and organised them in a particular way, nor *how* segmentation occurs in the ears of listeners, and the impact of the resulting syntactical structure. And although Ruwet never intended to provide a comprehensive account of how music works (since, for example, aesthetic issues are not the concern of his theory),[27] the main problem with his thinking is that it stops short of showing how non-structural elements are integrated with structural ones – of explaining how difference and sameness combine to form a coherent musical narrative over time.

This is an issue that music theorist Fred Lerdahl and linguist Ray Jackendoff tackle head on in their book *A Generative Theory of Tonal Music* ('*GTTM*'), which, inspired by Bernstein's Harvard lecture series, was published in 1983.[28] The two American authors synthesise ideas from a wide range of sources, including Chomskyan linguistics and cognitive psychology, to underpin their theoretical model. This identifies four types of hierarchy operating in tonal music, each of which relies in a distinct

way on our capacity to distinguish certain types of similarity and difference in sounds, and which work together to inform the musical intuitions
of *all* listeners who are familiar with a particular style. Lerdahl and Jackendoff's approach was driven partly by the desire to shift the emphasis in
music analysis from thinking only about how an elite perceive a particular
composition, *à la* Schenker, Babbitt, Forte, the American music theorist
David Lewin and others, to trying to understand how the *majority* of listeners familiar with a given style can *typically* be assumed to make sense
of what they hear – much more the epistemological territory of cognitive
psychologists.

Lerdahl and Jackendoff's search for the holy grail of being able to
explain how music works begins with the notion of 'groups', which are
said to occur when experienced listeners intuitively divide music into
imaginary chunks. The propensity of the mind to hear separate events
– notes or chords – as making up distinct, larger entities, like motifs,
which function within a structural hierarchy, forms a core part of the
theory set out in *GTTM*. An important difference between these and
Ruwet's notion of 'units', which are defined by the presence or absence
of *external* repetition, is that groups can also be determined by *internal* patterning, in accordance with the principles of Gestalt psychology.
These were first identified by the German experimental psychologists,
Max Wertheimer, Kurt Koffka and Wolfgang Köhler, and initially assimilated into musicological thinking by Leonard Meyer. The Gestalt effect
refers to the capacity of human (and non-human) brains to see – quite
literally – the wood from the trees, to recognise patterns and trends in the
innumerable individual items of perceptual information that assail us, to
discern larger entities from groups of smaller parts.

According to Lerdahl and Jackendoff, two internal types of grouping
are of particular significance in music, deriving from the principles of
'similarity' and 'proximity'. They illustrate these using visual analogies in
the form of squares and circles.

Groups of this kind have two defining characteristics: first, their
members have a property in common that is *not* shared with non-mem-
bers; and second, their members differ in at least one respect from each
other (otherwise they would be identical and perceptually indistinct). For

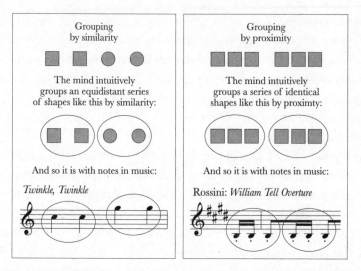

Figure 11 *Grouping by similarity and proximity in visual patterns and music.*

example, in *Twinkle, Twinkle*, the first two notes are identical in pitch ('C'), and this characteristic distinguishes them from the second pair (which are 'G's). However, the C's are set apart from one another by occurring at different times. Hence the notion of a 'group' (unlike Ruwet's concept of a 'unit') necessarily merges similarity and difference in a single structural entity.

But this sophisticated concept is only one element in Lerdahl and Jackendoff's theory of how music makes sense, which, like Schenker's, is hierarchical, whereby some notes are heard as being more structurally significant than others (which are 'ornamental' to a greater degree). For Lerdahl and Jackendoff, though, musical hierarchies are not just defined by patterns in the realm of pitch, but also through groups of notes' rhythmic and metrical qualities. Like Schenker, Lerdahl and Jackendoff take a reductionist approach, through which layers nearer the musical 'surface' are peeled away to reveal a structural core. In contrast to Schenker's procedure, however, there is no pre-determined outcome – no Ursatz serving as a common form of gravitational centre at the core of every piece.

Lerdahl and Jackendoff use the term 'elaboration' (and its opposite, 'reduction') to refer to the idea that one note or chord can be heard as being structurally subordinate to another.[29] To hear what this sounds like, consider Paul McCartney's song *Yesterday* – in particular, the opening three notes (to which the word 'Yesterday' is set). Although the music passes by quite quickly (the first two notes last only around half a second), the effect of this can be heard by mentally 'freeze-framing' the melody on the initial syllable 'Yes-'. It has a discordant quality (the pitch doesn't 'fit' with its harmony) that seems to want to resolve onto the '-ter-' that follows. In traditional Western music analysis the note to which 'Yes-' is sung is classed as an 'appoggiatura', a pitch that occurs on the beat and 'leans' into the main note, or to use the Italian metaphor, is 'propped up' by it. It is thought that the arresting quality of appoggiaturas stems from a feature of the auditory system whereby the harmonics to which they correspond, which are higher than those of the pitches in the chords that they elaborate, sound relatively dissonant. In Lerdahl and Jackendoff's terms, the appoggiatura *elaborates* on the main (harmony) note.

But appoggiaturas aren't just any notes that happen to clash with the harmony upon which they are superimposed. As Lerdahl and Jackendoff say: 'Structurally less important events are not heard simply as insertions, but in a specified relationship to surrounding more important events.'[30] In the case of appoggiaturas, what is that specified relationship? Tradition has it that they should be adjacent in pitch to the more structural notes that they ornament. That is, they should be *similar* to them. Hence, once more, Lerdahl and Jackendoff's theory ties *difference* into the musical narrative through acknowledging the implicit agency of (approximate) repetition.

The linguistic analogies of how music works proposed by Bernstein, and Lerdahl and Jackendoff, and the semiotic analyses of Nattiez and Ruwet are all founded in one way or another on repetition, which the authors identify as being active in different contexts, and fulfilling a range of syntactical functions. Repetition is considered to be a necessary element in music since, unlike verbal language, it lacks a framework of semantic meaning derived from external references. Hence music has no choice but to refer to itself. Seeking to explain how self-referencing in music works is the province of the last theoretical approach that we shall explore – another that is 'absolutist' in Meyer's terms. Our focus will be on the thinking of Arnold Schoenberg, who taught broadly conventional music theory at universities in California from the mid-1930s, despite being one

Figure 12 *Motifs of five, four and three notes from music in a range of styles.*

of the *enfants terribles* of early twentieth century music, notorious for his development of what became known as 'atonal' and, later, 'serial' music.

Explaining Music in its Own Terms: Arnold Schoenberg

Ask people what gives a familiar piece of music its identity, what sets it apart from all other pieces, and they are likely to think in terms of a distinctive fragment of melody – a sonic name-tag – for which musicians working in different areas have come up with their own, genre-specific terms. In the Western classical tradition, for example, a short, characteristic group of notes is called a 'motif'. In pop music, a brief, catchy phrase from the chorus of a song is known as a 'hook'; while in jazz, a repeated thematic fragment is referred to as a 'riff'. Whatever the style, these concise chunks of music have such a powerful individuality that they can come to stand for whole pieces in people's minds, potentially serving both as labels and prompts. And it takes far less material than one would imagine to define a unique musical idea: five, four or even three notes may be sufficient.

Given their apparent ubiquity and evident importance to the design of musical compositions, we should not be surprised that Arnold Schoenberg's influential book, the *Fundamentals of Musical Composition*,[31] begins by setting out how these 'potato prints' in sound function. According to Schoenberg, the motif determines the character of a piece, and must have sufficient rhythmic and melodic individuality both to be memorable and, therefore, recognisable. Like Ruwet, some years later, Schoenberg believed that musical structure is created by the repetition of motifs: they are both *necessary* and *sufficient* to bring unity, coherence and comprehensibility to compositions since they recur throughout them and contain all the material that is used. For Schoenberg it is axiomatic that repetition enables music to make sense, and so he makes no attempt to say how this process actually occurs, or how it is that repeating material is able to generate a kind of musical logic that the brain can grasp.

Nonetheless, this line of thought has an intuitive appeal, and although Schoenberg confines his reasoning to Western classical music, the repetition of motifs is in fact ubiquitous, appearing in all musical dialects: from the rhythmically complex dance music of the Ewe people of West Africa to the hypnotic bell-like patterns of sound emanating from the gongs and metallophones of the Javanese gamelan; from the stylised versions of the Kookaburra calls that feature in the didgeridoo playing of Aboriginal Australians to the measured Scottish Gaelic 'iorram' or rowing songs of the Isle of Mull.

To hear a simple example of this kind of repetition in action, consider the French nursery rhyme, *Frère Jacques*. Straightforward in design, it comprises four motifs, each reiterated immediately. What is the effect of this high level of recurrence? What is happening in experiential terms? How does the repetition of the first motif, for example – which comprises the four notes to which the words 'Frère Jacques' are sung – generate the melody's opening structure? And how does that in turn enable listeners to make sense of the music up to that point?

To seek answers to these questions we need to move beyond the world of music theory that Schoenberg inhabited, in which individual assertions and beliefs have the status of an incontrovertible type of knowledge that requires no defence, to the realms of philosophy and psychology. Here, evidence in one form or another has to be presented and interrogated to ascertain whether the views that are put forward hold up under scrutiny.

If music does indeed make sense through the recurrence of motifs,

Figure 13 Frère Jacques *comprises four motifs, each repeated immediately.*

as Schoenberg maintains, then it follows that a first step must be for listeners to acknowledge, at some level, that one short series of notes is a duplicate of another – even if they are not consciously aware of the fact. However, while the repetition of musical material is a straightforward enough concept to grasp (especially when, as in the case of *Frère Jacques* above, its existence is telegraphed in advance through seeing the score), in everyday contexts, in which explicit clues as to the way a piece of music was designed are likely to be absent, the brain has to work hard to discern what is happening.

One reason for this is the ephemeral nature of auditory perception, which means that sounds can be apprehended only through the narrow window of the present.[32] So, in order to make sense of music, fleeting impressions of notes have to be stored temporarily and then reconstructed in the mind to create the illusion of a continuous melody.[33] And to compare one motif with another – for example, to gauge how the first sequence of four notes to which the words 'Frère Jacques' are set relates to the second – means that the initial series must be mentally replayed at the same time that its successor is heard in order for the parallels between the two to be identified.

Schoenberg asserted that 'intelligibility in music is impossible without repetition'.[34] If this is true, then we must assume that the brain is constantly scanning incoming new musical material for patterns, without knowing for sure *what* is going to be repeated *when*. To facilitate this process, it seems that, in addition to remembering, *anticipation* must play a key role in the musical experience, working partly through internal patterning and partly in a more schematic, *probabilistic* way (for structural certainty can exist only in retrospect).[35] That is, potential continuations of a piece of music to which a listener is attending are being predicted all the time, and are judged to be more or less likely based on previous experience. Thus the brain is continually juggling freshly perceived sounds with memories of those heard in the immediate or longer-term past and expectations of what may occur in the future. Amazingly, the complex blend of mental processes underpinning the identification of repetition in music typically occurs without the need for conscious thought or explicit teaching. Our brains rapidly wire themselves up in the early years to undertake this demanding task without us, our parents or our carers being aware of it.

An issue that Schoenberg raises in the *Fundamentals of Musical Composition* is that music cannot exist through repetition alone, since this would cause nothing but an increasing sense of monotony. Even the most extreme manifestations of minimalist music, created in the 1960s by such American composers as Terry Riley, Steve Reich and Philip Glass, typically involve tiny increments of change through the gradual evolution of motifs during the course of a piece. But if it is true, as Schoenberg asserts, that repetition is necessary for coherence and comprehensibility, then presumably change would have the opposite effect, and give rise to disorder and confusion? Indeed, the composer himself states that altering every feature of a motif would produce something that was incoherent and illogical. What is needed, therefore, is for music to have sufficient variety to be interesting while at the same time having enough consistency to be intelligible: as our analysis of Ruwet's semiotic approach showed, sameness and difference must somehow work together to produce a musical message that is both pleasing and comprehensible. What is required is *variation*. But how does variation work? How can repetition and change co-exist in a meaningful way? How are they brought together in the mind of the listener?

Degrees of Repetition

To get some initial purchase on these issues, we will probe Schoenberg's contention that repetition may be 'exact' or 'modified', although even 'exact' repetition (so-called) can take various forms, provided the relationships between the notes in a motif are maintained.[36] This means that a melody can be 'transposed' to begin on a higher or lower note without affecting its identity. However, even if pitch and rhythm are duplicated precisely, other change is still possible within Schoenberg's definition of 'exact' repetition, since he feels at liberty to ignore other characteristics of musical sounds, such as loudness and timbre (or 'tone-colour'). He is able to do this because, as the French composer and conductor Pierre Boulez later observed, pitch and rhythm have together shouldered the burden of conveying the musical message in Western genres – forms of abstract communication in sound that other qualities, such as loudness and timbre, have merely served to articulate.[37]

The distinction between the *primary* conveyors of musical information (pitch and rhythm) and the *secondary* parameters of musical sound (loudness and timbre) is easy to detect in the melody of *Frère Jacques*: what gives the tune its unique musical identity is not the nature of the singer's voice, nor how loudly or quietly he or she sings, but the patterns of rhythm and pitch that unfold over the course of the song. Such patterning is both *necessary* and *sufficient* for the music to make sense. Hence we should not be surprised that the way in which the melody is processed in the mind puts greatest emphasis on pitch and rhythm too,[38] and the manner in which it is stored in memory and subsequently recalled tends to suppress the secondary (non-structure-bearing) characteristics of sound. So the differences that one would expect in timbre and loudness between discrete renditions of the song do not affect its capacity to convey an intrinsic musical meaning. To observe this phenomenon in action, consider your own memory of *Frère Jacques*. Unless a particular performance is strongly emotionally tagged (maybe your child sang it at a school concert, for example) or has been subject to a great deal of repetition (maybe the same child had a recording of it that was played at bedtimes), this information will probably have been lost.

Our relative indifference to tone-colour and dynamic is important, since melodies like *Frère Jacques* constitute shared cultural resources that can validly be taken up by anyone who wishes to sing them. The same is not true of all songs in other societies, however. For example, writing in the 1950s, the German musicologist, Marius Schneider, describes the 'personal song', widespread in ancient, totemistic cultures, which may be sung solely by the person to whom it belongs; it is only following its owner's death that another may venture a performance.[39] According to Schneider, the individuality of this music lies principally not in the design of melody but in the manner of performance – especially the timbre of the voice. Here, a central element of the music's meaning is its irrevocable association with the individual concerned. But in Western genres, where this is not the case, what functions do timbre and loudness fulfil?

During the course of an everyday rendition of an unassuming melody like *Frère Jacques*, timbre acts rather like a 'carrier wave': remaining more or less constant and bearing the message conveyed through pitch and rhythm, but not relaying any structural information in its own right. The brain's ready capacity to handle this kind of consistency of tone-colour must reach right back into our evolutionary past. It would have helped our forebears to identify that a given stream of sound emanated from a known fellow human (friend or foe?) or a particular type of animal (predator or prey?) amid the ever-changing complexity of the surrounding 'auditory scene', to use the term coined by the pioneering Canadian psychologist Al Bregman.[40] And the perceptual task would have been made easier, since then, as now, uniformity of timbre is usually reinforced with constancy or, at least, predictable change in loudness and the location of the sound source. (Parents know all too well the challenge of trying to focus on what their young offspring are saying as they scamper around their legs.)

Having consistency in at least some auditory dimensions reduces the considerable cognitive load imposed by trying to process a series of abstract sounds. Managing to make sense of the patterns made by pitch and rhythm is demanding enough, it seems: early work in the field of information theory by the American psychologists Irwin Pollack and Lawrence Ficks,[41] insightfully summarised by George Miller in his seminal paper, 'The magical number seven, plus or minus two', of 1956,[42] graphically showed the constraints of human perception with and between sensory domains. The more complex stimuli are, the greater the competition among their features for our attention. And as far as music is concerned, if qualities of sound such as timbre and loudness are a 'given', then that is a great help in ensuring that our pattern-junkie, though limited-capacity, brains aren't overwhelmed by the multidimensional musical message – as composers of 'integral serialist' music, such as Messiaen, Boulez and Stockhausen, working in the 1950s, discovered. By seeking to organise not only pitch, but also, simultaneously, other aspects of sound such as duration, dynamics and articulation through manipulating preordained series of values, it became evident that the effect was not one of complete orderliness, as one might think, but utter chaos, since the brain cannot process so much concentrated information in different auditory dimensions at once.

In fact, the changes in timbre and loudness that occur in music composed in more traditional ways are almost invariably subservient to the hegemony of pitch and rhythm. For example, rising pitch tends to signal greater emotional intensity, and this may well be reinforced with a *crescendo*. Consider, for instance, the main theme from Smetana's symphonic poem *Vltava* – his depiction of the river Moldau – in which the levels of loudness mirror the pitch contour of the opening motif, enhancing its effect: the ear hears a wave of sound slowly rise before falling back rather more quickly.

On other occasions, the impact of the repetition of motifs is *transformed* through dynamic change. A celebrated example occurs from bar 16 in the first movement of Beethoven's *Pastoral* Symphony, where a short five-note motif in the first violins (harmonised by the remaining strings and horns) is heard no fewer than nine times in succession. What is the musical function of this apparent tautology? Surely such a high degree of recurrence would be tedious, irritating or even comical?

But no, Beethoven's music taps into a primitive, autonomic response, whereby loud sounds increase the body's state of arousal, having a pronounced psychophysical impact that can include an increased heart rate, deeper breathing and changes in skeletomuscular tension.[43] Effects such as these are liable to be evoked by the gradual rise to a climax – *forte* – that Beethoven dictates should occur midway through the sequence of motifs, at which point the bassoons briefly add weight to the texture. Then listeners are gradually allowed to relax again as the music fades to *pianissimo* ('*pp*'). As Bernstein states in *The Unanswered Question*, Beethoven creates 'the metaphor of approaching and receding' in a narrative that,

Figure 14 *Dynamics become the main focus of attention with repeated motifs in the first movement of Beethoven's* Pastoral *Symphony.*

remarkably, can be interpreted in both an abstract and a representational way.[44] In either case, it is as though the role of carrier usually fulfilled by the loudness of the sounds, and that of message-bearer, normally accomplished by pitch and rhythm, are reversed: to use the language of information theory, the high degree of redundancy in the chain of identical melodic motifs frees the ear to focus on the change in dynamics.

Step changes in loudness, less frequently, timbre, and, even, occasionally, the location of the sound source, which coincide with the repetition of motifs, tend to have a rhetorical function. For instance, following the model of the late Renaissance polychoral masterpieces of Giovanni Gabrieli written at the end of the sixteenth century for the magnificent Basilica of Saint Mark in Venice, composers of the Baroque period (1600–1750) would sometimes make use of an 'echo' effect, whereby a motif or theme was immediately reiterated at a lower dynamic level. The sense is one of a pause in the forward momentum of the musical narrative to reflect on what has just happened, before things move on again. A playful example occurs in Purcell's vocal quartet *May the God of Wit Inspire* from his masque *The Fairy Queen*. Here, the repeated reduction in dynamics – literally, a twofold echo – explicitly conveys the meaning of the lyrics.

Figure 15 *The repetition of motifs in the second movement of Schubert's* Unfinished *Symphony gives a sense of suspended animation.*

A particularly beautiful instance of stepped changes in timbre, working in combination with staged dynamics, can be heard in the slow movement of Schubert's *Unfinished* Symphony. The recapitulation of the second theme is underway – typical of Schubert with its poignant vacillation between a tragic version in the minor mode, and the warmth and tenderness of a variant in the major key. This concludes with a lyrical figure, played successively by the clarinet, oboe and flute, whose limpid calm the listener knows, from having heard a comparable passage earlier, in the exposition, is about to be overwhelmed by a loud and tempestuous rendition of the melody by the full orchestra, back once more in the minor. Through his threefold insistence on the motif, it is as though Schubert himself is putting off the moment before the storm breaks, leaving the music for a few seconds in a state of suspended animation.

All these examples of repetition and change working together in a musically coherent way illustrate an important facet of perception, without which music would make no sense at all. It is this. While the different aspects of sounds – pitch, timbre and loudness – can be separated conceptually in the process of creating, performing or analysing music, they are not typically heard in a discrete way: rather, each note merges into a single percept, meaning that the structural effect of simultaneous patterning in different auditory dimensions can quite literally be more than the sum of its parts. This fusion occurs through a cognitive function that psychologists call 'binding', whereby the different features of an object, whose perceptual processing is initially managed separately in the brain, are brought back together to form a unified mental image of something.[45] In music, binding is an important way in which sameness and difference can be amalgamated to create a structural whole. In particular, the sense of structure evoked through the way in which just two dimensions of sound (pitch and rhythm) are arranged, usually transfers to the others (including timbre and loudness), giving the impression that a stream of musical notes has a comprehensive, multifaceted coherence, and enabling the concept of 'exact' repetition, as mooted by Schoenberg, actually to embody certain types of change.

Intervals and Transposition

The excerpts from Beethoven and Schubert show pitch and rhythm being duplicated precisely, against a backdrop of changes in loudness and timbre. However, almost all music involves more substantial development of material than this, the most common form being 'transposition': the process through which entire motifs are shifted up or down in pitch, while rhythm remains unchanged. Like the repetition of motifs at the same pitch, the use of transposition appears to be universal in music.

Now it may well be that you are already familiar with the tunes shown in Figure 16, and that, in the past, they intuitively made sense to you without your being aware that they involved motifs being transposed. Indeed, the children's song *Hickory, Dickory Dock*, which originated in the oral tradition, could quite possibly have been improvised in the first instance by people who had no knowledge of music theory and without the conscious thought that certain motifs are transposed versions of others. At the same time, it is evidently easy for listeners, irrespective of their musical background, to develop an explicit awareness of transposition once their attention has been drawn to it, and Schoenberg argues that this is one of the ways in which composers organise musical sounds to make them comprehensible. But how does the brain subconsciously make sense of transposition in the course of day-to-day listening, when the ear is not directed to it?

There is strong evidence that, from an early age, the mind regards a tune that has been transposed as being in some way equivalent to the original. This was shown many years ago in an ingenious experiment undertaken by the Canadian psychologist Sandra Trehub and her

Figure 16 *Examples of the transposition of motifs in Western music.*

co-researcher Hsing-Wu Chang with babies that were only five months old.[46] The very young children were first habituated to a short series of six tones (by playing it to them 30 times!), and then heard either the stimulus in transposed form, or a scrambled version of that transposition. The latter consistently resulted in a rapid heart deceleration (a well-established autonomic reaction to a new experience) whereas the former did not. Therefore, we can conclude that the infants' brains must have been focusing on features in the original series and the transposition that were the same. What were these similarities?

The answer to this question lies in the fact that it is not *notes* that convey the essential information about a melody, but the *perceived differences between them*. It is these differences that the babies' brains were recognising as invariant features in the transposed melodies. In relation to pitch, such differences are called 'intervals'. In Western music, despite its wide range of styles and genres, only a few different sizes of interval are typically used (although singers and performers whose instruments admit variation in pitch, such as string players, often widen these slightly or make them a little narrower for expressive effect).[47] Research such as Trehub's shows that this limited set of intervals automatically becomes modelled in the brain early in infancy through the hundreds of hours of musical exposure to which children are subject. And while the notion of

Figure 17 *Examples of melodic intervals.*

intervals may appear to be a remote, abstract concept for those without formal musical training, differences in pitch can in fact easily be brought forward into consciousness, since they are embedded in each of the tunes that every individual will have learnt. For instance, try humming the opening two notes of the pieces in Figure 17. The first, *Nessun Dorma* by Puccini, begins with the smallest possible interval (with no change of pitch); thereafter the tunes commence with successively wider transitions until the last, *Somewhere Over the Rainbow* by Harold Arlen, which leaps up using the largest interval that is commonly found in melodies (the 'octave').

With the exception of the interval that initiates *Nessun Dorma*, all these differences in pitch are 'ascending' – implying a move from a lower note to a higher one. This polarity can be reversed, whereby the second note is lower than the first: think, for example, of the opening descents of *Yesterday*, *Swing Low Sweet Chariot* and *Eine Kleine Nachtmusik*. Each interval, in its rising and falling forms, has a distinct 'feel' – a personality of its own – which can vary somewhat according to melodic, harmonic and rhythmic context in which it is heard, and which makes an important contribution to the *meaning* of music. It is intriguing to think that something with no physical correlate – the perceived difference between two pitches – has the capacity to evoke an emotional response. For example, the acerbity of the augmented 4th that kicks off *The Simpsons Theme* perfectly captures the sharp satire of the cartoon series; the opening minor 7th of *Somewhere* yearns for resolution; and the minor 3rd with which *Greensleeves* begins conveys 'Alas!' melodically, adding depth to the lyrics.[48]

The relationship between pitches and intervals is both conceptually and psychologically complex. At its heart lies the apparent paradox that while it is intervals that are core to the musical message, these can only be reified – brought into existence – when they are anchored on, and so expressed through, particular pitches, which are themselves of less importance. To observe this process in action, think again about the melodies listed in Figure 17. Prepare to sing, for example, *When the Saints Go Marching In*. How did you know which pitch to start on? You probably hadn't given it a thought up to now. That's because, rather like loudness and timbre, this information isn't usually held in memory – or, at least, only in an approximate way. So, when people sing a song in the shower or the bath, most of the time they are effectively creating the pitches afresh, from scratch. These may be somewhat higher or lower than the ones used in previous renditions – the amateur Pavarottis performing their ablutions probably wouldn't be able to tell.

Indeed, the notion of standardising the pitch to which all instruments should be tuned is relatively recent: it was only in 1955 that the International Organization for Standardization (ISO) decreed that the 'A' above 'middle C' should be fixed at 440Hz, and even today, this is not adhered to universally. Moreover, so-called 'period performances' naturally adopt the pitches to which the relevant historical instruments (or copies of them) are tuned. So, by modern standards, Bach's B Minor Mass is often heard a semitone lower than its title suggests, in B flat minor! And aside from circumstances such as these, from time immemorial, singers have changed the pitch-range (or 'tessitura') of songs to suit their voices. Here the burden of making the necessary transposition lies with their accompanists, in whom the ability to play a piece in different keys is a welcome though generally unsung skill.

The context in which Schoenberg refers to transposition in *The Fundamentals of Musical Composition* is not between different performances of the same piece, however, but *within* works – as in the examples shown in Figure 16. His claim is that transposition is one of the techniques that composers adopt (more or less consciously) to ensure that the music they create makes sense. This assertion is made within the wider frame of reference that repetition is necessary for music to be comprehensible. It follows, therefore, that transposition must include an element of *invariance*, and this is provided by the intervals between (successive) notes being repeated. Add to this the fact that the pitches through which a given interval is realised differ when it is transposed, and we have *sameness* and *difference* bound together in a single musical gesture.

This fusion of repetition and change, made possible by the fact that it is intervals that matter more than individual pitches in cognitive terms, is crucial for the way that music works. If it were *not* the case – if the onus were on discrete pitches to convey the musical message – then the design of pieces would have to be highly constrained if they were to make sense to the majority of listeners. Transposition would result in incoherence. And for the 99.99 per cent of people who do not have absolute pitch, works would need to be of limited duration (or be extremely repetitive), since motifs that were more than a few moments apart – beyond the reach of working memory – would be forgotten. To put it simply: music as it currently exists would largely be nonsensical.

Coda

A brief survey of musicological thinking of the last hundred years provides some answers to the question of how music works, but, inevitably, these raise more questions, which can't immediately be resolved. Notwithstanding the gaps in our understanding, it is possible to construct a line of reasoning to explain what *is* known of how music works and to clarify what *isn't*.

There is general agreement that music will make sense if its constituent sounds are organised or *structured* in some way. Some believe that structures arise as a reflection of *external* factors (with no consensus as to what these may be, with possibilities ranging from the spiritual to the temporal), while others contend that musical organisation is *internally* driven (through a kind of logic, as yet unspecified, which appears to be unique to music) – though, it seems, the two need not be mutually exclusive. For example, Schenker's graphs illustrate his belief that the divinely conceived 'chord of nature' can be prolonged and elaborated through human influence to create musical structures, extended in time. As a consequence of the internal/external division, there appear to be at least two forms of musical meaning: a 'referential' type, in which the disposition of musical sounds point listeners to things in the world beyond; and an 'absolute' kind, where an affective response is evoked purely through the nature and arrangement of the sounds themselves.

But what *is* musical 'structure'? The diverse theories of how music works in absolute terms all acknowledge the centrality of *repetition* in musical organisation, either implicitly (as in the symmetry of Schenker's Ursatz) or explicitly (as in Schoenberg's explanation of music's reliance on recurring motifs). Yet there must be more to music than repetition alone, otherwise all the sounds in a piece would be sucked metaphorically into an auditory singularity – a musical black hole. Therefore *difference,* or change, is essential too. However, if sameness yields structure, then (following Schoenberg's thinking) difference alone must give rise to disorder.[49] Hence there is a potential problem.

So, for music to work, repetition and change must be linked systematically, whereby the effect of structure is somehow transferred from sameness to difference, and a synthesis emerges. To achieve this, music relies on two characteristics of auditory perception. This first is 'binding'. Sounds are multidimensional, having distinct qualities such as pitch, loudness and timbre, and a location in time and space. These can vary more or less independently, and are processed with differing degrees of separation in the brain. However, the individual perceptual strands are rapidly reintegrated in our stream of consciousness, so that we experience the sensation of a single auditory entity: one sound with different qualities that reflect a common physical source. Through this mechanism, a sense of structure in one domain (say, pitch) can be transferred to the others. This explains why, when we hear people singing a tune, for example, the vocal sounds they produce appear to be organised in their entirety, even though loudness and timbre do not figure in the song's structural make up (and why different individuals can sing the same melody in different ways without compromising its identity or structural integrity).

The second way that sameness and difference in music can be connected is through the brain's capacity to extract *relative* information from the auditory environment by comparing two sounds or more. Every note not only has qualities on its own account (it may be half a second in length), it also has a perceived existence in relation to other notes (it may be twice as long as the one that preceded it). These abstract items of information, mined from beneath the perceptual surface by our order-seeking brains, have a mental existence of their own, divorced from any particular context. So one note can be a given interval higher or lower than another, for example, irrespective of the pitch of either. This means that it is possible for a relationship between two sounds to be repeated between a quite different pair of notes. And in this way, sameness and difference can be locked together in cognition.

In summary: musical meaning that is derived internally (or, to use

Meyer's term, 'absolutely'), from the fabric of music itself, arises from coherent combinations of repetition and change ('variation') that work together to produce structure. Although variation is conceptually straight-forward, psychological research has shown that detecting it is cognitively demanding, requiring sophisticated sound-processing abilities as well as advanced skills in auditory learning, recall and anticipation. Such abilities typically develop purely through exposure to music and by informal engagement in music-making activities in the early years, leading to a kind of musical understanding that exists purely on an intuitive level. It is also possible, though, through formal education, for such intuitions to be overlaid with a gloss of conceptual knowledge, and this is what, for centuries, music theorists have done.

This line of thought takes us some way towards understanding how music works, but it stops short at a critical point. *How* does repetition convey a sense of structure (thereby enabling music to make sense)? And beyond this, how is it that abstract patterns of repetition and change in sound are able to convey meaning? It is to the first of these issues that we next turn our attention.

2

The Zygonic Conjecture

DURING THE TWENTIETH CENTURY, a number of writers went further than merely accepting that repetition is a primary structural force in music, by attempting to say *how* it enables music to make sense. For example, the British essayist Basil de Sélincourt, in an article published in the first volume of the now venerable journal *Music and Letters*,[1] compares the growth of a musical composition to that of a flowering plant, 'with its multitude of leaves and blossoms and intertwining stems and branches: where not only the leaves repeat each other, but the leaves repeat the flowers, and the very stems and branches are like un-unfolded leaves.' Unlike Schenker, however, Sélincourt did not seek to imply that there was a direct relationship between nature and music. On the contrary, it was his contention that:

> The value of repetition in music belongs of course to the peculiar
> inwardness of the art. A musical composition must be content to
> be itself. The reference and relations into which analysis resolves its
> life-current need point to no object, no event; they take the form of
> the creative impulse which is their unity and they repeat one another
> because iteration is the only outward sign of identity which is available
> to them.[2]

So in Sélincourt's view, music appears to have an inner compulsion for coherence, which finds expression in repetition, which in turn somehow generates a sense of agency. Sélincourt does not elaborate on *how* this may come about, however.

The Austrian musicologist Viktor Zuckerkandl takes a further step along this conceptual path in his book, *Sound and Symbol*.[3] Published in 1956, the same year as Meyer's *Emotion and Meaning in Music*, it remains, unjustifiably, in my view, much less well known. Zuckerkandl's ideas are partly indebted to Schenker, although, like Meyer, he also draws on Gestalt psychology, as well as the phenomenological thinking of Edmund Husserl and Martin Heidegger.

Zuckerkandl commences his discussion of repetition informally, observing that

> music can never have enough of saying over again what has already been said, not once or twice, but dozens of times; hardly does a section, which consists largely of repetitions, come to an end, before the whole story is happily told all over again.[4]

Here, he is merely adopting a type of description that is typical of many other thinkers, from 'traditional' theorists such as Stewart Macpherson and Wallace Berry to composers such as Carlos Chávez and Igor Stravinsky.[5] But Zuckerkandl takes a further step, and advances a more analytical, psychological argument:

> nothing in the physical world corresponds to the play of forces in tones, for the reason that these forces are not active in the tones at all, but *in us*, who hear. They have their origin in us – in the feelings that hearing tones arouses in us and that we then project out of ourselves into the tones.[6]

That is to say, the sense of agency generated by repetition doesn't originate in musical sounds themselves, but in the minds of listeners. At this point, Zuckerkandl's line of thinking stops, begging the question *how* does repetition in music generate a sense of agency between notes?

The American composer Edward Cone, in an article entitled 'On derivation: syntax and rhetoric'[7] inches towards an answer. In seeking to explain how repetition can produce a sense of structure in the minds of listeners, he uses an algebraic analogy, in which 'x' and 'y' can stand for any elements of music:

> y is derived from x (y ← x), or, to use the active voice, x generates y (x → y), if y resembles x and y follows x.

The new insight here is the addition of the concept of *derivation* (and its opposite, *generation*). Cone's contention is that by repeating something in music – a motif, a theme, a chord – listeners are given the impression that the new material is *derived from* the old. It is this sense of derivation that must surely form the basis of the inner logic of music, an understanding of which would enable us to explain how music works: how repetition enables pieces to make sense, and how, in the absence of semantic meaning, music offers a coherent medium of communication.

So, in summary: Schoenberg argues that repetition is the source of internal musical structure, which makes it comprehensible. In short, this can be expressed as:

$$\text{repetition} \Rightarrow \text{musical structure} \Rightarrow \text{music makes sense}$$
$$(\text{where '}\Rightarrow\text{' means 'leads to'}).$$

Following the thinking of Sélincourt, a sense of *agency* can be added in to the equation (which, according to Zuckerkandl, exists purely in the mind of the listener):

$$\text{repetition} + \text{agency} \Rightarrow \text{musical structure} \Rightarrow \text{music making sense}$$

Cone takes us a step further, asserting that repetition and agency give rise to the perceived *derivation* of one musical feature from another. That is to say:

$$\text{repetition} + \text{agency} \Rightarrow \text{derivation} \Rightarrow$$
$$\text{musical structure} \Rightarrow \text{music making sense}$$

However, there are still key items of information missing from chain of contingencies – the links between the elements:

How does repetition cause a sense of agency?
How do repetition and agency work together to evoke a sense of derivation?

How does a sense of derivation give rise to musical structure?
How does structure enable music to make sense?

The key to unlocking this puzzle would seem to be the notion of agency, since it is that which connects repetition with derivation, and without which neither musical structure nor comprehensibility could follow. What does agency mean in this context? Based on the thinking of Zuckerkandl, it could reasonably be defined as 'a perceived quality of musical sounds, through which one note is felt to have an effect on, or influence over, or the capacity to control another or others'.

But how can this be? Surely, it is the composer, or conceivably the performer, who *controls* musical sounds, who decides what should occur, and when? This form of influence is apparent in the use of music notation or through verbal instructions, spoken or written, when one person dictates, more or less precisely, the nature and timing of the musical sounds that another should play or sing. But this is not the type of agency to which we are alluding. Zuckerkandl and Cone refer to a form of *perceived influence* between sounds that is evident to listeners and must therefore be implicit in the way that music is heard. This is something that infants can comprehend, and, as the account of Anthony showed, even children with learning difficulties can grasp. It is a feeling that occurs as we listen to music that we can *all* understand intuitively without the need for verbal explanation or explicit musical understanding. So, how does this sense of 'perceived influence', this notion of *agency in repetition* work?

Derek

After much searching, I discovered the answer to this question, not from the academic literature or from esteemed colleagues working in the field of musicology, but in the course of my everyday work at Linden Lodge School where, during the 1980s, having started as a volunteer, I went on to serve as Head of Music. At that time, a new generation of children was working its way up the school – every bit as interesting and, for teachers, in some ways more challenging than their predecessors, as they had higher levels of cognitive disability in addition to their visual impairment. Among them was the young Derek Paravicini.[8]

As a seven-year-old, Derek was the most prodigiously musically talented child that I'd ever encountered, with or without special needs. By the age of eight, he had already amassed a repertoire of thousands of pieces of music that were immediately at his disposal on the piano: all learnt rapidly by ear, and each one available to him with complete fluency in any key. Though it was unorthodox, he had the most extraordinary technical facility, with the capacity to dart up and down the keyboard with great rapidity and accuracy, often seeming to flick the notes, his fingers as much in the air as they were in contact with the keys. His tastes were truly eclectic, from Bach and Beethoven to the Blues and the Beatles, though he had a natural affinity for early jazz, particularly the 'stride' style of Fats Waller. Irrespective of the composer, though, his playing had – and continues to have – a joyous vitality that finds expression in his tendency to add notes to melodies, to enrich harmonies and to fill out textures, creating whirling worlds of sound that are utterly, uniquely Derek.

When he was nine, Derek's remarkable talents were the most wonderful secret waiting to be told, known only to close family and friends. Within just twelve months, though, his face was to be familiar across the UK, following two appearances on Derek Jameson's show *People* that aired during prime time on BBC1. Before his tenth birthday, he played at the Barbican Hall in London with the Royal Philharmonic Pops Orchestra, entertained at a private function at Buckingham Palace, and appeared on *Wogan* in Britain, and on other chat shows and news bulletins all over the world.

Yet Derek, who had been born prematurely at 26 weeks, was totally blind and had severe learning difficulties – disabilities that manifested themselves in a restricted understanding of the world around him, limited expressive and receptive language, and little or no capacity to manage independently in everyday life. Acquiring new concepts and skills outside the musical arena was a slow and painstaking process, both for Derek and for those who were trying to help him. Later, he was to receive both a diagnosis of 'classic' autism and international acclaim as one of the greatest 'savants' ever to have lived – with a most extreme combination of abilities and disabilities, which I subsequently characterised as being different sides of the same, twice-exceptional coin.[9]

As a baby, we can imagine that it was his relentless focus on the perceptual rather than the functional qualities of sounds that led to the development of his extraordinarily refined, universal sense of absolute pitch, which came to exist at the expense of an appreciation of what the same sounds potentially could indicate (as signals of everyday events) or symbolise (as words). Similarly, we can suppose that it was Derek's obsession with making music, to the exclusion of virtually all other activity, that fired his ferocious talent, but which also meant that he didn't develop the usual skills and understanding that would have enabled him to function in other areas of life as most children do. As a consequence, everyday tasks that for most people are routine (such as getting washed and dressed) were quite beyond him, while learning to play complex music on the piano just by listening to it, which most adults would find inconceivably difficult, was, for Derek, as natural as breathing.

I started to work with him when he was just five years old – three years after he had started to teach himself the piano – the beginning of a long journey of exploration for both of us, which today, over thirty years later, continues with no end in sight. In the early stages of our unorthodox teacher-pupil relationship, I soon came to realise that there was little point in trying to *explain* to Derek what needed to be done, since words for him were largely unfettered by conceptual understanding: rather, they seemed to float, unattached from meaning, in his auditory universe, mixing on equal terms with everyday sounds and music. I sometimes thought that the world for Derek must be like an immense, rambunctious orchestra, constantly playing a captivating kaleidoscope of different sounds, which were there to be relished for their own sake rather than providing any practical information or demanding action. So, despite his musical abilities, working with Derek was a huge challenge: the devastating combination of blindness and learning difficulties meant that he had no explicit understanding of his fingers or his thumbs as discrete entities, for example, nor an awareness of which hand was his left and which the right. And, for him, most words were at best meaningless, at worst confusing or even threatening. So how could one possibly teach him the piano?

The answer seems obvious in retrospect, though it took me a while to work it out. The important point was that Derek *did* have a language, through which he could communicate fluently, willingly and with great aplomb. Music. The way to teach Derek, I discovered, was not through words, but through music itself. Initially this involved many hours of games in which Derek gladly copied whatever I played on the piano. I didn't have to tell him what to do: quite intuitively, he echoed whatever I produced with astonishing speed and accuracy, and with an exuberance that never waned. When boredom was a distant memory for me, Derek still wanted more. His sense of AP meant that, for him, every note on the piano, every musical sound, every hum of an electric motor, every chink of glass or clink of cutlery, every buzz of every bee, did not merely come across as high or low or somewhere in between, but had a distinct tonal character of its own. Although, when we first met, Derek had no idea what the names of the notes on the piano were (A, B, C sharp, *etc.*), to him, each one of the 88 keys sounded distinct. And, best of all, they were always the same; faithful friends in a confusing world.

Every morning, I would collect him from breakfast in the dining hall, telling him that it was time for his piano lesson. And on each occasion, with his characteristic echolalia and confusion over pronouns, he would reply 'It's time for your *piano* lesson', with a lilting, singsong quality to his voice.

Once in the classroom, I invariably had to assist him in negotiating his way up onto the piano stool, but even before he was sitting down, he'd wriggle free of my helping hands and start to play an ascending C major scale in octaves. He'd use both hands to karate chop the keys, and would sing as he went: 'Thumb, second finger, third finger, thumb, …' This ritual was repeated each morning, and I would always smile wryly, knowing that I still had a long way to go to bring any semblance of conventionality to his technique.

Then, beginning with his left hand, I would physically guide his fingers, which would curl and uncurl wilfully, as I attempted to direct them into the shapes and patterns of movement that the likes of technical aficionados such as Carl Czerny and Charles-Louis Hanon would have recognised. That would still give free rein to his right hand, though, and he could never resist providing harmonies for the rising scale that was

Figure 18 *Helping Derek, aged 8, with his fingering*

sounding in the bass. But it was a distinct improvement on his self-taught martial-arts approach to the piano, which had already seen one instrument consigned to a higher place (an outbuilding in a North Downs summer camp for disabled children).

At an appropriate point towards the end of each lesson, I would quietly ask 'Copy game?'

'Copy game?' he would punt back, echoing my intonation (an octave higher). It was as though the challenge had already begun.

I enjoyed testing Derek with notes at the extremes of the keyboard, which were both perceptually and (given his blindness) particularly kinaesthetically challenging. So I might play, for example, the lowest C sharp on the piano, *staccato*.

Instantly, Derek's hand would shoot out like a boxer's left jab, and he would somehow manage to get all four fingers and his thumb lined up to hit the narrow note with a short, percussive *bonk*, before his hand returned to his lap with equal agility and speed.

Despite having seen him do it hundreds of times before, observing Derek perform feats like this always left me in awe. Here was someone who, at breakfast, hadn't been able to find a slice of toast on the table in front of him, yet now, sat before the piano, could locate a note that was a little more than a centimetre across at arm's length, without hesitation – in a fraction of a second – and with uncanny accuracy.

Next I might play a cluster of two or three adjacent notes at the same time – perhaps at the upper reaches of the keyboard, as quietly as I could. Again, whichever ones I chose, Derek would respond in a flash, and, typically ignoring the dynamic niceties of my musical offering, would catch the keys with a perfect right hook. Often, his hand would remain aloft for a while, trembling with an excitement that would spread down his arms to his whole body, and culminate in a visceral spasm of unalloyed joy. Evidently, musical notes for him were so much more than neutral daubs of sound in the auditory landscape; it was as though each one was an animate being, capable of friendship, and thereby able to arouse a powerful emotional response when encountered after a period of separation, however brief.

I can remember thinking that Derek's reactions to my prompts were so immediate and so reliable that it was as though there were imaginary strings between my fingers and his – a virtual connection between each of the notes that I had chosen and the ones that he had played. In the moment before he had responded to me, Derek had, in theory, all 88 options available to him. But, by choosing to copy what I had done, he had in effect allowed my notes to *control* his. Not through verbal instruction, nor compliance with notation. Not through physical direction, nor visual reproduction. I had dictated what notes should occur next solely through the medium of sound itself.

Then, in the course of one copy game, late in 1987, it occurred to me that, in the language of Cone, Derek's notes were metaphorically *derived* from mine, and mine had effectively *generated* his. What I had witnessed was repetition with perceived intent: *imitation*. It was this that caused a sense of agency, which repetition alone did not. So:

repetition + intent = imitation

And a new chain of contingencies formed in my mind: imitation provides a sense of agency, which leads to the perception of musical structure, which enables music to make sense.

imitation ⇒ agency ⇒
musical structure ⇒ music making sense

This struck me as being a potentially powerful idea, though also somewhat disconcerting, since it meant that what makes music 'music' is not just the physicality of the notes, but the *intent* with which they are executed by performers and discerned by listeners. And since intent, as a form of belief, is generated in the mind – a product of human consciousness, which has no physical correlate – it had to be the case, I reasoned, that, without people, music could not exist. There would merely be patterns of kinetic energy expressed as molecules jostling to and fro. Apparently the vivid nature of perception – crucial for our functioning and survival – beguiles us into thinking that music exists beyond ourselves in a material way. But that is just an artefact of our egocentricity.

Building a New Theory of How Music Works

While the experience of Derek's copy game had given me a new insight into the question of how music works, this was only in one, highly idiosyncratic, context. In order to ascertain the potential relevance of my observation to the way in which musical understanding functions more generally, I realised that it was necessary to deconstruct what had occurred in some detail – to map out each stage of the interaction, and thereby ensure that every step in the sequence of events was captured, enabling me to ascertain precisely how each one related to the next.

Immediately after the two notes had been played and heard, it seemed reasonable to conclude that in my mind (explicitly) and Derek's (implicitly) there must be the following:

- a representation of the first C sharp,
- a representation of the second C sharp,
- an imaginary relationship between them, encapsulating the

Figure 19 Step 1 *was my decision to play a particular note – the lowest C sharp on the keyboard, with the aim of Derek copying what I produced.*

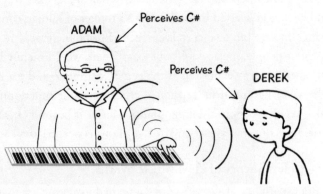

Figure 20 Step 2 *was the perception by Derek and me of the C sharp that I'd played.*

Figure 21 Step 3 *was the decision by Derek to copy the C sharp. This implied a voluntary constraint on his freedom (potentially to play any of the 88 notes on the piano keyboard) in response to my stimulus.*

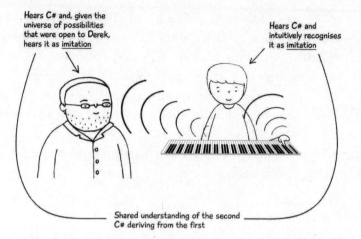

Hears C# and, given the universe of possibilities that were open to Derek, hears it as <u>imitation</u>

Hears C# and intuitively recognises it as <u>imitation</u>

Shared understanding of the second C# deriving from the first

Figure 22 Step 4 *was for Derek and me to hear the low C sharp being played. Given the universe of 88 possible notes, I heard this as imitation, and I assumed from his pleasurable reaction that Derek did too. That is, we both heard the second C sharp as deriving from the first.*

sense that the first had generated the second (or that the second was derived from the first) through imitation.

Clearly, a crucial issue in this analysis is the precise nature of the perceived relationship between the notes. What it evidently does *not* represent is any kind of material connection between my pitch and Derek's: there is no direct *causal* link that made the second C sharp the same as the first. Rather, it is as though, when listening intuitively to this tiny musical fragment, we had both willingly suspended our disbelief, just as people do in hearing a story, reading a novel or watching a play. Here, however, the disbelief did not pertain to an imagined world conjured up through words, but to the *impression of one note influencing another*. It seemed that the complex chain of causation that *did* exist between my

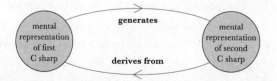

mental representation of first C sharp

generates

derives from

mental representation of second C sharp

Figure 23 *Imagined relationships between the two C sharps.*

brain and Derek's, which extended out into the physical world of the two pianos, had been mentally transferred to the notes themselves, rather as in Zuckerkandl's conjecture, made some fifty years earlier. There are echoes here, too, resonating even further back in time, of Arthur Schopenhauer's early nineteenth-century notion of music as being a direct embodiment of the 'will' that all things have to survive and to procreate. The tendency to endow inanimate objects – notes – with sentience, must surely be one of the most extraordinary characteristics that distinguishes us from other living creatures; that marks us out as being human.

* * *

This explanation of how a combination of repetition and intentionality – imitation – creates a sense of musical agency, through which one note is heard as generating another, appears to be satisfactory as far as it goes. But to what extent does it reflect the everyday experience of creating, re-creating or listening to music?

The notion of imitation is widely used by musicians in referring to the time-honoured technique[10] through which one part duplicates another in contrapuntal textures (in which different melodic lines occur at the same time). This approach finds its simplest expression in children's rounds: tunes in which young singers are intended to join in at different times, such as *Frère Jacques*, *London's Burning* and *Row, Row, Row Your Boat*, causing a polyphonic structure to be built up, in which the voices fit together in a harmonious way. Is this procedure underpinned by the same kind of repetition with intent that I had encountered in Derek's 'copy game'?

Consider, for example, *Row, Row, Row Your Boat*. Hum through the first phrase and pause at the point where the second part is supposed to enter. Think about (or sing) the first note of Voice 2. How did you know what it was supposed to sound like? Because you are aware (having heard the song before) that it should be the same as the opening note of Voice 1: the design of the round demands, whatever pitch Voice 1 starts on, Voice 2 must do the same, through imitation. In other words, the first pitch of Voice 2 is metaphorically controlled by that of Voice 1, and,

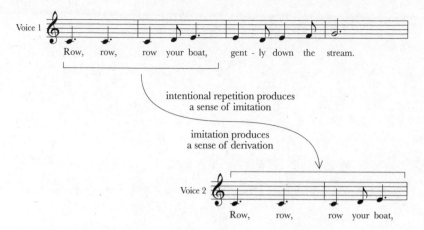

Figure 24 *A sense of derivation produced through voices imitating each other in* Row, Row, Row Your Boat.

by participating in the round, Voice 2 forsakes all the other notes that conceivably *could* have been sung. So, as with Derek's 'copy game', here is an example of intentional repetition producing a sense of agency. The principle does indeed appear to be the same in rounds.

We can further surmise that the effects of generation and derivation that are experienced (if only subconsciously) by the performers of rounds in a *proactive* way may be perceived *reactively* by listeners who are not part of the performance process, but who are nonetheless familiar with the general style and genre of the music, by mentally re-living, as it were, the imitative process.

So (thanks to the unknowing Derek) I stumbled across an explanation of just *how* repetition can create the illusion of musical structure in the mind, the element that is absent in the thinking of Schoenberg, Sélincourt, Zuckerkandl, Ruwet and the rest – even in Cone's reasoning, which comes so close. The new factor is the recognition of the potential role of perceived *intentionality* in musical repetition, giving the impression of one note controlling another. It is my belief that, from this sense of control, a feeling of agency is generated, which in turn gives rise to perceived structure.

* * *

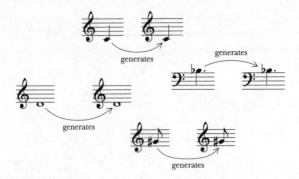

Figure 25 *Consciously repeating a note produces a sense of derivation through imitation.*

But are Derek's 'copy game' and the children's rounds special cases, since they involve at least two people, between whom there is manifestly a desire to replicate musical sounds? Can the same principle be extended, say, to a melody that is performed by one person?

To test this out, let us imagine that we are setting out to compose a simple tune. For the sake of argument, let's choose a mid-range note: 'middle C'.

What next? If we were to repeat the C, would it convey a sense of intentionality? Try singing or playing (or even just imagining) one note and then another the same. Do it slowly enough to give yourself time to reflect on the two sounds. Does the pitch of the second note appear to derive from that of the first? Try starting with a different pitch, and perform the same exercise. And then another. To me, each time I do this, it is rather like playing the 'copy game' on my own – whereby I provide both the model and its replication – and, since I can access memories of them in retrospect, I sense that there must be discrete representations of the pair of notes concerned, connected via an imitative relationship.

To see how this principle may extend to listening (rather than composing), reflect on your reaction to the openings of the following pieces, whose melodies all begin with two notes that are the same. Do you hear the second as being a copy of the first? When I listen to the tunes (or mentally replay them in my head), and contemplate what I am hearing, I *do* hear intentionality in the initial repetition, and therefore a sense of agency operating between their opening notes.

Figure 26 *Hearing a sense of derivation through imitation in familiar melodies.*

* * *

This phenomenologically-inspired approach to understanding how music works is unique in its capacity to probe what is a personal experience. But there are potential problems too. It may be that suggesting a certain mode of listening – drawing attention to specific features in the auditory landscape – affects the way in which the fragments of music are perceived. That is, the very act of introspection is likely to be a confounding factor in our thought experiment. Being asked whether one hears a given note as imitating another (rather than simply repeating it, with no sense of derivation) is rather like being guided to see a particular image in a Rorschach blot. Once one's perceptual faculties are led in a certain direction, it is difficult to avoid them going down that route. Similarly, one could argue that just because listeners *could* hear a passage of music in a certain manner, doesn't mean that they typically *do* (even subconsciously).

Nonetheless, it seems reasonable to assume, where successive notes are the same, that this repetition would normally be acknowledged at some level in cognition, otherwise it is difficult to see how listeners could make sense of music at all. And, if asked, they would surely be able to identify repetition overtly where it occurred. But do they generally perceive intentionality?

One way of tackling this question is to consider whether there are circumstances in which two sounds of the same pitch could plausibly be heard *without* them being considered to be connected imitatively – where there was no sense of intentionality in the repetition. What are the scenarios in which this may occur? Possibilities include sequences of everyday sounds that are alike. Consider, for example, the ticks of a clock. Although they may not have a readily discernible pitch, to my ears, these tiny pinpricks of sound provide a clear example of repetition that is not imitative: as I listen to the grandfather clock in the hall, I experience no sensation of intentionality existing between the ticks. Rather – and here it is striking just how important belief systems are in perception – I have the sense (informed by a sure knowledge) that the similitude of the ticks is driven by an external agency that they share in common: the clockwork mechanism.

But what about the chimes of the clock, which are ostensibly more musical in sound? As I listen to them now, I lean towards hearing each of the 'dings' following the first as imitating the one that preceded – in other words, as a kind of basic music – even though I know that, like the ticks, they are controlled mechanically. Indeed, I am reminded of Mussorgsky's tone poem *Night on the Bare Mountain*, in which a representation of the village church bell tolls to herald the coming of dawn. But mentally putting this to one side, and listening again, I find that I can hear the chimes the other way too: as an automated series of sounds, between which no sense of derivation exists.

It is worth reflecting on this ambiguity in a wider context. *Most* of the similarity that we perceive as a result of human endeavour appears to stem not from imitation, but from sets of things having been created through the same process. For example, the six HB pencils lying in an unopened packet on my desk are (virtually) identical not because any one is a copy of any other, but because they were all created by a single machine. And the same is true of the muddle of unwashed mugs nudging against my computer keyboard, of the ring binders on the shelves to my right, of the small, dark-red bricks in the Lutyens building (the architectural centre-piece of Linden Lodge School) opposite my house, of the series of street lamps in the road beyond ... the list is potentially endless.

Is the same true of nature? Peering through my study window I can see the late autumnal yellow leaves clinging on to the branches of the old oak tree at the end of the drive. The leaves share a close resemblance, not because any one of them exists as a replica of any other, but because they all grew from the same genetic blueprint in a (more or less) common environment.

It is interesting to note that, across the ages – from the ancient Judeo-Christian myth of God creating humans in his own image (Genesis 1:27) to the notion of 'autopoiesis' introduced some 2,500 years later by the Chilean biologists Humberto Maturana and Francisco Varela to define the self-maintaining chemistry of cells[11] – people have recognised that self-replication is integral to life. Put simply, every living thing on the planet is the product of another or others that are similar. And although the cost of existing within a relatively rapid evolutionary system has been the individual genetic compromise inherent in sexual reproduction, whereby the features of two entities are merged to create variation rather than to duplicate either one of them exactly, the principle of species perpetuating themselves through re-creation seems to be one that is deeply embedded in the human psyche. We can speculate whether it is through people (subconsciously) mimicking this natural process that musical structure (as defined here, in which one note is heard as generat-ing another through imitation) first arose. There is no way of knowing for sure, and rather than falling into the trap that ensnared and then corrupted the thinking of postmodernist musicologists such as Susan McClary who asserted causal relationships between phenomena in the 'real world' and in music merely on the grounds of shared surface fea-tures, it has to remain an intriguing speculation, albeit one with roots reaching down into the history of human thought as far as back as Aristotle.

A more prosaic question remains, though: the status of the clock chimes. What is it about these, in contrast to the ticks, that enables me to hear them as being imitative? The answer must presumably lie in the difference in the sounding quality of the ticks and the chimes. With their defined pitch and sustained sound, the chimes have an inherently more 'musical' ring to them than the perfunctory ticks. And it may be the case that sounds I have learnt to associate with music somehow prime my brain to process them in a particular way, which doesn't apply to other (non-musical) noises in the environment.

Some composers have enjoyed toying with this very ambiguity through using mechanical sounds to create music (by treating them imitatively): imbuing everyday sonic objects with new, aesthetic meanings by stripping away their functionality and placing them in an unfamiliar, artistic context, while at the same time, breathing new life into the notion of 'music' by extending listeners' auditory palettes. Consider, for example, Antheil's *Ballet Mécanique*, which incorporates the roar of aeroplane propellers, passages in Varèse's *Ionisation*, which use high and low sirens and an instrument termed a 'lion's roar', and the first of Schaeffer's *Études des Bruits*, which consists of transformed locomotive sounds. However, for more traditional listeners for whom the noises of a train will remain forever just that, we can assume that the music-syntactic processors in the brain will not be sparked into life.

Conversely, if I were to hear two successive musical sounds that were the same by chance (for example, on account of a child randomly hitting notes on a keyboard), I would be hard pressed *not* to hear one as a consequence of the other, even if I were aware of the arbitrary nature of their aetiology. And a further scenario comes to mind: that of a child playing notes on an instrument with only a single pitch, such as a chime bar. Again, it is difficult to imagine *not* hearing the results as imitative with regard to pitch, and therefore as music.

So, what constitutes music is in the ear of the beholder: it is perfectly possible for a series of sounds that were *not* intended to be heard musically to be perceived as such, while one person's sweet melody may be pure noise to another. However, the fact that, within cultures (and very often between them), most people would agree as to what amounts to music and what does not, is a fair indication that the types of sounds and the kinds of sonic organisation that trigger the ear to search for intentional repetition are common across broad groups of people. How the human brain learnt that musical sounds should be processed in a particular way – both ontogenetically (in our development as individuals) and phylogenetically (in our evolution as a species) – is clearly a crucial question that will be addressed in due course.

* * *

The notion of a special form of perceived relationship between sounds – a type of mental connection that makes music what it is, that has no physical correlate – is, by definition, abstract and so runs the risk of being somewhat fuzzy in conceptual terms. It is helpful, therefore, to have a label for the cognitive link between sounds through which a sense of intentional repetition is evoked, and a way of representing such relationships on the page. While undertaking research for my PhD as an external student at the University of London, I came across the Greek prefix, 'zygo-', which refers to a yoke, a union or the presence of two similar things, and it seemed to me that the idea of two notes that are the same being metaphorically yoked together in the mind perfectly captures the idea of repetition and intentionality. A suitable noun already existed too: 'zygon', which was previously defined as 'a connecting bar', and, more specifically, 'an H-shaped fissure of the brain'. To this I added a further definition: 'a perceived relationship between aspects of two sounds that are the same or similar, and through which one is heard to derive from the other through imitation.' From this I derived the adjective 'zygonic', and used the term 'zygonic relationship' to distinguish it from imagined connections between sounds that were *not* imitative.[12]

To represent zygonic relationships visually, I use a letter 'Z', placed over an arrow, indicating the direction in which imitation is felt to take effect. To indicate that *pitch* is the feature concerned, I add the superscript 'P'.

Zygonic relationships can function *proactively* in the creation of new musical structures, or *reactively* when these are recognised by listeners.

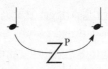

Figure 27 *Illustration of a zygonic relationship of pitch: a mental connection between two pitches that are the same, and through which one is felt to derive from the other.*

Consider, for example, the following melodies that open with a repeated pitch:

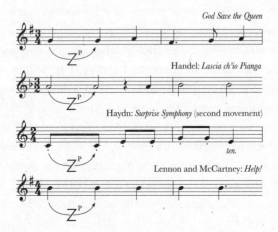

Figure 28 *Examples of zygonic relationships of pitch assumed to function reactively in pieces that use repeated pitches.*

There is clearly a lot more to music than pitches that are the same, though, and to see how zygonic theory can be extended, we will briefly return to my interactions with Derek.

Connections between Connections

In the previous chapter we saw that while individual pitches are important in music, it is the differences between them – 'intervals' – that give melodies and chords their identity. So a tune can be sung or played starting on any note, and will remain recognisable (indeed, most listeners would not notice if an entire piece were played in the 'wrong' key). *Relativity* holds sway in music, even for people like Derek, with his acute sense of absolute pitch, for whom each note sounds distinct.

From the very beginning of our work together, I aimed to foster and develop Derek's natural capacity for transposition: playing the same music, but starting on different notes. This is an invaluable skill both for technical reasons (since the layout of the keyboard is asymmetrical, moving a piece to a different key demands a high level of kinaesthetic awareness and physical agility) and because it achieves certain musical ends too. For example, it means that the accompaniments to songs can be subtly shifted up or down to suit the pitch range of different voices. When I first encountered Derek at home, he was already doing this instinctively when accompanying his belovèd but ageing Nanny, whose voice was somewhat past its prime, in songs of her youth (from the 1930s): he would repeatedly change key *mid-piece* if necessary to accommodate her sometimes erratic 'warbling' (as he was wont to call her vocal efforts).

To analyse the mental processing that transposition entails, consider the scenario in which I would teach Derek a melody and then have him perform it in a different key. Let's say I was introducing him to *When the Saints Go Marching In*. I might play the first line, thus:

Figure 29 When the Saints *beginning on C.*

And then ask Derek to play it starting F. Derek would be likely to respond with:

Figure 30 *Derek's version of* When the Saints, *beginning on F.*

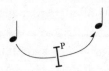

Figure 31 *Illustration of an 'interval': the perceived connection between two pitches that are different.*

So what is happening? Just what is Derek copying?

Here, the intentional repetition – the imitation – is not of notes but *intervals*. Zygonic theory can be used to explain how this works, and for that it will be helpful to represent intervals visually. I do this by using the letter 'I' (for 'interval'), superimposed with an arrow.[13] Here, a *half* arrowhead is used, in order to symbolise change (in contradistinction to the *full* arrowhead used to show repetition). Again, the superscript 'P' is used to show that the relationship pertains to pitch.

To listeners attending to music in a 'non-formalist' way (to borrow from Meyer's nomenclature), intervals simply pass by on a perceptual level, as differences in auditory sensations. But from the point of view of seeking to understand how music works, it can be useful to categorise them in terms of size, and to include this information in their representation as relationships – particularly since the way that standard Western music notation works means that this detail is not conveyed explicitly, but can only be inferred from reading a score (see Figure 17). The labels that musicians traditionally use to describe interval sizes are governed by a complex set of rules pertaining to the perceived function of the pitches on which they are anchored, and readers without that specialist knowledge who wish to know more should consult any standard text on music theory.[14] Suffice it to say that the interval between the first two notes of *When the Saints* (to the words 'O when') is called a 'major 3rd' – information that can be placed near the arrowhead (see Figure 32). It is this, and this alone, that Derek imitates (the pitches that he uses are different from mine).

So we can say that a zygonic relationship exists between the interval that I played and Derek's. Clearly, this imaginary connection that the brain constructs is rather different from a zygonic relationship between

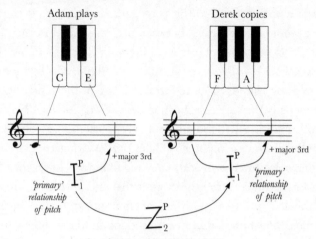

Figure 32 *Derek's imitation of the* difference *between pitches (rather than the notes themselves) results from a 'connection between connections': a* secondary *zygonic relationship of pitch between intervals that are the same.*

two notes of the same pitch; it works at a more abstract level, comparing *differences* between things, rather than the qualities of things themselves. By perceiving a relationship *between relationships*, it is as though we have gone two steps beneath the perceptual surface. Surprisingly, perhaps, this level of abstraction is commonplace in cognition. For example, as I glance out of my study window, I can see that the distance between two of the fence posts that define the boundary of my garden is the same as that separating a second pair; while, in a purely conceptual way, I can under-stand the equivalence of the father-son relationship that I have with my son Tom and that which my colleague, the music psychologist David Hargreaves, has with his son Jon.

It is useful to be able to distinguish relationships of this order with those that directly connect entities that we can perceive, and so the latter ('connections between things') I call 'primary', and the former ('connec-tions between connections') I term 'secondary'. This information can be included on the representation of relationships using a suitable subscript ('1' for primary and '2' for secondary).

Just as primary zygonic relationships (between pairs of identical pitches) are not confined to the 'copy game' scenario, so it is with secondary zygonic relationships (between intervals). And in the same way that the direct imitation of pitches is found in children's rounds (such as *Row, Row, Row Your Boat*), so the imitation of intervals (but not pitches) occurs in some 'canons': a more formal version of the genre. Among the most famous is the three-part canon *Non Nobis Domine* ('Not unto us, O Lord'), traditionally (though probably spuriously) attributed to the English Renaissance composer William Byrd. With deceptive simplicity, the second voice enters two beats later and four notes lower than the first; the third part comes in four beats after that and lower still. The effect is one of timeless beauty as, with no conscious effort, the ear instinctively grasps the connections between connections and hears how voices travelling 'horizontally' in time fit together 'vertically' in chaste Renaissance harmonies. The ingenuity of canons like this one is that all their material derives from a single line of music, in contrast to the more familiar scenario of a tune with a separate accompaniment. In Byrd's piece, the melody *is* its own accompaniment: an organic, parsimonious form of construction that lies at the heart of canons' aesthetic appeal (see Figure 33).

The imitation of intervals is not limited to that occurring *between* voices; on the contrary, I have never encountered a tune in which most of the differences between successive pitches do not recur, often repeatedly; it seems to be something that is fundamental to the way in which melodies are designed and understood. However, a sense of derivation linking differences in pitch is easiest to hear when entire motifs are transposed. This is because the impression that one interval is imitating another is reinforced by being part of a sequence of similar connections. This musical intuition appears to have been transferred from our common sense understanding of the world: the more features that two things or events have in common, the greater the probability that these similarities did not arise by chance, and the more strongly we believe that one was the cause of the other (or that they share a common root).

For example, consider the scenario in which a teacher is watching a group of young children playing outside, running and jumping and chasing one another. She notices that one child spins right around, and then another does the same. Was the second copying the first? It is hard

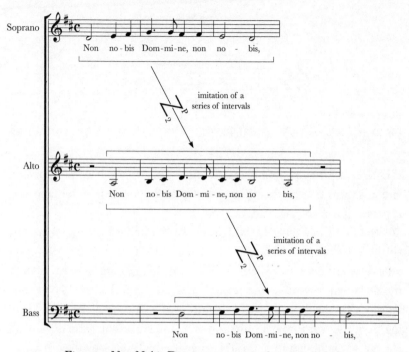

Figure 33 Non Nobis Domine: *a canon in three parts, which relies on the imitation of intervals through secondary zygonic relationships of pitch – 'connections between connections'.*

to say, since all the children are engaging in physical activity, and there are only so many different movements that they can make. But now the first child hops three times on his left leg and performs a star jump. Again, the second child does the same. This leaves the teacher in no doubt that one child is seeking to replicate what the other does.

And so it is in music – although in a melody, the sense of one motif imitating another usually passes by without our consciously being aware of it. However, by listening attentively it is possible to hear the process in action, and to this end, we will revisit one of the tunes that was cited in Chapter 1 as an example that makes use of transposition: the children's song *Hickory, Dickory Dock* (Figure 16). First published in London in the mid-eighteenth century, this is, ostensibly, a very straightforward little piece. As with all music that has stood the test of time, though, whatever the style and genre, when one starts to analyse how it works – even, in

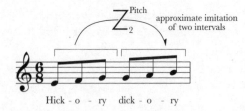

Figure 34 *Transposition in a melody functions through 'connections between connections'.*

this case, just the opening phrase – a host of subtleties become apparent, and it is these that might explain our continuing interest in the song as it is passed down the generations.

The first three notes (to which the word 'Hickory' is sung) mark out two intervals that are subsequently replicated – approximately – starting on a different pitch (for 'dickory'). This opening gesture is successful as a musical micro-narrative since it combines unity and change: it is my contention that the second motif is heard (usually subconsciously) as deriving from the first through imitation of its intervals, while also expressing change – it is higher in pitch. This engages the listener by fluently combining the strictures of musical logic with the freedom demanded by development. Interestingly, the structure of the music reflects the rhyme of 'Hickory, dickory', although here the nature of the change (the initial consonant) and the way it is integrated with repetition (the remainder of the word) are quite different. Together, though, the verbal rhyme and musical transposition are locked together to form a succinct auditory Gestalt that is both persuasive and memorable.

Taking a step back from accounts such as this, it seems paradoxical that a process so complex, which requires a considerable intellectual effort to understand, is usually accomplished by the brain apparently effortlessly and without our being aware of it. Even someone with severe learning difficulties, like Derek, can formulate connections between connections of pitch – secondary zygonic relationships – in a fraction of a second, it seems, with no effort at all, and wholly unknowingly. And he didn't need teaching how do to it. To put it another way, if Derek and the rest of us *didn't* have the capacity to abstract rules and other information from what we perceive, even our large human brains would quickly become overwhelmed; sets of relationships and instructions on how to use them require a fraction of the processing load of 'front line' perceptual data, and they can be stored much more efficiently too. So although it may seem as though we have a kind of record library in our minds – a private playlist to which we have unfettered access – it isn't really like that. The music collections that we harbour do not principally comprise representations of sounds, but are more like MIDI files: instructions as to how to re-create pieces, potentially in different contexts. We will discuss this in more detail in Chapter 5.

In music, the coding of sounds as information abstracted from the perceptual 'surface' also enables us to recognise (and enjoy) different performances of the same piece (since a series of similar relationships and rules apply to both, despite potential differences in the notes themselves). And it enables us to access our musical library in other ways too – searching by any feature that we choose. For example, if a listener were asked to think of tunes that begin in the same way as *When the Saints* (that is, with the interval of a 'major 3rd' between the first two notes), this should be achievable relatively easily (examples that spring immediately to mind include *Kumbaya*, *Michael Row the Boat Ashore* and Stevie Wonder's *Sir Duke*). The identification of appropriate melodies is possible because we can search for and locate songs that begin with the instruction that can be conceptualised as 'ascend a major 3rd'. If we had no option but to scour through memory traces of melodies and harmonies each represented as a series of absolute pitches, it would be a far more onerous task – every piece requiring a separate calculation to determine its opening interval. As we shall see, a comparable principle applies in relation to rhythm: pieces can be played at different speeds, yet still be regarded as 'the same thing' because their temporal data are stored primarily as ratios.

* * *

There exists another device, similar to transposition, through which composers can connect one motif coherently to another, and which also involves systematic change: 'inversion'. This entails intervals, in effect, being turned upside down. Inversion is possible since differences in pitch

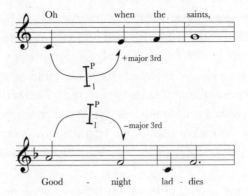

Figure 35 *Melodic intervals of the same size but opposite polarity.*

have a certain 'polarity', whereby they can either ascend (move to a note that sounds higher) or descend (go to one that sounds lower). So, for example, the interval with which *When the Saints* begins is the same size as that which opens *Goodnight Ladies*, though the two have opposite polarity (the first rises, the second falls).

Inversion features widely, though unobtrusively, in melodies from all styles and genres. It appears to be a form of musical development that the ear learns to detect effortlessly,[15] in the same way that the visual system intuitively grasps the notion of mirror images, without needing to understand the mathematics involved at a conceptual level. Take, for example, the opening three-note motif of *Hickory, Dickory*: if, instead of transposing it, we invert it, the consequent musical structure is no less difficult to follow (see Figure 36).

In terms of musical structure, inversion works through the *size* of an interval being imitated but not its *direction* (which is reversed). The mental connection through which this transformation occurs is called an 'inverse' zygonic relationship, which is illustrated with a 'minus' prefix placed before the 'Z'.

Sometimes composers use inversion more overtly, calling attention to this special form of relationship, by using a distinctive rhythm, for instance, or by giving a particularly prominent place in the musical texture to the motifs concerned. Brahms provides a striking example in the opening of the second movement of his 4th Symphony, when the

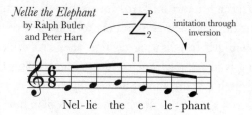

Figure 36 *Melodic inversion.*

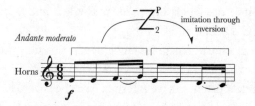

Figure 37 *Melodic inversion heralds the opening of the third movement of Brahms' 4th Symphony.*

horns introduce the main theme unaccompanied. Although the pitches are the same as those used in *Nellie the Elephant*, the effect couldn't be more different.

Frameworks of Pitch

Inversion and transposition may seem simple enough in principle, but there are nuances in the patterns of intervals used that add another layer of meaning to almost all music. These small irregularities, evident in the transformations shown in Figures 34, 36 and 37, enable each pitch to be perceived as fulfilling a unique role in relation to every other; within the shell of structural repetition, they provide the means for the melody to operate teleologically – seeming to drive towards a goal, to strive for closure, in a way that stylistically attuned listeners instinctively understand.

To fathom how this process works, it's necessary to appreciate that composers' choice of pitch has traditionally been highly constrained. And this is not just to do with writing music for instruments that have more or less fixed tuning systems (such as the piano). Even the repertoires of those with intonation that can vary (like the violin) still usually employ one of only a few basic *frameworks* of pitch. In performance this configuration is often bent (though never buckled) for expressive effect, through the introduction of devices such as 'portamento' (sliding from one note to another) and 'vibrato' (a pulsating change of pitch). But for now the important thing is to acknowledge the deeper underlying regularities in the domain of pitch that are almost universally present in music.

There are various analogies that can help to explain how pitch frameworks operate. One way is to view the pitches that are available to composers as a kind of preordained alphabet – indeed, this is the thinking behind the pitch nomenclature used in English and some other languages: A, B, C, D, E, F and G.

But whereas we can recognise any letter in isolation through having learnt the alphabet as a child, and know where it sits in relation to its neighbours, unless listeners have AP, they *won't* be able to identify a given pitch, nor, therefore, know where it belongs in a series. So how do most listeners manage?

As is so often the case, the solution that a human brain (or, more likely, several brains) came up with, unwittingly, no doubt, over a period of time in prehistory is startlingly simple yet brilliantly effective: cross-culturally, frameworks of pitch evolved that were based on intervals of two (or sometimes three) different sizes, configured in an asymmetrical pattern. This notion is so readily and intuitively apprehensible that children in the early years can grasp how pitch frameworks function merely through exposure to music in a particular style. The crucial thing is that sufficient *difference* is present to enable the position of a given pitch on the framework to become apparent relatively quickly in the course of a piece, while there is also enough *similarity* to avert cognitive overload, since the intervals only differ marginally and tend to be used repeatedly within a framework.

The most frequently used pitch framework in Western music[16] forms the 'major scale', which can be heard by playing the white notes on a piano up or down from any 'C' (see Figure 38). Once the nearest 'C' to the right or left of the first has been reached, the scale can be repeated – to the limits of the keyboard in either direction. This is possible since notes that are eight scale-steps apart (an 'octave' in musical parlance) have a special acoustic affinity, brought about by their close relationship within

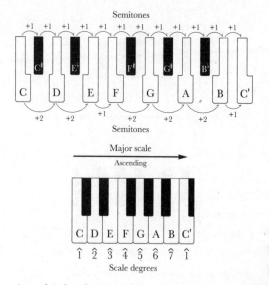

Figure 38 *The major scale is based on an asymmetrical pattern of two different intervals.*

the harmonic series (see Figure 3). Given that the intervals between adjacent notes on the keyboard (black or white) are all the same (each comprising a 'semitone'), it follows that the major scale, ascending, is defined by the following intervals, expressed in semitones: +2, +2, +1, +2, +2, +2, +1.

Following Schenker, musicians label the pitches that form a scale by using numbers with carets: $\hat{1}, \hat{2}, \hat{3}, \hat{4}, \hat{5}, \hat{6}, \hat{7}$ (see Figure 38). These are known as scale 'degrees'. Due to the effect of octave equivalence, degrees work in 'base eight': that is, they repeat every eighth note. So a pitch that would otherwise be labelled as $\hat{8}$ appears as $\hat{1}, \hat{9}$ is designated as $\hat{2}$ and so on. In its descending form, $\hat{7}, \hat{6}, \hat{5}, \hat{4}, \hat{3}, \hat{2}, \hat{1}$, the intervals that comprise the major scale are inverted and played in reverse order: −1, −2, −2, −2, −1, −2, −2 semitones.

Generally speaking, music that uses a pitch framework corresponding to the major scale is held, in Western cultures at least, to elicit a positive emotional response: in everyday terms, it sounds happy. There are a number of theories as to why this should be so,[17] including the framework's potential derivation from the harmonic series, thereby affirming intervals that are present in natural sounds. In particular, degrees $\hat{1}, \hat{3}$, and $\hat{5}$ are particularly strongly represented in the overtone series,

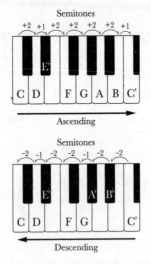

Figure 39 *The ascending and descending forms of the melodic minor scale (beginning on C).*

and, as Figure 3 shows, these form a 'major' chord – a harmony that has such a powerful identity for listeners steeped in the tradition of Western music, that it brings to mind the framework of the major scale as a whole, and means that there is an intimate relationship between melody (successions of pitches) and harmony (their simultaneous aggregation into a single percept).[18] Whatever its origin, the capacity of pieces that use the pitch framework based on the major scale to evoke positive emotions is constantly reinforced in Western culture through association with events (such as weddings) and scenarios (in films, for example) that are cheerful and reassuring.

The other pitch framework that is generally (though much less frequently) used in Western music is based on the 'minor' scale, which is generally thought – and experienced – to elicit sadness. Again, this reaction appears to arise from a combination of an innate response and cultural reinforcement.[19] The disposition of the minor scale is rather less stable than the major, with alternate rising and descending forms (and possible combinations of the two). The version that ascends is the same as the major scale, but with the third degree moved down by one semitone: +2, +1, +2, +2, +2, +2, +1. The critical relationship here is that between $\hat{1}$ and the 'flattened' $\hat{3}$ – an interval that musicians term a 'minor 3rd'. It is this that gives the scale its special character.

The variant of the minor scale that descends is, as the nineteenth century German theorist Hugo Riemann observed,[20] an exact inversion of the major scale: −2, −2, −1, −2, −2, −2, −1. Moreover, by starting this descent on 'A', the scale uses only (and all) the white notes on the keyboard: the same set of pitches as the major scale starting on 'C'. This shows that there is potentially a good deal of overlap between major and minor pitch frameworks, a correspondence that plays a crucial role in the capacity of Western music to convey a complex mix of emotions within a short space of time.

The fact that both major and minor pitch frameworks have an asymmetrical design (whereby each pitch occupies a unique position in relation to others) has important consequences not only for our ability to understand music, but also the way it functions aesthetically. Crucially, as we have already observed, the asymmetrical design of scales enables each degree to be perceived as fulfilling a distinct *function*. This is what musicians mean by the concept of 'tonality'. The functions associated with each scale degree are defined and reinforced through the idiosyncratic patterns of transitions that occur in music between the pitches pertaining to frameworks. For example, $\hat{7}$, particularly when it is harmonised with a 'dominant' chord (that is built on $\hat{5}$), typically rises to $\hat{1}$, which, in this context, tends to be harmonised with a 'tonic' chord (constructed on the first degree). This combination of melody and harmony, typical of traditional Western classical music, is known as a 'perfect cadence'. Examples are shown in Figure 40. The powerful impact of perfect cadences derives from composers imitating them, time and time again, evoking a strong sense of closure in listeners familiar with the style (rather as the word 'Amen' does in Jewish, Christian and some Islamic prayers).

The asymmetrical design of pitch frameworks has other effects too: for example, while all the intervals are small enough to be processed as single steps on a 'ladder' of pitch, the fact that there are differences between them means that when motifs are transposed, they can be regarded both as the same as the original (in the sense of maintaining a particular sequence of changes of scale degree) yet transformed (since the precise nature of

Figure 40 *Examples of perfect cadences.*

the intervals concerned is likely to vary). I believe that it is this capacity for reappearances of a motif to be at once congruent with another, yet differ from each other, that underpins much of music's ability to form an emotional narrative in sound. In particular the fact that a motif based on a major harmony can be transformed to the minor, *yet remain in the context of a pitch framework based on the major scale*, and *vice versa*, is of central importance to the perceived expressivity of Western tonal music.

A visual analogy can be found in photo-mosaics that use many small faces to create a single big one. It is perfectly conceivable that the miniatures, of which the large image is constructed, may be mainly or even entirely of people looking sad, while the bigger, composite picture depicts someone with a happy expression. So, there is a mismatch between the detail and the whole. In music, as the emotional narrative moves through time, this contrast enables composers to take the ear on a journey of tonal conflict and resolution.

Take, for example, the opening of Bach's 1st Prelude of Book 1 of *The Well-Tempered Clavier*, BWV 846, in C major (which the nineteenth-century French composer Charles Gounod subsequently used as the basis of his *Méditation sur le Premier Prélude de Piano de S. Bach*, better known as the 'Ave Maria'). The whole piece comprises a series of broken chords, but

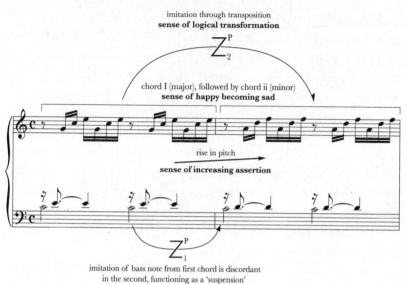

Figure 41 *The subtle combination of similarity and change in the opening of Bach's Prelude, BWV 846 produces a sense of yearning at once simple yet complex, immediate yet profound.*

it is only the first two iterations that will concern us here. The underlying harmonies are C major (chord 'I') and D minor (the chord on the second degree, labelled 'ii'), which, as we have seen, are liable to evoke contrasting affective responses: in broad terms, major sounding 'happy' and minor 'sad'. So listeners are presented with a motif that is likely to come across at first as positive and cheerful, but which is almost immediately transformed into something that is potentially rather melancholy. However, this change is tempered by the fact that the pitch of the top line (the melody in Gounod's version) rises, a move that is generally felt to be assertive – to give a positive sense of change[21] – while the lowest note, which is concordant in C major, is held over or 'suspended' under the chord of D minor, forming a dissonance that has a sense of needing to be resolved. To my ears, this intricate fusion of similarity and difference, of major becoming minor, imbues the music with a sense of yearning – a complex emotion that, amazingly, is evoked by a series of abstract sounds through the blend of regularity and irregularity inherent in the design of the major scale.

Beyond the mixed emotions elicited by the first two bars, it is of interest to observe, as the piece unfolds, that a little under half of the first forty-six appearances of the prevailing broken-chord motif, which lead the listener up to the final, sustained 'dominant pedal' (a long bass note on the fifth degree of the scale, against which a series of different harmonies are heard) express minor or 'diminished' harmonies – chords that are made up entirely of minor 3rds. In my view, Bach's repeated reference to these more wistful chords that can be created within the pitch framework based on the major scale contribute significantly to the prelude's emotional depth. Without them, we can speculate that the music would have been unable to offer a persuasive reflection of Bach's inner world, in which complete happiness (which would be depicted through unrelenting major harmonies) would have been a chimera.

Later composers, such as Schubert, exploited the major-minor dialectic in a more overt way, moving beyond the juxtaposition of individual motifs in different modes to setting contrasting pitch frameworks side by side. The song cycle *Die Winterreise*, a bleak but mesmerising masterpiece of despair, completed just before the composer's death in 1828, sets twenty-four poems by Wilhelm Müller, which begin by depicting the physical journey of a man seeking to escape from the loss of love and end metaphysically by portraying the futility of life. In Song 5, *Der Lindenbaum*, as the poet-narrator's thoughts vacillate between the warmth of happy memories and the icy reality of his current plight, the sweet contentment of the major mode is transformed into the sour despondency of the minor. This is achieved by maintaining all the pitches in the melody save the crucial third degree, which falls a semitone – a change that is reinforced in the accompaniment, which sees a hymn-like serenity replaced with restless unease. Hence, unlike the initial transition in Bach's C major prelude, where the transposed second version of the motif is heard as a *development* of the second (and the sense of the music moves on), here the effect is one of adversity *supplanting* good fortune, and emotionally there is a disjunction in the musical narrative (see Figure 42).

If the shift from major to minor has tragic consequences, the opposite – a move from minor to major, from dark to light, can be triumphant (as in the last movement of Beethoven's 5th Symphony), or it can be

Figure 42 *Schubert uses a change of mode (from major to minor), combined with repetition, to produce a sense of sadness* supplanting *happiness in* Der Lindenbaum.

bittersweet indeed. For example, in the first song of the *Winterreise* cycle, Schubert uses this device to create a moment of exquisite tenderness as the journeyman switches his attention from wandering across snow-covered fields to the thought of his loved one, asleep and dreaming. There is a temporary feeling of warmth as a small flame of memory flickers into life, but the listener who knows the song senses that it won't survive the chill wind of fate for long. This awareness, which is not shared by the narrator, adds a sense of pathos. The last verse of the poem, describing how the wanderer wrote on his lover's gate 'Gute Nacht' ('Goodnight'), is heard twice – and set to music that remains in the major mode. Perhaps there is hope after all? No. With its ultimate breath, the melody bows to

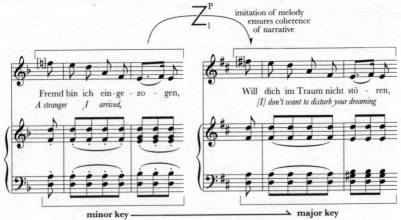

the change from minor to major mode is ostensibly positive, but, to the knowledgeable listener, who has an awareness of what is in store for the poet-narrator (the final change back to the minor key), it gives a particular sense of pathos

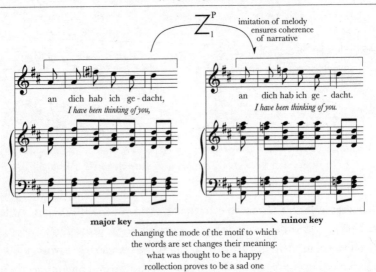

changing the mode of the motif to which the words are set changes their meaning: what was thought to be a happy recollection proves to be a sad one

Figure 43 *The change to major in* Gute Nacht *is poignant given the broader context of the minor mode.*

the inevitable, and the final line 'An dich hab' ich gedacht' ('I have been thinking of you') is repeated in the minor, cutting through the blended musical-poetic narrative with a jagged sense of despair from which there can be no recovery. The die for the rest of *Winterreise* is cast.

* * *

The imitation of intervals evidently fulfils a crucial role in the understanding of music, both in the way that entire pieces are represented in memory, enabling us to acknowledge different performances as distinct versions of a single conceptual entity, and, within the course of a single composition, as the structural means through which transposition occurs. As we noted above, however, the process of repeating the difference between one pitch and the next (irrespective of whether the intervals concerned ascend or descend) lies behind the moment-to-moment structure of most melodies: it is a form of organisation that is ubiquitous in music, and is reflected in the structure of the pitch frameworks that inform composition. There is also a tendency in almost all genres for small intervals to occur much more frequently than large ones.[22] My own study of the first movement of Mozart's Piano Sonata, K. 333[23] (of which more later) shows a broadly typical distribution, with over 60 per cent of melodic intervals comprising a single scale-step. But how much of this duplication is likely to be heard as imitative?

To get to grips with this question, we'll consider the opening of the sonata: a largely unaccompanied descent of six notes – each separated from the next by a fall of one scale-step. The issue is this: does the second interval sound as though it derives from the first, the third seem to stem from the second, and so on? In my view this *is* the case, for the same reason that one sound followed by another (in a musical context) will evoke a sense of imitation. To think the opposite would imply a belief that the pattern arose by chance, with no sense of human agency. But this is clearly not the case, and so I believe that the brain interprets the structure underpinning a scale such as the one used by Mozart as a chain of *secondary zygonic relationships of pitch*.

A visual analogy would be a teacher watching a pupil sketch an abstract design. Looking over his pupil's shoulder, the teacher watches as she draws a small star, then another, and then another, whereby the distance between the second and the third is about the same as that separating the first and the second. What is the teacher likely to think? It seems improbable that he would regard the pattern made by the stars as

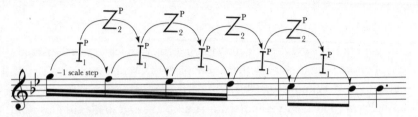

Figure 44 *Each melodic interval in the opening of K. 333 is heard to exist in imitation of the one that precedes through connections between connections – secondary zygonic relationships of pitch.*

occurring by chance. And we can assume that the addition of further stars would strengthen his belief that the sequence was generated imitatively.

An intriguing and important question is whether – in the case of the musical scale or the sequence of stars or, indeed, any other comparable artistic creation – a sense of derivation extends beyond successive relationships to those that are separated by other notes (or stars). For example, in the opening of Mozart's sonata, is the interval between notes three and four, as well as being perceived to imitate the interval between notes two and three, also heard as echoing the difference between notes one and two? And what about that between notes five and six? Even a relatively short sequence of notes can theoretically harbour many relationships.

Hence a potential *network* of connections may be activated in the mind upon hearing any series of intervals that are the same. This in turn implies two assumptions, which are fundamental to zygonic theory. First, the interval between two pitches may be thought to exist in imitation of *any number of others*. And second, such an interval may itself be the subject of imitation *any number of times* (see Figure 45).

Now it may be that some connections are more salient than their neighbours on account of the relative prominence of the notes to which they pertain in domains other than pitch (such as loudness). In this case we can surmise that their imitative effect would be more powerful too. However, other things being equal, it seems probable that the greater intervals' separation in time, and the more intervening material that exists between them (with its potential for cognitive interference), the weaker the imitative effect is likely to be.[24]

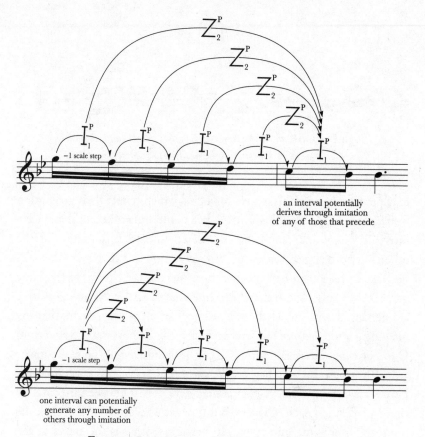

Figure 45 *Potential networks of imitative relationships exist between intervals that are the same.*

But does there come a point at which the zygonic effect disappears altogether? Consider, for example, identical intervals that are separated by some margin, such as the ones between notes four and five, and fifteen and sixteen in K. 333.

Focussing on these out of the usual listening context, it feels as though there must be some logical connection between them, since the likelihood of two differences in pitch that are the same occurring by chance is so remote. But intuitively it doesn't seem plausible to assert that one exists directly in imitation of the other. Rather, the perceived relationship between these intervals appears to be more like the connections that we

Figure 46 *Intervals from a single melody that are the same, between which direct imitation seems unlikely to be perceived.*

may perceive between the leaves on a tree, which reflect their generation from a shared genetic blueprint. What is the musical equivalent? Two intervals where one cannot be considered to exist in imitation of the other, but both appear to derive from a common source.

This scenario can be explained by returning once more to the 'copy game' – but this time we will imagine that both Derek and Anthony are playing it with me at the same time. Let us assume, again, that my opening gambit is *When the Saints*, which I ask the boys to transpose from C to A (using a musical prompt). They both successfully copy the major 3rd with which the song begins. We can presume that imitative connections – *secondary zygonic relationships of pitch* – exist between the interval that I played and each of theirs. But now let us place an observer in the room to witness the interaction. In her mind, what is the status of the connection between the intervals that Derek and Anthony played? She will be aware that neither interval derives from the other, but both stem from a single source. So she may perceive what I call an *indirect* zygonic relationship between them.

Indirect zygonic connections of this type are of enormous importance in music; without them, the art form simply couldn't function. We've already noted that in the construction of a piece of music, it is essential that listeners should not be overloaded with too much information. Responding intuitively to human perceptual constraints, composers tend to position pitch and rhythm in the foreground of a piece, with other auditory features, including loudness and timbre, used mostly for background continuity. We will examine these secondary aspects of musical design in the light of zygonic theory shortly, and set out the major role that indirect imitation plays in their formulation. For now, though, we will demonstrate how, even within the domain of pitch, there are different organisational strata functioning simultaneously, and show how some that exist in the background rely on imitative relationships functioning *indirectly*.

A basic level of consistency is guaranteed through composers drawing on the same small stock of intervals, derived from a common pitch framework, over and over again, while at the same time using those same intervals to construct more substantial melodic shapes that stand out as the basic building blocks of music: motifs. These acquire individuality through aggregations of intervals working together as single units (and, as will become apparent, operating hand-in-hand with rhythm). So, in music, as far as pitch is concerned, the background and the foreground are *made up of the same thing*. Each interval has the capacity to fulfil a dual function.

Once more, an analogy will help to make clear what is occurring. Consider the mosaic shown in Figure 47. It is made up of twelve different tiles, which recur throughout. The general pattern that they make is more or less immediately apparent to the eye intent on seeing detail. However, taking a broader view, it is evident that the tiles also cluster together in the mind to form larger shapes, which are themselves repeated. In Figure 47, their identity is reinforced through shading.

Seeing the mosaic reminds us that musical motifs may be structured in two ways through *direct* relationships: internally, when adjacent, or nearly adjacent, pitches or intervals imitate one another, as in the opening of K. 333, for example (see Figure 46), and externally, when a sequence of pitches or intervals is replicated: see, for instance, Bach's Prelude in C Major (Figure 41) and Schubert's *Gute Nacht* (Figure 43). But what is the source of the *indirect* relationships that are presumed to link intervals that are the same, and which are widely separated in time? The answer can be found in the construction of a pitch framework that is held in our minds. Where do pitch frameworks originate? From the pieces of music that we hear. And how are they reinforced? Through our constant exposure to music that uses them. Therefore, we can surmise that, generally speaking, we hear all intervals that are the same as echoing one another on account

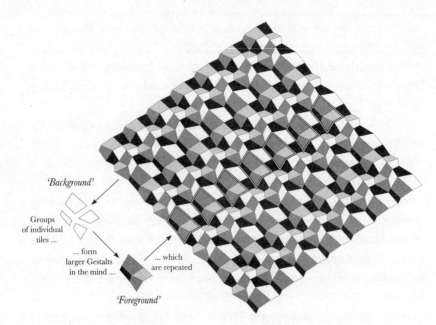

Figure 47 *The tiles of the mosaic function to create 'foreground'
and 'background' patterns in the mind.*

of a weak imitative force that constantly operates in the background of
our musical experience.

Rhythm and Metre

So far, our discussion of zygonic theory has focussed on pitch, and how
a single, universal principle – that of imitation – appears to underpin a
range of different types of musical structure. We now move on to consider rhythm, which is typically the other main load-bearing dimension
of music.

Ask classically-trained Western musicians about rhythm, and they
will often talk in terms of note-lengths or 'durations': semibreves, minims,
crotchets, quavers and the like in UK English – whole-notes, half-notes,
quarter-notes and eighth-notes in the US. This is because of the way
that notation works: players and singers can tell when a note is supposed
to begin based on the length of the one that precedes; when one note
ends, the next usually starts. However, this is not how *listeners* intuitively

perceive things; it is the point at which notes begin, or their 'onsets', that are of most importance. This is why it is possible to *clap* a rhythm that was intended for performance on instruments with a sustained sound, or for voices, without compromising its identity.

Like pitch, 'onset' – or the point in time when a note begins – is what may be termed a 'variable' of the sounds that make up music. As the name suggests, a variable is a perceived quality or feature whose appearance is not fixed. For example, pitch exists on a theoretical continuum, ranging from the highest imaginable sound to the lowest. But onset is rather different. It defines a note's location in the dimension of time. And although, in the case of simultaneity, onsets can be the same, once a particular onset has occurred, it can never be repeated. So, it would seem reasonable to assume that zygonic theory, whose central premise is that structure occurs through imitation, cannot apply in this domain. However, although the point in time when a given rhythm occurs cannot be replicated, the rhythmic pattern itself can. So just what is it that is being duplicated?

To address this question, let us return once more to Derek's 'copy game' and ascertain what would have occurred if I'd played a short rhythm and he had echoed it. Let us imagine that the rhythm comprised the first six notes of the Christmas carol *O Come, All Ye Faithful*, passing by at a moderately brisk pace, where each crotchet beat lasts for half a second. How would Derek have imitated what I played? First, we can assume that he would have constructed a temporary model of the motif in his mind, to which he subsequently had access, and which included information about the length of time between the beginning of each note and the next. Music psychologists term such relationships 'inter-onset intervals' (or 'IOIs'). Although in Derek's mind such relationships would have existed at a purely intuitive, unthinking level, in order to assist our analysis, it is reasonable, nonetheless, to view them through the lens of conceptual understanding. Hence the IOIs may be defined in terms of seconds, for example, although such units of time would have had no meaning for Derek (beyond their phenomenological impact). The fact that Derek reproduced these IOIs implies that imitation must have occurred through connections between connections: secondary zygonic relationships. And

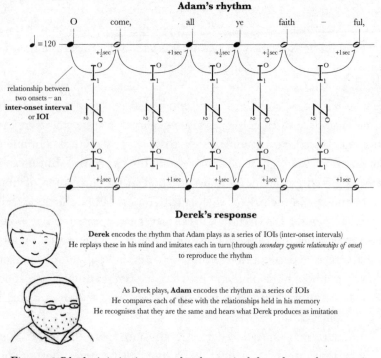

Figure 48 *Rhythmic imitation created and recognised through secondary zygonic relationships of onset during a rendition of the first line of* O Come, All Ye Faithful.[25]

in recognising that Derek copied what I did, we can surmise that I must have re-created a form of these relationships in my mind too.

So we have a process that in some way corresponds to transposition in the realm of pitch. But here, it is the onsets of notes that are transposed – shifted forward – in time. It is remarkable, and a characteristic that appears to be unique to music, that the same logical principle lies behind the way that organisation works in different domains, with structurally equivalent, but perceptually distinct, results.[26]

The similarities between the ways in which pitch and rhythm are structured do not end with the repetition of motifs. Just as melodic intervals are frequently imitated in the course of melodies, so it is with IOIs, where, by a considerable margin, the ratio 1 : 1 dominates rhythmic design.[27] That is to say, by far the most common scenario in music is for an IOI to be followed by another one that is the same. The opening of

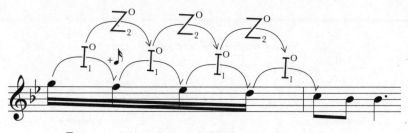

Figure 49 *A chain of identical IOIs that opens Mozart's Piano Sonata, K. 333, deemed to exist through imitation.*

Mozart's Piano Sonata K. 333, discussed above in relation to the structure of its descending scale (see Figure 44), also provides a typical example of a chain of identical IOIs, each of which may be heard as being derived through the imitation of those that precede.

Astonishingly, the 1 : 1 ratio characterises almost 80 per cent of successive IOIs (equating to around 1,270 relationships) in the melody line of the first movement of K. 333 taken as a whole, and so, as with pitch, we have a form of 'background' organisation that is held together with indirect zygonic links. And, as is the case with pitch, these innumerable imitative relationships plug into an imaginary framework of equally-spaced time intervals, constantly being rolled forward in the mind as music is performed or heard: facilitating memory, framing understanding and fuelling expectation. Furthermore, just as not every pitch has to be present for the brain to recognise an underlying framework such as the major scale, neither does every IOI need to be anchored to a note that is physically present for a regular beat to be established in the mind of the listener.

Consider, for example, Erik Satie's *Première Gymnopédie* for piano. A dotted minim is used to open the bass line, which is followed, after a crotchet rest, by a chord whose duration is a minim. This pattern is repeated a further three times before the melody, in crotchets, enters in the right hand in bar 5. The ear has a strong tendency to hear a regular beat in music, yet in the introduction to the *Gymnopédie* one does not exist. So what does the musical mind do? It *imagines* a pulse where one is not present. This process is achieved by a process of extrapolation: through taking the IOI that exists between the opening bass note

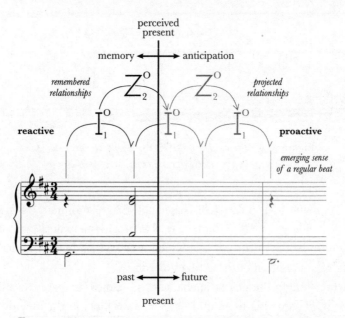

Figure 50 *The sense of a regular beat emerges through the projection of imitation into the future in Erik Satie's* Première Gymnopédie.

and the first chord, and projecting it into the temporal space created by the minim through a secondary zygonic relationship. That is, the minim chords become mentally subdivided into two crotchets, and a regular three-beat pattern is heard.

In many styles, this 'main beat' of a piece (to which listeners instinctively tap their feet or clap their hands) can be subdivided, forming a potential hierarchy of faster micro-beats, nested within slower ones. Musicians call this phenomenon 'metre'. To hear this in action, consider *Rockin' All Over the World* by Status Quo. Here, there are *four* readily detectable beats occurring at the same time, each in a ratio of 2 : 1 with the next nearest in the hierarchy (see Figure 51).

In other styles, the relationship between beats at different metrical levels may be conceived, to a greater or lesser extent, as being *additive* (rather than *divisive*).[28] In the past, Western musicologists regarded music from their own tradition as being largely 'divisive' in metrical terms, whereas sub-Saharan African and South Asian rhythms were thought primarily to be additive. However, this stance has since been

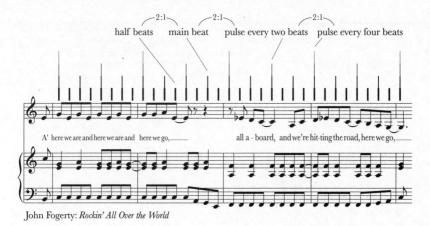

John Fogerty: *Rockin' All Over the World*

Figure 51 Rockin' All Over the World *expresses a hierarchy of four pulses in the ratio 2:1.*

criticised as a post-colonial oversimplification,[29] and a conception of metre as groups of pulses (even or uneven) taken to offer a truer, more inclusive model.[30] [31] Consider, for example, Dave Brubeck's *Blue Rondo à la Turk* (1959), which begins with the quavers in each bar grouped as 2+2+2+3. After three iterations this pattern is replaced with 3+3+3, followed by a return to 2+2+2+3. So the bars are the same length (nine quavers), but the way they are parsed, into even and uneven groups, alternates. Arguably, it is this metrical switching that gives the music its special character.

Whatever one's view, the phenomenon of 'metre' may be modelled by thinking of the musical framework of time as wrapped around a rotating cylinder. A regular point of reference is provided by an added emphasis being applied (physically or perceptually or both) to one or more of the pulses. Unfurling this imaginary cylinder yields a notional 'two-dimensional' framework (Figure 52), upon which notes can be positioned in pitch and time, such that every location is at once *distinct* yet *replicable*. Frameworks with this dual characteristic are fundamental to music, since, as we have seen, pieces rely on repetition for structure and, ultimately, meaning. From a cognitive perspective, the music psychologist John Sloboda contends that such frameworks are a *necessary* feature of music, since they enable musical understanding to get off the ground.[32] It

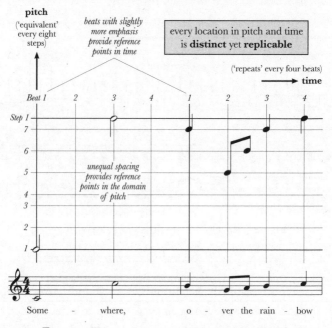

Figure 52 *The imaginary two-dimensional framework of pitch and time that lies in the background of music.*

is certainly the case that frameworks are a universal feature of virtually all traditional styles and genres, and children typically grasp the pitch-time frameworks that are pertinent to their culture from around the age of four (sometimes earlier, sometimes later). This enables them to sing short songs with which they are familiar from beginning to end, in time and in tune (see Chapter 4).

The crucial thing is that faster beats do not exist independently of slower ones; they are locked into a shared framework through a process of synchronisation. The points at which beats on different levels in the hierarchy coincide are emphasised in perception, and they appear to have a greater stability than their neighbours, functioning as 'anchors', upon which pieces almost invariably end. So metre can be understood to function in some ways like tonality in the domain of pitch. And just as composers can create a sense of the unexpected in relation to pitch, through setting up patterns whose continuation is thwarted or by selecting relatively unusual transitions between scale degrees, so comparable

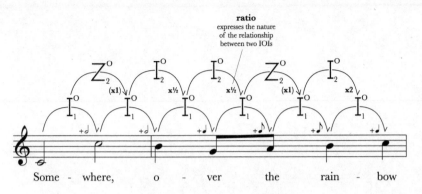

Figure 53 *Rhythms are stored in long-term memory as ratios at secondary level.*

effects are possible by toying with the expectations generated by metre – by shifting the onsets of notes so that they occur just before or after the main perceived pulse, for example. Musicians term this sense of rhythmic tension 'syncopation', and Status Quo use it to great effect in the chorus of *Rockin'*, repeatedly adding punch to the word 'like' by having it occur a fraction of a second before the beat (just in case listeners had any doubt as to the band's fondness for rock'n'roll).

The pitch content of melodies is stored in long-term memory largely as intervals, which represent the perceived *differences* between notes (rather than the notes themselves). With regard to rhythm, the brain primarily encodes music in an even more abstract way, as the *ratios* that can be heard to exist *between inter-onset intervals*: that is, as secondary relationships – connections between connections. These are usually judged in relation to an underlying beat. So in my mind (and yours), the rhythm of the opening phrase of *Somewhere Over the Rainbow* is reduced in long-term memory to a series of five ratios: x1, x½, x½, x1, x2.

Having a cognitive representation of rhythm at this level of abstraction is essential, since it enables us to hear a piece of music played at different speeds or 'tempos', without each rendition sounding like a completely different musical entity. So, as a performer plays a piece by ear (without the use of notation) and a listener, who is familiar with the music, attends to the new rendition, unlikely though it may seem, their brains are processing imitative connections between connections *between connections*;

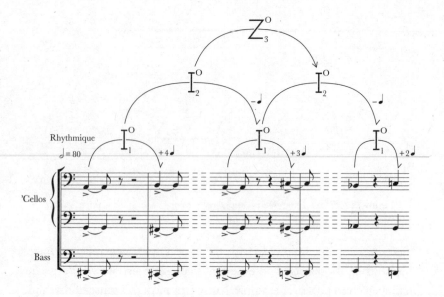

Figure 54 *Hearing the regularity of the accelerando in* Pacific
231 implies cognitive processing at the tertiary level.

or, in my terminology, '*tertiary* zygonic relationships'. We can surmise that these function proactively in the minds of performers, and reactively in the case of listeners. And although, in general, listeners' memory for tempo appears to be more accurate than that for pitch,[33] once more, it is *relativities* that are of principal importance in conveying a piece of music's identity and enabling it to make sense. Originally, in the 1939 film *The Wizard of Oz*, Judy Garland sang *Somewhere Over the Rainbow* at around 160 beats per minute. In contrast, Eva Cassidy's version, recorded at the Blues Alley jazz and supper club in Georgetown, DC in 1996, was only half that speed (and also contained some rhythmic variation). Listening to the two renditions, it is evident that the role of 'absolute' tempo is largely an aesthetic one: playing a piece significantly faster or slower (or higher or lower) can – as here – markedly change its affective impact. But its underlying structure, and so its comprehensibility as music, will remain intact.

There is one further role that the imitation of onsets at the tertiary level plays in music, and that is in passages that speed up (through 'accelerandi') or slow down (by virtue of 'ritardandi') in a regular way. Often,

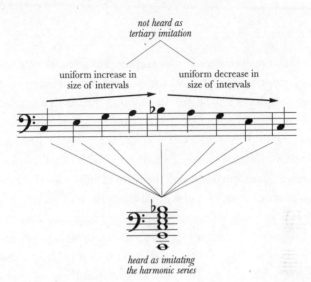

Figure 55 *Uniform change in intervals in a common walking bass pattern is likely to be heard harmonically rather than through tertiary-level imitation of pitch.*

changes in tempo are just shown through verbal indications in the score, though occasionally composers notate the variation with some precision – as in Arthur Honegger's symphonic movement *Pacific 231*. As the train starts to move, a series of chords representing the chuffing of the engine become incrementally closer in time. Listeners who intuitively grasp this linear acceleration are processing imitation at the level of *connections between connections between connections* (see Figure 54).

It is interesting to note that, as far as music is concerned, this depth of abstraction appears to represent a universal limit of human perception. As we have seen, tertiary relationships have a role to play in the way that onset is sometimes structured, and they are also theoretically available in the domain of pitch. For example, a widely-used 'walking bass' pattern in Blues and rock comprises a series of intervals that decrease regularly in size. However, this uniform change is more likely to be heard to derive from the harmonic series (see Figure 3) than as a result of tertiary imitation of pitch (Figure 55). It seems that connections between intervals of pitch (*secondary* relationships) have proved sufficient to meet composers' needs to date.

* * *

Although we have considered pitch and rhythm separately up to now, in reality they work hand-in-hand in music, together defining motifs and themes, and playing a crucial role in enabling the ear to track the evolution of material as it occurs. A short, characteristic rhythm is typically more memorable than a series of melodic intervals, so, provided there is little or only modest change in a pattern of IOIs, pitch can be subject to substantive transformation, and the ear will still make the connection between a particular motif and a modified version of it. This practice is commonplace in many styles and genres of music, so much so that it can become formulaic. The advantage of substantial rhythmic repetition, as writers of popular songs are well aware, is that it enables a melody to be grasped quickly and easily. Take for example, the song *You Are My Sunshine*, first recorded in 1939, which soon became a part of mainstream American popular culture. The first six phrases all derive from the same straightforward rhythmic pattern (which is simplified slightly at the end of the fourth line to give a sense of temporary repose). The last four bars develop the material from the opening, acting like a miniature coda, and bringing a sense of closure. Observe the way that lines 5 and 6 mirror lines 3 and 4 at the heart of the song. So, this unassuming little melody unfolds to reveal a surprisingly sophisticated structure A B : B A – the 'chiasmus' (Figure 56; see also Figure 9).

Rather more rarely, pitch is treated as an invariant feature while rhythm is transformed. There are many beautiful examples in Richard Strauss's late Oboe Concerto, whose three movements are constructed from the same stock of short melodic ideas, which are remodelled in all manner of ways. For example, one pattern comprises four repeated pitches followed by a leap up of a third and then a descent of four scale degrees. Different rhythms characterise the motif's appearance in each of the movements. It is easy for the ear to follow the connections between themes thanks to the taut logic of Strauss's writing, in which one has the sense of not one note being wasted in the transparent, contrapuntal textures devised for the small orchestra that accompanies the oboe (Figure 57).

In conjunction, pitch and rhythm provide such a wealth of musical

Figure 56 *The first six phrases of* You Are My Sunshine *all use the same rhythm with varying patterns of pitch.*

information, that both can be changed at the same time in myriad different ways without compromising a sense of coherence. For instance, as we saw in Handel's *Harmonious Blacksmith* variations for harpsichord (see Figure 5), extra notes can be added between those that already exist. Or

Figure 57 *Patterns of intervals are repeated in combination with rhythmic transformation in Richard Strauss's Oboe Concerto, ensuring the movements are integrated thematically.*

the opposite process can occur, whereby material is stripped away from a motif, in a process that Schoenberg called 'liquidation'.[34] Beethoven was among those who favoured this technique, and a telling example is to be found in the first movement of his 5th Symphony, when the famous 'fate knocking on the door' motif heard at the outset is pared down more and more until only a single chord remains. This alternates between the wind and the strings in an extended passage that gets quieter and quieter. What will happen next? Abruptly, in bar 228, the full orchestra interrupts proceedings with a full version of the 'knocking' motif, loud and contrasting – shocking, even. It is as though Beethoven, having led listeners incrementally further and further away from the opening figure, while still clinging on to its essence, suddenly forces them to turn round, Orpheus-like, and see just how far they have come, confronting fate head on, as it were.[35]

Timbre, Loudness and Location

No theory of how music works would be complete without some reference to timbre and loudness. We have already noted that these dimensions tend to function as carriers of the main musical message that is conveyed by pitch and rhythm. Nonetheless, both timbre and loudness are inescapably present in every note that is played, and, as features that are core to the nature of sound itself, composers have to be mindful of their impact.

In a good deal of music, the structural effect of timbre and loudness is somewhat neutral; compositions that were intended for one instrument or ensemble can generally be played by others with little or no loss of comprehensibility, although aesthetically, things will inevitably change to varying degrees and according to listeners' personal preferences. For example, playing music of the Baroque period that was intended for the harpsichord on the piano may set the purist's teeth on edge, but others may appreciate the dynamic variety that is possible on the modern instrument. But no one would seriously contemplate performing, say, the dramatic opening of Tchaikovsky's 4th Symphony for horns and bassoons on the celesta, since the emotional force of the music is bound up with the *fortissimo* sounds of the wind.

With both timbre and loudness, moment-to-moment consistency tends to be the order of the day, and so there is a good deal of repetition. Although this typically appears to pass by with little attention being paid to it, we can assume that the brain is constantly monitoring what is occurring, since any change is noticed immediately. To use an analogy of the font used in a book, once the eye is settled into reading, it takes a difference in the typeface or its size for the printed text itself to be brought into perceptual focus.

So for most of the time, we can consider the networks of potential connections that the brain may make between the timbres and levels of loudness in a piece that are similar or the same to function *indirectly*: the sounding qualities of no one note are held to derive particularly from those of any other, but, taken as a whole, the cumulative effect of continual background imitation is powerful.

To hear what is involved with respect to timbre, consider four pieces of music by Bach, each written for a single instrument: two for harpsichord (the first and second of the Partitas), one for violin (the first Sonata) and one for 'cello (the first Suite). The pieces are uniform in timbre, which can be heard in terms of three different types of indirect imitation: *within* each piece, *between* two pieces that use the same timbre (the Partitas), and between any one of the four pieces and others that share a similar uniformity of timbre, and are regarded by the listener as existing within the same stylistic milieu. Much the same principles apply to more complex works that use sets of *different* timbres, such as a symphony orchestra, a

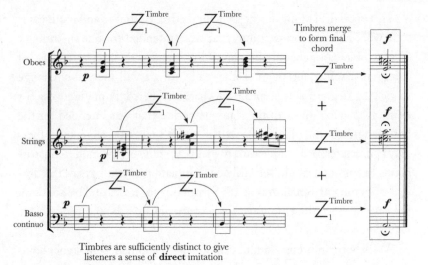

Figure 58 *Direct imitative relationships of timbre that occur at the end of the second movement of Bach's* Brandenburg Concerto No. 1, *BWV 1046.*

wind quintet, a rock band or a jazz trio. Imitation of timbre, within and between works, is still the order of the day.

It would be unusual for the relationship between the timbres of any two notes to be perceptually prominent enough to be heard as being directly imitative, although occasional examples do exist, such as the compelling – not to say ethereal – exchanges between three solo oboes, the upper strings, and the harpsichord, bass and bassoon at the end of the slow movement of Bach's *Brandenburg Concerto No. 1.*

More commonly, such connections work in conjunction with the repetition of motifs and themes, borrowing a sense of derivation from them. For example, in Schubert's *Unfinished* Symphony, the unusual sound of the oboe and clarinet playing in unison above quivering violins and lent impetus by a rhythmic pizzicato motif in the violas, 'cellos and basses, adds a peculiarly melancholy quality to the drooping first main theme. And when the passage returns in the recapitulation, it is this distinctive use of timbre and texture, as much as its melodic and harmonic qualities, that take the mind and the emotions straight back to the beginning of the symphony – rather as someone's scent can trigger memories and feelings more viscerally than a visual image.

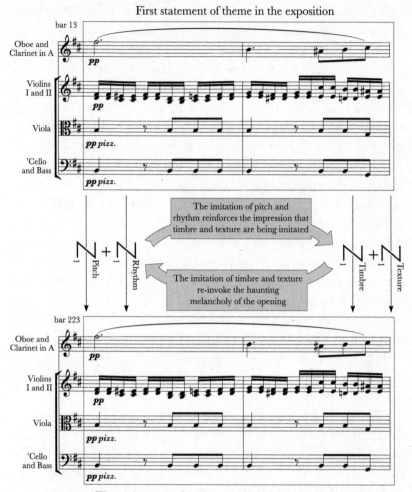

Figure 59 *The imitation of pitch, rhythm, timbre and texture working together in the first movement of Schubert's* Unfinished *Symphony.*

The examples from Bach and Schubert both employ the imitation of timbre at the *primary* level. Occasionally, in traditional Western music, *secondary* zygonic relationships may be invoked – when a change of timbre is repeated on different instruments, for example. An example is to be found in the sinuous first movement of Bartók's *Music for Strings, Percussion and Celesta*, when, following the climax, the violins, violas and 'cellos successively add mutes (from bar 67) as the music recedes towards the relative tranquillity of the opening once more.

It was Schoenberg who first suggested, within a Western music-theoretical framework, that timbre could function structurally, on a par with pitch, in the intriguing musings that conclude his *Harmonielehre* (*Theory of Harmony*).[36] However, despite his own efforts and those of his contemporaries and successors, extending from the meticulous miniature scores of Anton Webern to the brash organised soundscapes of Edgard Varèse and flamboyant sonic gestures of Karlheinz Stockhausen that led in turn to the world of modern electronic music, the domination of the pitch-rhythm pairing has not been seriously challenged. Paradoxically, it is in the ancient techniques of Australian aboriginal didgeridoo playing that the notion of timbre as the dominant organisational force in music seems to have become most firmly established in the minds of mainstream music consumers. And here, once again, it is repetition that holds sway, both in steady-state sounds and rhythmic patterns of regular change ('ee–oo–ow', 'ee–oo–ow'): elementary forms of structure that are perceived through *primary* level relationships. *Secondary* connections (between changes in timbre anchored on different absolute values) are harder to discern, since the quality of a sound can vary in a number of different dimensions, such as hard/soft, sharp/dull and pure/rich.[37]

Turning to loudness, the position is rather more straightforward, since variability is possible in only one respect, and both step changes and gradual modification are commonplace. Loudness is arguably the quality of sound where 'absolute' values matter the least: in evolutionary terms, it has been essential that the nature of a noise – whether an animal growling as a sign of hostility, for instance, or calling to attract a potential mate – is recognisable as such at different distances (and hence at a wide range of volume levels), and so it is with music. Consider, for example, the differences in loudness experienced by listeners seated at the front of a concert hall as opposed to the back, or even listening to a transmission of the event at home over headphones. So what counts are comparisons – at both primary and secondary level (of repetition and regular change) – *within* a listener's experience of a performance, rather than primary relationships *between* performances, whether of the same piece or different ones. What is important in listening (say) to a performance of Ravel's *Boléro* is that the loudness level is heard to increase from beginning to end, irrespective of its start and end points.

There is a final variable of sound that we should consider: the location of its source. Generally, in Western music, performers (and members of the audience) remain static, though there are obvious exceptions, such as opera singers, actors in musicals, and players in marching bands. Nonetheless, the fact that the place from which music is heard to emanate typically remains stationary can be regarded as an important feature in the music-structural 'background' (along with consistency in timbre and loudness). Moving the source of the sound (for example, through electronic means) would not compromise a piece's capacity to make sense, although it would be distracting, and therefore almost certainly have a negative aesthetic impact.

Some pieces depend for their full effect on having sounds emanate from more than one location. Music conceived in terms of two distinct sources ranges from the antiphonal singing characteristic of some African cultures[38] to the sixteenth- and seventeenth-century Venetian technique of *coro spezzato* or 'divided choir', and, in the modern era, Henry Brant's *American Debate* of 1976, for wind and percussion in two groups. Composers have sometimes demanded *three* distinct groups of players, notably in pieces such as Stockhausen's *Gruppen*, which requires a different conductor for each instrumental unit. An even greater number of ensembles are specified on occasions: Berlioz's *Grande Messe des Morts*, for instance, calls for an exceptionally large orchestra including four brass bands. Whatever the situation, to the extent that composers emulate each other's practice, and the manner of performance is derived from earlier renditions, so it is conceivable to regard the location of the sound as being derived through imitation.

Coda

Pieces of music tend to have a complex life cycle. This is because the humans who invent them generally want their creations to spread, virus like, to inhabit minds other than their own. So although a composition need theoretically only ever exist inside the head of its creator, this would be the exception rather than the rule; for with the composer's demise, the piece would also cease to be, and a fragment of immortality would be lost and gone for ever. But to reach other minds, music has to assume a physical form – typically, longitudinal pressure waves in the air – and venture out into the wider world. The great majority of such waves will never find a home and dissipate in the environment. A tiny proportion, though, will reach the ears of listeners and effect a transfer of musical information, before themselves disappearing in a puff of entropy. But by then, they will have done their job, and passed on the musical DNA of a piece to another host.

Apart from sound waves, other proxies are available to music too, which can offer more or less permanent representations or analogues of pieces outside a human brain. Historically these have included arrays of lines and shapes drawn or printed on paper; tiny, irregular grooves impressed on wax cylinders and subsequently circles of vinyl; minute series of magnetic fields set up on metal-coated tapes; spirals of minuscule bumps moulded onto polycarbonate disks; and, most recently, sequences of electrical charges stored in the floating gates of countless transistors that are only nanometres across. These technologies have revolutionised the preservation of music and meant that its transmission is more wide-spread than ever before; the number of people able to hear a piece has increased from hundreds or perhaps thousands in the middle ages to millions in the early part of the twentieth century, and billions today. Within moments, a performance made available on the internet can have spread all over the world.

But more than this, computers have now moved far beyond merely being able to store and transfer musical ideas: using the rules and param-eters set by their programmers, they can create new pieces that make sense to us and are even capable of evoking emotional responses. Music no longer has to start life in a human brain. This is despite the fact that the computers responsible for producing the materials cannot themselves understand what they are doing or feel the impact of their work. And while they lack the intuitive capacity of humans to innovate in such a way that the truly novel pieces they create still make sense and are aes-thetically pleasing, computers can at least be programmed to ensure that the music they generate uses structures that are perceptible, which (surprisingly) is more than composers have always done. Here, the problem has sometimes been that the cognitive constraints on musical design are much tighter than our capacity to conceptualise what is theoretically possible, and so there is potentially a mismatch between music as conceived by composers and perceived by listeners.

These perceptual limitations are summarised in a set of principles that I refer to as 'the magical number 2±1'[39] (in deference to George Miller's seminal paper on the limits of perceptual categories – see p. 40). As we have seen in this chapter, making sense of music is all about comparing notes, and the '2±1' refers to the three levels of relationship through which comparisons can potentially be drawn. Their possible configurations, which we have explored in some detail, can be summarised as follows.

The brain may compare a quality of one sound, such as its pitch, timbre and loudness, with the same quality in another. Such comparisons, between characteristics of the perceptual 'surface', are made through mental connections called *primary* relationships. They can be depicted using an arrow with the letter 'I' for interval. Relationships through which one feature of a note is thought to imitate another that is the same or similar are called 'zygonic', and are labelled with a 'Z'.

Mental connections between primary relationships – whether zygonic or not – are commonplace in music. These are called *secondary* relationships. Again, they may convey a sense of imitation, and so be classed as zygonic.

Connections between secondary relationships are also used to form certain types of musical structure. They are referred to as *tertiary* relationships. They invariably convey a sense of imitation, so they are *always* zygonic. They may connect secondary (and primary) relationships that are themselves imitative (though they need not be).

So, the main forms of musical structure that exist are these:

Comparing Notes: Primary Level

Pattern of relationships	⌒ I	Z
General comments	The perceptual acknowledgement of how a quality of one note stands in relation to the same quality of another.	The cognitive acknowledgement that a quality of one note imitates another that is the same, which typically occurs intuitively in the course of listening and improvising; however, it may be conceptualised in composition or analysis.
Pitch	Differences in pitch are the building blocks of melody and harmony – found in almost all music (apart from some chants).	The imitation of pitch plays a crucial role in musical structure with respect to events (notes), groups (motifs) and frameworks (modes).
Onset	Differences in onset enable music to exist over time.	The imitation of onset results in simultaneity: used in almost all music that has a texture of two parts or more.
Timbre	Differences in timbre are characteristic of some (though by no means all) music, both simultaneously and successively.	The constancy of timbre, occurring through indirect imitation, is found in almost all music, ranging from entire sets of pieces to individual motifs, where homogeneity is almost invariably used to reinforce structures of pitch and rhythm.
Loudness	Differences in loudness are found in much (though not all) music.	Although dynamic contrast is a significant affective component in some styles, the loudness levels of successive notes tend to be the same or similar; indeed, extended periods may occur at the same dynamic level or within a relatively narrow dynamic envelope: indirect imitation is indicated.

Table 1 The function and effect of *primary* relationships in music

Comparing Notes: Secondary Level

Pattern of relationships			
General comments	The perceptual acknowledgement of the difference that may exist between two primary relationships.	The cognitive acknowledgement that one primary relationship imitates another that is the same or similar.	The cognitive acknowledgement that imitation at the primary level is itself imitated at the secondary level.
Pitch	The differences in intervals are normally perceived intuitively but may be conceptualised in music theory.	The imitation of intervals underpins: regular patterns of ascent and descent; the transposition of motifs; and the distribution of identical intervals in pitch frameworks.	Exists where one series of repeated pitches is believed to imitate another.
Onset	Ratios between IOIs are fundamental to the creation and perception of rhythm.	The imitation of IOIs underpins the creation of a regular beat and equal subdivisions of it.	The imitation of simultaneities.
Timbre	No known examples	The imitation of differences in timbre is rarely found, though may occur with the successive addition or removal of mutes, for example.	The indirect imitation that underpins the constancy of timbre that is characteristic of many passages and pieces.
Loudness	No known examples	The imitation of regular change in loudness, such as in crescendi and diminuendi.	The indirect imitation that underpins the consistency of loudness that is characteristic of many passages and pieces.

Table 2 The function and effect of *secondary* relationships in music

Comparing Notes: Tertiary Level

Pattern of relationships		
General comments	The cognitive acknowledgement that one secondary relationship imitates another that is the same or similar.	The cognitive acknowledgement that imitation at the secondary level is itself imitated at the tertiary level.
Pitch	Recognised in music theory,[40] though probably not usually perceived by listeners.	A few rare examples are to be found, for example when a chromatic scale (comprising intervals of a semitone) is transformed into a whole tone scale in bars 349–361 of Glinka's *Russlan and Ludmilla* Overture
Onset	This level of imitation underpins accelerandi and ritardandi, and augmentation and diminution, and playing music at different speeds.	Imitation of the very consistency of regular beats within and between pieces.
Timbre	No known examples	No known examples
Loudness	No known examples	No known examples

Table 3 The function and effect of *tertiary* relationships in music

It is worth reminding ourselves that the relationships we have identified and discussed are purely *hypothetical constructs* – in the American cognitive linguist George Lakoff's terms, metaphorical representations of particular 'link schemata' through which structure is believed to be modelled, typically subconsciously, in the imaginary 'musical space' we keep in our minds. But is the theory – 'zygonic theory' – correct?

When I first set out my ideas in the 1990s,[41] there was a good deal of evidence (as we saw in Chapter 1) scattered throughout the diverse music-theoretical and analytical literatures that repetition was central to the way in which music is organised, though no one had articulated just *how* duplicating an aspect of a sound could generate the conceit of structure and intuitively enable us to make sense of music. The notion that the (subconscious) acknowledgement of *imitation* may play a part in music cognition through giving the impression that one sound may derive from another was implicit – but only implicit – in the findings of some music-psychological and psychoacoustical research. Among these was the auditory 'continuity illusion', whereby a continuous sound that is physically interrupted (and entirely masked) by noise appears to continue.[42] How is the gap filled? By the listener generating imaginary new material from the sound that was discontinued through imitation; in this case using primary zygonic relationships of pitch, timbre and loudness. Other work, on expectation in music, through which listeners showed that they are able to gauge the probability of what was likely to come next in a foreshortened series of sounds, was similarly indicative of listeners' capacity to derive new material from old through the imitation of pitches or intervals.[43]

In the decade since the publication of the last main exposition of zygonic theory (*Repetition in Music: Theoretical and Metatheoretical Perspectives*) a good deal of related empirical work has been undertaken both at the Applied Music Research Centre at the University of Roehampton, which I lead, and with colleagues at Goldsmiths College and University College London. Research was initially undertaken in the field of music theory and music psychology, and much of this is reported incidentally in *Comparing Notes*, including work on the cognitive constraints that impact on our understanding of music, similarity perception, expectation, creativity, memory and the perception of hierarchies in pitch and in relation to the onsets of notes.[44] The zygonic approach has been used in epistemological discourse, to clarify the distinction between the modes of thinking characteristic of music theory, music psychology, music education and music therapy.[45] Subsequently, the focus has shifted to explore potential applications of the theory in day-to-day experience of music, including the investigation of patterns of influence and interaction in the context of group improvisation; chronicling how children develop musically in the early years; analysing the impact of visual impairment and autism on young people's evolving musicality, and accurately describing the skills of musical 'savants'.[46] There are also a number of projects in train that are investigating the extent to which the zygonic principles of structure deriving through imitation may have a wider relevance in other art forms, including drawing, painting, sculpture, mime, dance, stories, poems and plays.

Whatever the verity of the zygonic conjecture, the imitative relationships through which I contend that musical structure is created and perceived can at best offer only a highly simplified version of certain cognitive events that we can reasonably surmise take place during participation in musical activity. However, while simplification is always necessary to make headway in theoretical terms, some idea of the complexity involved can be gleaned by appreciating that the single concept of a zygon bequeaths a vast perceptual legacy, with many potential manifestations: between, for example, pitches, harmonies, timbres, loudnesses, durations, IOIs, tonal regions, textures, processes and forms that are the same; over different periods of time; and within the same and between different pieces, performances and hearings. Zygonic relationships may function reactively, in recognising musical structure that has just been heard, or proactively, in projecting what the future may hold. They may function between sounds that are remembered, currently being perceived or just imagined.

Given this variety, there is, of course, no suggestion that zygonic relationships, in their manifold forms, model a single aspect of cognitive processing or have a particular neurological correlate. In seeking to understand the world, animal brains – including our own – had to evolve to be able to recognise and process common attributes of the environment (such as similarity) in many different contexts. One of the fascinating areas for future research will be to ascertain how elements of cognition that originally developed for survival evolved into music-processing abilities (as the music theorist and psychologist David Huron and others have started to do)[47] and, conversely, how music itself evolved to take advantage of cognitive capacities that weren't designed with music in mind (through the process that biologists call 'exaptation')[48] – issues to which we return briefly at the end of the next chapter.

3

How We Construct
Musical Meaning

CHAPTER 2 OFFERED AN EXPLANATION of how music makes
sense by showing how it is structured through different forms of imitation. But that is only the beginning of the story of how musical *meaning*
works, which is the subject of this chapter.

The problem that has beset philosophers and psychologists over the
years is that the notion of 'meaning' in general, and 'musical meaning'
in particular, is – to say the least – elusive. Why? Because the concept is
abstract, subjective, and difficult (if not impossible) to express satisfactorily through language. As the American actor and musician Martin
Mull purportedly once said, 'Writing about music is like dancing about
architecture.'[1] That is, words can never really do justice to the immediate sensation of musical sounds, nor the feelings that they are capable of
arousing. And even when one accepts the inevitable constraints of verbal
expression, the very idea of musical meaning evades clarification: just
when it seems as though the concept has finally come comprehensively
into focus, another view pushes its way unbidden into the frame, and the
picture no longer appears to be as clear or persuasive.

In cases like this, when an intellectual problem appears to be intractable, analogy can sometimes offer a fresh perspective, revealing, for example, underlying coherence where none was directly visible. With this in mind, and given that verbal utterances are arguably music's nearest conceptual neighbour, conveying ideas and feelings through humanly organised sounds over time, we will use *language* as a basis for comparison throughout this chapter.

Structure in Music and Syntax in Language

Giving an account of musical structure is rather like describing syntax in language, which explains how verbal utterances are organised, the different functions that words can fulfil in relation to one another, and the rules through which they can be combined – but syntax is *content free*. Hence, two sentences using exactly the same grammatical structure can mean entirely different things. For example:

The little girl kicked the ball angrily.
The greedy boy drank the soup voraciously.

Indeed, in linguistic parlance, a sentence may be 'well-formed' – that is, grammatically coherent – but nonsensical. For instance:

The thoughtful chair eyed the tree churlishly.

And so it is with music. It is possible for two passages to have the same perceived structure (as defined by their internal patterns of imitative relationships), but have different pitches, 'inter-onset intervals' (IOIs), timbres and levels of loudness. Hence they will be likely to elicit different responses in listeners. They will *mean* different things. But how does this work? In language, the element that can vary in utterances with the same syntax is semantics – what it is that the words represent. Language means something, ultimately, because words act as symbols. They point to things beyond themselves, and it is their capacity to arouse mental images and feelings that imbues them with significance. But notes typically don't refer to objects, actions or ideas that are external to the fabric of music itself. On the contrary, they tend to be self-referencing. Notes relate to other notes. So wherein does musical meaning reside?

Responding to Sound

My starting point is the intuition that *all* musical sounds and combinations of sounds can potentially evoke an emotional response. While this conjecture may not seem plausible to someone, say, perfunctorily pressing a key in the middle range of the piano, which produces a note that probably comes across as being rather neutral emotionally, consider that some responses are more powerful and so easier to detect than others – particularly those elicited by qualities of sound that are at the extremes of a given perceptual range. Take, for example, the hushed, sustained, spine tingling low Cs played on double basses, contrabassoon, bass drum and organ that open the introduction to Richard Strauss's *Also Sprach Zarathustra* (popularised in Stanley Kubrick's *2001: A Space Odyssey*). Or listen in sheer awe to another C – this one near the top of the human vocal range – in choirboy Roy Goodman's 1963 pellucid recording of Allegri's *Miserere* with the choir of King's College, Cambridge. Our reactions to these musical sounds may be particularly strong, but they are not unique. And while we can take time out, as we are doing here, to reflect on how different notes affect us, such responses are typically unthinking and, research has shown, rapid, occurring in less than a second.[2]

This position accords with the observations and reasoning of Francis Sparshott, who, working in the field of philosophical aesthetics, asserts that, interaction with the wider cultural and physical environment notwithstanding, music (in a pure state) 'functions in a special world in which the items are wholly musical objects ... [which] are designed to stand in precisely defined and conceptually elaborated relations to each other, and are engineered with no other purpose than to reward perceptive attention.' And just as our perception of the world at large is saturated with affect,[3] so too the way in which we engage with musical artworks is typically at an affective level, with an aesthetic current in our stream of consciousness flowing in response to pieces as they unfold over time, feature by feature.

Moreover, empirical studies in the field of music psychology over many years have indicated that the general features of music, such as register, tempo and dynamic level relate more or less consistently to certain emotional states.[4] For example, passages in a high register can feel exciting[5] or exhibit potency,[6] whereas series of low notes are more likely to promote solemnity or to be perceived as serious.[7] A fast tempo will tend to induce feelings of excitement,[8] in contrast to music of a slower pace that may connote tranquillity[9] or even peace.[10] Loud dynamic levels are held to be exciting,[11] triumphant[12] or to represent gaiety,[13] while quiet sounds have been found to express fear, tenderness or grief.[14] Conversely, as Leonard Meyer asserts, 'one cannot imagine sadness being portrayed by a fast forte tune played in a high register, or a playful child being depicted by a solemnity of trombones'.[15]

However, while many of these basic physiological responses may be elicited by hearing music, they are certainly not exclusive to it: *any* succession of sounds, natural or humanly created, may invoke primitive feelings of the types described. This is only part of the picture, though, since in musical contexts, these elemental responses are likely to be overlaid with more sophisticated reactions. For example, psychologists Patrik Juslin, Anders Friberg and Roberto Bresin contend that at least some of our responses to music may derive ultimately from the cues used to express emotions vocally in early nonverbal communication and speech.[16] These are present cross-culturally,[17] suggesting a common root in the evolution of our species (that is, through 'phylogenetic' derivation), and apparently embedded in our development as individuals ('ontogenetically') in the vocal interactions that occur spontaneously between babies and their caregivers.[18] And then there are responses that are specific to *musical* sounds and combinations of them – in particular, those with close connections to the harmonic series. For example, as we have seen, in Western cultures, other things being equal, major chords tend to evoke a sense of happiness and minor chords sadness.[19]

Structure and Content in Music

Whatever the ultimate derivation of human responses to musical sounds – whether as a physiological reaction to their fundamental qualities, or through memories of the shared emotional engagement that early vocal interaction can bring, or as an auditory response to combinations of notes that have an affinity with the harmonic series – according to zygonic theory, they fulfil a similar function in pieces of music by supplying its 'content'. In effect, this stands in place of the semantic meaning of language: instead of a series of mental images elicited by different verbal symbols, listeners to music will have a range of affective experiences generated in response to qualities of sound in the domains of pitch, time, timbre and loudness, each of which can potentially vary.

However, content alone doesn't make music. One could imagine creating a succession of sounds, each of which evoked a distinct emotional response, rather like a line of separate words that all denote different (and unrelated) things:

cancer azure network flying New York oak childbirth blind

But the discrete sounds wouldn't constitute music, any more than the sequence of unconnected words adds up to speech. These need to be logically connected, and this requires two things. First, the relationships between words must represent credible connections between the entities, actions or ideas that they represent: 'the thoughtful chair eyed the tree churlishly' is meaningless to the extent that one cannot imagine furniture having sentience, senses or sensibilities. Second, the way that words are related must conform to the syntactic conventions of the language in which they are situated. Hence the meaning of the utterance, 'The cat fierce the dog chases old.', is, to put it mildly, ambiguous, since the customary word order in English, which determines subject and predicate, is not followed. Nor is it clear which adjective qualifies which noun.

In language, then, meaning has an impact on syntax, and *vice versa*; the two are inextricably linked. And a comparable position exists in music. According to zygonic theory, logic in music – its syntax – is dependent on a class of relationships through which a quality of sound pertaining to one note is felt to derive from an identical or similar quality of sound belonging to another, and this is held to occur through imitation. In this way, one note is felt to influence or control another. So, as in language, the content of music is determined by what composers (and to an extent performers) wish to convey, and, as in language, composers have to use structure to get their message across – and, inevitably, that structure is also integral to whatever is communicated.

Like syntax and semantics in language, musical structure and content are intimately and intricately related. Both are ultimately defined by the attributes of the sounds in question, which, like the threads in a woven fabric, function to hold things together as well as creating aesthetically pleasing effects. Just as content is inconceivable without structure (for, as we have observed, that would be tantamount to chaos), so structure cannot *physically* exist without content, although in an *abstract* sense it can, consisting as it does entirely of zygonic relationships. However, as soon as structure becomes reified in a particular context, it fuses with content, the two becoming one.[20] Take, for example, a very simple structure functioning in one domain: a single zygonic relationship of pitch. This can have widely varying musical consequences, from the joyful insistence of the repeated notes that mark out the fugal theme in Mozart's *Magic Flute* overture, to the arresting opening of Beethoven's Violin Concerto, with its repeated strokes on the kettle drum; from the rousing introductory trumpet fanfare of Mendelssohn's *Wedding March*, to the contemplative mood of Lennon's song *Imagine*.

One important consequence of the relationship between structure and content in music is that contrast can be achieved without compromising coherence. This is possible since notes are multifaceted, and are therefore potentially connected in the mind through numerous parallel relationships, any of which may but need not be imitative. Consider, for example, the first entrance of the soloist in the second movement of Bartók's third piano concerto, which follows a passage for strings and clarinet. The general effect is one of contrast, engendered by marked differences in register, timbre and dynamics. However, coherence is discreetly maintained through the continuation of the beat and a descending pattern of pitch (see Figure 60).

Contrasts such as this are arresting precisely because they occur with relative infrequency in most styles (in relation to the example shown, both the preceding 15 bars and the great majority of those that follow are characterised by homogeneity of musical content). This may in part be a consequence of the demands of structural coherence, through which passages are typically replete with imitation, in turn leading to the saturation of textures with values that are similar or the same.

Inevitably, then, in aesthetic terms, music has a tendency towards

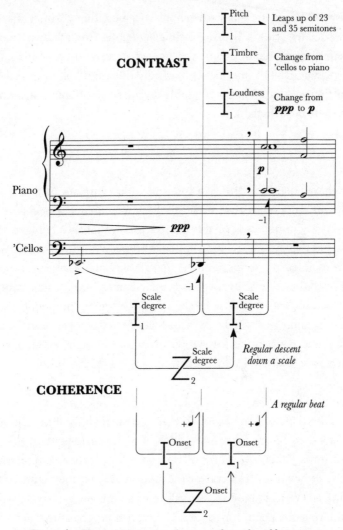

Figure 60 *The multidimensional nature of sound enables contrast*
to function within a framework of musical coherence.

affective evenness or gradual change; sudden contrasts appear to be the
exception rather than the rule. In fact, if they *were* the rule (rather than
the exception) the ear would become inured to them, and they would
lose their impact. This observation bears on a general characteristic of the
relationship between structure and content in music and our aesthetic

response to it: there are many more notes in a piece than distinct affective states associated with it. By implication, *most* notes (though by no means all) seem to reinforce or colour the state that currently pertains rather than replacing it with one that is markedly different. Just as in real life, unremitting vacillation between highly divergent emotional states would appear to be unsustainable.

* * *

So, we have identified the two indispensable elements in music that enable it to function as a medium of self-expression and as a channel of communication: the emotional responses that we intuitively make to all sounds and the 'zygonic relationships' that the brain formulates between features of notes (or groups of notes) that are similar or the same, through which imitation is acknowledged. These elements are music's 'content' and 'structure', and they fuse in the mind to form a compound that is 'musical meaning', to which we feel an 'aesthetic response'. But how do structure and content work together over time to generate an abstract narrative in sound – to lead the ear through an affective journey?

Meaning in Language

This will be explained by way of an example: an analysis of the children's song *Twinkle, Twinkle, Little Star*, which, as we saw in Chapter 1, was used by Mozart as a theme for a set of variations for piano, K. 265. First, we will look at how the lyrics convey meaning, and what the nature of that meaning is. We will take the perspective of an imaginary listener who is encountering the poem for the first time, with no access to the written text, hearing it being recited by a child.

The lyrics comprise the first verse of an early nineteenth-century poem, *The Star*, written by the English poet and novelist Jane Taylor, published in 1806.

> Twinkle, twinkle, little star,
> How I wonder what you are!
> Up above the world so high,
> Like a diamond in the sky.

It is traditionally sung to the French melody *Ah! Vous dirai-je, Maman,* which first appeared in print in 1761, before the poem was written. Since the music is longer than the words, the opening lines of the lyrics have to be repeated at the end.

From the outset, things are unusual. The word 'twinkle' rarely appears in English (apart from its appearance in *Twinkle, Twinkle, Little Star!*) and its rarity is compounded here by a relatively uncommon syntactic context: the 'imperative' form of the verb, through which the speaker is commanding something (as yet unknown) to twinkle. If the first 'twinkle' was unusual, its immediate repetition, were this everyday speech, would have been truly exceptional, since the same word rarely occurs twice in succession. Such a construction is almost entirely rhetorical. However, in children's rhymes, repetition is comparatively common, as is the imperative mood: 'Row, row, row your boat', 'Baa, baa, black sheep'. Add this to the fact that the words function rhythmically, and our listener may quickly become aware (if he or she wasn't already) that here is something other than prose or day-to-day spoken language: rather, here is a sequence of words that children can just experience for their own sake and enjoy learning and chanting with others – the repetition of 'twinkle' functioning quasi-onomatopoeically, indicating how the star's scintillations continue over time. The next word is 'little', which is an adjective whose full import, along with 'Twinkle, twinkle', is waiting to be realised. This realisation occurs with the fourth word – 'star' – which is the thing being addressed. It completes the first main idea of the poem: we now know that there is a star, that it is little, and that it is being told to twinkle.

But who is the narrator? Although, in the next line, a first-person perspective is used – 'How *I* wonder what you are' – it is not clear who the 'I' is meant to represent. Is the child reciting the poem intended to function like an actor, reciting a third party's script? Or is it a (Georgian) adult's fantasy view of what children think? Maybe the child is being used as a more or less unwitting conveyor of a message that is largely for adult consumption. In any case, the second line has an intricate syntactic structure, which is by no means easy to decode. It takes the form of an 'exclamative' sentence – one that expresses emphasis or strong feeling. This means that the initial adverb ('how') is not used with its familiar interrogative intent, but to stress an idea. The object of the main verb 'wonder' is a further clause ('what you are'). Hence in generative grammatical terms, this implies a further (second) level of dependency on the main subject, the star.

Line three, 'Up above the world so high', is characterised by a sequence of words that is not characteristic of colloquial English. Clarity of meaning has been sacrificed to maintain the trochaic metre of the first two lines (comprising stressed followed by unstressed syllables) and the rhyming pattern of paired lines. That is, there is a conflict between semantics and poetic structure. This is resolved by transposing the words 'so high' from where they would naturally occur at the beginning of the sentence ('So high up above the world') to the end. The result is that naïve ears may hear 'so high' as referring to the world rather than the sky.

In line 4, 'Like a diamond in the sky', the use of figurative language, first employed in the personification of the star, is extended through its comparison with a precious stone. For our adult listener, the imaginative leap from attributing a human sense of self to an inanimate astral object, to likening it to a precious stone, is likely to cause few problems. Moreover, the simile involving the diamond is multi-layered: here is something that not only glistens, but also connotes value and eternity. Such analogies may well lie beyond the comprehension of the child reciting the poem, however.

Finally, there is the repetition of the first two lines, something that, as we have observed, was not present in the original poem. This reinforces the earlier signals that 'here is language beyond the everyday': 'here is art'. The reprise adds a sense of completion to the rhyme, which goes beyond mere repetition of the words, since they are imbued with a new depth of meaning. Our listener now knows that the twinkling star is high up and looks like a diamond.

In summary, the way that words are used in *Twinkle*, despite it being a children's song, is highly complex, and it illustrates the ten main elements of language that work together to form meaning.[21] First, there are *semantics*, through which human ideas, feelings and experiences are represented by distinct but largely arbitrary chunks of sound ('words'). Second, there is *syntax*: the rules, determined by convention, through which words can be juxtaposed. Third, there are figures of speech such as *simile* and *metaphor*, through which imagined comparisons between two things are drawn, offering fresh insights to one or both. Fourth, there is the position in time – the *standpoint* – from which existence or action is described (which informs the tense of the verbs used). Fifth, there is the *source*, the personal perspective of the narrative that is adopted (first, second or third person). Sixth, there is *sequence*: the order in which words, and groups of words, are presented in time. Seventh, there are the *sounds* that words and combinations of words make – their auditory qualities, including rhyme, alliteration and metre. Eighth, there is the *spoken quality* of the passage concerned: the tone of voice with which words are enunciated. Ninth, there is the question of *shared knowledge*: the commonality of experience between the sender and receiver of information that is required to enable communication to function. And tenth, there is the *social context*: the relative status and linguistic competence of the participants in using language.

These result in a system of communication through sound whose principal function is to share everyday information about oneself, others and the wider world. The vast majority of verbal language is improvised and ephemeral, although it can be elevated to serve as art, in which case it is typically planned, recorded, learnt and reproduced, and valued for its aesthetic qualities. Language's principal method of conveying meaning is through symbolic representation, though with powerful (and sometimes contradictory) secondary, connotative meanings arising from context and manner of expression. It relies on a shared experience and understanding of what is being represented; inevitably, there will always be differences in the message as sent and received, but there is generally sufficient conceptual overlap for speaking and listening to be regarded as an accurate and reliable mode of communication. Language contains very little immediate repetition, but is nonetheless tightly structured, based on the capacity of words to fulfil a limited number of discrete functions in relation to one another – functions that are ultimately determined by the way we perceive and represent the world. It is largely learnt informally, and never completely, in a process that can potentially continue all our lives; in English, it is estimated that well-educated native adults generally understand around 17,000 'base' words – a small proportion of all those that exist.[22] Language is employed by all people (who function 'neuro-typically'), both as generators and receivers of verbal messages. So as a means of communication, it is universal, though it varies in detail from culture to culture. With these characteristics in mind, we now move on to consider how the *melody* of *Twinkle, Twinkle* functions: how it makes sense, how it conveys meaning, and what the nature of that meaning is.

Meaning in Music: The Art of Simplicity in Sound

Music is sometimes referred to as a language, though whether it actually is or not has been the subject of keen philosophical debate.[23] At the most basic level, music shares with speech the characteristic of being a form of human communication that occurs through streams of sound. And in both instances, these streams are 'chunked', typically subconsciously, in cognition: in the case of language, into phonemes, words, phrases and sentences; while in music the segmentation over time comprises notes, motifs, phrases and melodies. Beyond this, though, there are key differences, prime among which is the matter of semantics: if one takes 'language' to mean a medium through which *concepts* can be symbolised and conveyed, then music fails the test, since notes generally do not stand for anything – they have no meaning beyond their capacity to evoke emotional responses. As a result, a number of other features of language, which rely on the fact that words have symbolic meanings, cannot apply to music. For example, as we have observed, syntax, which gives language its structure, depends ultimately on its semantic content: what a word means determines its function. Then, in the absence of meaning, a narrative cannot have a position in time (past, present or future) or be understood as stemming from a particular source (first, second or third person). And simile, metaphor and comparable figures of speech are not available. So what does this leave?

Try reading the following aloud:

> Hwæt! We Gardena in geardagum, þeodcyninga, þrym
> gefrunon, hu ða æþelingas ellen fremedon.

Assuming that you are not a scholar of *Beowulf*,[24] you will not have the option of processing these words meaningfully as language: you can only assimilate them as a series of pure sounds, which (a) have auditory qualities and (b) occur in a particular sequence. These are the two core characteristics of music. But how do they relate to musical structure and content, enabling them to generate meaning over time?

To answer this question, we will return to *Twinkle*, this time to the melody. Again, we will adopt a phenomenological approach, in an effort to gain some insight into the mental processing that is likely to be involved in making sense of this brief series of forty-two notes, and extracting meaning from them.

Hum the first note to yourself (at whatever pitch feels comfortable) and then stop. Now just *think about* the second note. In your imagination, what does it sound like? It should be the same as the note that you just hummed. So we can assume that your brain calculated what the second note should be by recalling the first and issuing a 'copy' instruction. And in the absence of 'absolute pitch', that is how the opening of the *Twinkle* melody is stored in most people's memories – as a rule saying: 'whatever the first note is, imitate it to produce the second'.

Now hum the two notes. Hear how the second *derives from* the first, which is used to *generate* the second. This occurs through the mental connection that we have labelled a 'zygonic relationship', functioning *proactively*. We can presume that a comparable *reactive* relationship will be mirrored in the mind of someone listening to the two notes, who recognises the repetition and senses the imitation. Although your focus was probably largely on pitch, it is likely that *all* the qualities of the first note were imitated in the second: pitch, loudness, timbre and duration.

So much for this initial chunk of structure – the simplest possible form of musical organisation. But how does this relate to the *meaning* of the music at this point? Unlike the opening notes of Strauss's *Also Sprach Zarathustra* and Allegri's *Miserere*, those that begin the *Twinkle* melody probably won't convey much feeling at all. You probably chose to start on a pitch in the mid to lower range of your voice (in subconscious anticipation of the jump up that is about to come). This very ordinariness means that the note's capacity to evoke an affective response will be limited: if anything, as we have observed, it is likely to elicit a sense of emotional neutrality – something that will doubtless be reinforced by a moderate degree of loudness, an unexceptional vocal timbre and a relatively short duration. Moreover, the repetition of these unremarkable qualities means that the opening of *Twinkle* will most likely come across as an introductory statement of something more substantial that is about to unfold, rather than having any particular affective significance of its own.

What happens next? It would be possible for the same note to appear for a third time. However, while exact imitation is the source of musical logic, if a message is to convey information and so engage the interest of fellow humans, it has to be more than the same thing heard over and over again. Indeed, we are programmed to ignore most unchanging, moderate stimuli in the environment, since, ultimately, they are unlikely to be of importance for our survival.[25] Generally speaking, it is sounds that are very high or low that we need to be worried about, especially if they are loud or getting louder. And while the balance between sameness and difference varies in music within broad parameters, to begin a tune with three notes the same would be the exception rather than the rule (though see Figure 87).[26]

In any case, whoever originally created the *Twinkle* melody decided that change was the order of the day at this point, and introduced a leap of five scale-steps, forming an interval of a 'perfect 5th'. As we saw in Figure 3, this occurs between harmonics 2 and 3 of 'natural' sounds, giving the two pitches an acoustic affinity and a strong sense of defining a major chord of which the lower note is the 'root'. This means that if, for example, the first two notes of the *Twinkle* melody were a C, the third would be a G, and the two different pitches together would, for a Western listener, imply the harmony, and the pitch framework, of C major.

Hence although the 'G' could not be described as 'structural' in terms of pitch at this point in the melody (since it is not generated through the imitation of the two Cs heard previously), its appearance will sound commonplace to listeners familiar with the Western musical 'vernacular', and suggest that the tune is likely to be embedded in a recognised style

What is a listener's affective response likely to be upon hearing the ascending interval from (let us say) C to G? To get some idea, hum the first two notes of the tune and *think about* the third. As you imagined

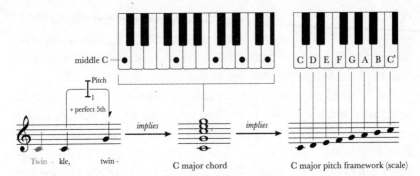

Figure 61 *To the suitably encultured listener, the second interval of* Twinkle, Twinkle *brings to mind a major chord and, from that, the pitch framework of the major scale.*

Note 3, did you feel a slight physical rise in tension in your throat as your vocal cords prepared to sing at the higher pitch? You may have sensed an accompanying elevation – albeit a very small one – in your level of emotional arousal too. As we observed in Chapter 2, just as individual notes have the capacity to evoke responses, so do the differences between them, and a rise in pitch is likely to provoke an increase in affect. This gives a feeling of movement, of progression: the musical journey is now underway. (Stopping the song after Note 3, even if the *Twinkle* melody were not familiar, would give a distinct sense of more to come.)

At this point, the creator of the tune faced a structural issue. How could the leap from C to G be connected logically into the musical narrative, which up to that point had comprised a pair of notes the same? Whoever composed the melody intuitively knew how this circle could be squared: by reiterating the *pattern* that linked Notes 1 and 2. That is, the very repetition of the opening is itself repeated, five notes higher, a form of imitation that occurs through a connection between a connection – a *secondary* zygonic relationship (see Figure 62).

It is interesting to observe that, by chance, the repetition of repetition in the melody is matched in the lyrics, as 'twinkle' is itself repeated. We have already suggested that two 'twinkles' hint at the *ongoing* nature of the star's scintillations. And the tune incorporates both repetition and change in the same gesture (as only music can). Hence the *blended* meaning of the words and music together suggest that, while the twinkling of the star is unchanging, the way we view it is nonetheless shortly to evolve. Since words and music were written quite separately, this blended meaning was not part of the original thinking of either the composer or the author. This is, of course, irrelevant to the listener's experience, however.

So far, we have discussed how content and structure pertaining to pitch combine to create meaning in the first four notes of *Twinkle, Twinkle* – but what about the other main feature of musical design: rhythm? The first three notes, equally spaced in time, are sufficient to set up a steady beat in the minds of listeners, enabling them to predict the likely *when* of subsequent events, which greatly assists their perception and understanding of the *what*. As we showed in Chapter 2, this occurs through the imitation of 'IOI's ('inter-onset intervals') projected into the future (via secondary zygonic relationships).

Hence, the *Twinkle* melody appears both to *create* in the mind of those who hear it (and who are familiar with Western mainstream music) and subsequently *to be governed by* the imaginary 'two-dimensional' framework in the domains of pitch and time that is characteristic of virtually all music (see Figure 52).

Turning now to notes 5 and 6 of *Twinkle, Twinkle*: these extend the principle set out by notes 3 and 4, moving another step up the major scale (to the 6th degree), while utilising the 'repeat the note' pattern once again. So, once more, both coherence and change are simultaneously assured.

Again, there is consistency of duration, and loudness and timbre are likely to remain more or less constant too. In terms of the *meaning* of the musical narrative at this point, the ascent raises the tension a fraction more. Partly this is due to the increased 'height' of the pitch, and partly because it occupies a place in the major scale that is functionally further away from the one that is perceived to be the musical 'home' of the piece – the first scale degree, $\hat{1}$, or 'tonic' (notionally C), which is the note with which the *Twinkle* melody begins. However, with the end of the first line of words approaching ('star'), the music needs a point of temporary repose (rather than a sense of complete closure) and 5th degree of the scale, $\hat{5}$, or 'dominant' (notionally G) has the necessary qualities. It is the first pitch that does *not* fulfil the function of $\hat{1}$ to occur in the harmonic series (see Figure 3); hence to the listener it has a sense of being near to

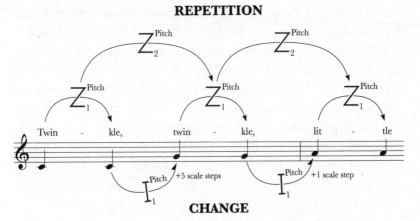

Figure 62 *Repetition of repetition binds changes of pitch coherently into the unfolding melodic narrative.*

$\hat{1}$ yet distinct from it, and most musical narratives in the Western classical tradition head towards the key associated with $\hat{5}$ (the 'dominant') as their first main departure from $\hat{1}$ (the 'tonic'). To hear this process in action, sing the first six notes ('Twinkle, twinkle, little …) and *imagine* the seventh. Can you feel the sense of physical and emotional relaxation as you prepared to sing 'star'? And afterwards having arrived somewhere new without being too far away from the musical 'home' of the opening notes?

Here, the rhythm is necessarily different too, since 'star' has only one syllable. This means that the repetition that was responsible for the music's logic up to this point is not an option. However, coherence is assured since the new appearance of $\hat{5}$ echoes those that occurred earlier. And the longer note at this point reinforces the intuitive pause in the words.

In summary, the first line of the music of the *Twinkle* melody takes the listener on a miniature musical journey: the changes in pitch give the illusion of movement up the major scale, before a small descent to a point of temporary repose. This effect is engendered through familiarity with many other pieces of music that use the same pitch framework in statistically similar ways. The abstract narrative in sound is coherent because we hear individual notes as deriving from one another through imitation.

Notice that although there are seven different musical events, there are only four different pitches and two different note-lengths. This high degree of 'redundancy' (to borrow a term from information theory) is a consequence of musical events having to refer to themselves to make sense. The position with words, however, is very different: because their meaning resides in things beyond themselves, the amount of repetition they engender – even in poems, such as *Twinkle, Twinkle, Little Star,* where reiteration is used to add another, rhetorical layer of meaning – is, as we have observed, generally much less. As we shall see, this has important consequences for children's early musical and linguistic development.

* * *

In music, the ends of phrases are of particular interest and importance, since they are potential turning points, where melodies could head off in a number of different directions, according to the shape of the piece that the composer wishes to create. Should we have the same thing again, for example, or something different? If so, how different should it be? If it is *very* different, how will the music be made to sound coherent? In fact, the capacity of one phrase to join logically with a range of others is fundamental to the process of composition, and a vital element in our intuitive understanding of musical structure.

In *Twinkle, Twinkle,* following the first phrase, with its assertive move from tonic to dominant – 'away from home' – mere repetition would seem a backward step: rather, there is a sense of the musical narrative needing to continue, perhaps leading the ear to a new tonal destination or maybe taking it back to $\hat{1}$, to the melody's starting point. Therefore, we are in the realm of *difference* that nonetheless needs to offer a coherent extension to what went before. This is achieved simply, yet subtly, through two kinds of musical logic operating in tandem: repetition of the rhythm of the entire first phrase alongside a continuation of the descending pattern of pitch with which the opening line ended. Together, these structural devices work to produce an abstract narrative in sound that is both coherent and aesthetically satisfying: the initial leap up unleashes a sense of energy, which is followed by a more measured return to the tonic down the steps of the scale, and a feeling of repose. The essence of this

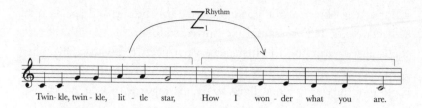

Coherence is assured through the rhythmic repetition of the entire first line
working in tandem with a descending scale that returns to the tonic (C)

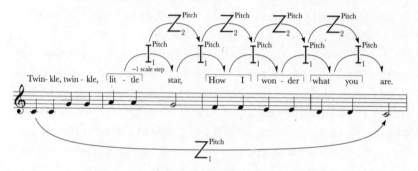

Figure 63 *Structural connections ensure aesthetic unity
in the first two lines of* Twinkle, Twinkle.

melodic design – of an 'arch' in sound that rises then falls – is clearly one
that the human brain finds particularly pleasing, since it is found time
and again in the music of many cultures.[27]

We have now arrived at the end of the first section of *Twinkle, Twinkle*.
It is a self-contained musical miniature with sufficient variation in pitch
to give a sense of setting out from a particular point, moving away from
it and returning, while, at the same time, every note is coherently related
to at least one other through imitation. This repetition of one form or
another locks the diversity together, giving the fourteen separate notes a
powerful sense of perceptual unity.

However, as we know, this is not actually the end of the musical
journey. The music starts up again in what listeners familiar with the
music will recognise as the 'middle section'. Aesthetically, this demands
to be something different, yet also to belong to the same whole. We have
already seen how the text, which has reached the same point in its structure, achieves this need for variety within unity. The first two lines identify

a star as the object of the poem, describe this briefly, and speak of the subject's contemplation of it. Lines three and four proceed with the same topic, also continuing the first person perspective. Hence they cohere with lines one and two. However, they move on to cast the subject's perception of the star in a new light, by comparing it with a diamond.

What does the music do to achieve a comparable aesthetic end? How does the composer indicate to the listener that what he or she is listening to belongs to the same narrative while telling a different part of the story? Is it possible for the second section of the music to 'comment' on what went before in the same way that the words do?

The *Twinkle* melody achieves this in a way that is at once straightforward yet subtle. With the word 'up', the tune returns to the 5th degree of the scale, the goal of the first line, thereby taking the listener to a place that is at once familiar and yet indicative of more to come. What will happen this time? As the end of line two provided a sense of completion, the ear demands something else, and this is achieved by transposing the whole of the previous line of music up one step.

This works since, while the notes themselves are *different*, the relationships between them are *the same*, following an identical pattern. Aesthetically, the effect is also similar in some respects, yet with a fundamental difference, since the music ends not on the 1st degree of the scale, but the 2nd (see Figure 64). This means that the line ends with the feeling of being close to home, but not there yet. You can gauge this effect by singing the tune up to the end of line three ('Up above the world so high') and then stopping. Do you have a sense that the music yearns for something more? Now sing the tonic (the 1st degree of the scale). Can you hear how that note produces a sense of fulfilment? If so, this is for two reasons. First, because, as we have observed, the great majority of pieces end with the tonic, which means that it can be a strong indicator of closure. Second, the melody moves down in steps from the 5th degree: $\hat{5}, \hat{4}, \hat{3}, \hat{2}$... and so there is an *expectation* that the pattern will continue, and that the 1st degree will follow.

However, listeners' expectations are to be frustrated, since the fourth line ('Like a diamond in the sky') begins not with the tonic, but by jumping back to the dominant (the 5th degree), and then doing what

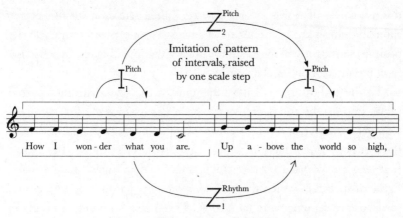

Figure 64 *The development of musical ideas through the simplest of means characterises lines 2 and 3 of* Twinkle, Twinkle.

music does best – repeating what has gone before. The notes of line 4 are identical to those of line 3, but in terms of *meaning*, listeners may interpret this repetition in different ways. For example, it is possible to hear line 4 as an affirmation of line 3 in musical terms, as though the performer were declaring: 'Did I mean what I just said? Yes I did – and I'll say it again!' This way of understanding the music can be emphasised by singing the fourth line slightly louder than the third, rather as people sometimes speak more loudly to underline a point whose significance they suspect may have been missed the first time round.

Line 4 of the *Twinkle* melody can also be heard as an *echo* of the third, particularly if the repeat is sung more quietly than the original. With this interpretation, it is as though the performer is *reflecting* on the musical meaning of the line 3: 'Did I mean what I just said? I *think* so. Let me listen carefully one more time.' So repetition can have different *rhetorical* significance in music, just as it can in language.

Whichever interpretation is adopted will spill over into one's under-standing of the text: the first stressing the diamond-like nature of the star, the second putting more weight on its position above the world. Either way of reading the connection is reinforced by the repetition that occurs at the end of the lines in the form of 'sky' rhyming with 'high'. Because the two series of words are in any case linked semantically, this correspondence in sound is not necessary to ensure coherence: contrary to the position in music, where repetition is essential for things to make sense, in poetry it is an optional extra.

By the end of line 4 ('Like a diamond in the sky'), with its repeated move down to the 2nd degree of the scale, the urge for musical closure is stronger than ever, and what follows is one of those magical moments, in the form of a dual function, which can only occur in music. The closest that language comes to it is in the figure of speech called 'anadiplosis', a figure of speech in which the word or words used at the end of a phrase (or clause or sentence) are used to start the next. An example occurs in line 8 of Milton's poem *Lycidas*: 'For Lycidas is dead, dead ere his prime'. In music, though, the repetition isn't necessary, as the twofold function can be implied in a single note through elision.

To hear this in action, sing 'Like a diamond in the sky' and then the first note of the next line 'Twin-' (the tonic). This provides a satisfactory conclusion to the descending patterns presented in lines 3 and 4, but at the same time sets in mind a repeat of lines 1 and 2, and so generates an urge for the music to continue (see Figure 65).

And so the *Twinkle* melody comes to an end as it began, with a repetition of the first two lines. The corresponding text is repeated too. The coherence of the music – the sense of derivation through imitation – is clearly audible. But what narrative meaning can possibly be engendered through repeating half the material of the song? What new information can be added by saying so much of the same thing again?

The metaphor of a journey, which starts from home, moves away and then returns, which was invoked to explain the sense of the first two lines (with their movement from the tonic to the dominant scale degrees and back again) seems appropriate once more, though here it is writ on a larger scale. It is as though the first two lines ('Twinkle, twinkle, little star, How I wonder what you are') represent 'home' at a deeper structural level, while the second two lines ('Up above the world so high, Like a diamond in the sky') personify 'being away', and the last two lines (a repeat of 'Twinkle, twinkle') depict 'home' again. Hence the design of the song as a whole can be heard as an extension of the narrative set out

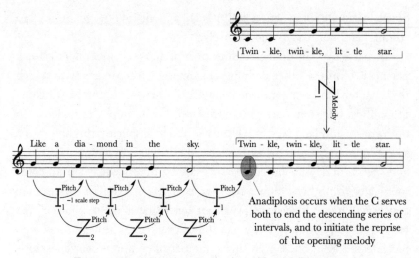

Anadiplosis occurs when the C serves both to end the descending series of intervals, and to initiate the reprise of the opening melody

Figure 65 *The end of the second section of* Twinkle, Twinkle, *and the beginning of the third, overlap.*

in the opening lines. But as the action takes place over a longer period of time, the sense of return is stronger, and the final descent to the tonic feels more complete.

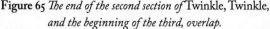

Thus within a short and ostensibly unremarkable children's song lies an intricate and enduring musical message – enduring because it is at once so simple and yet so subtle. Although most music is far more complex than this, the underlying principles are essentially the same.

What a stroke of human genius – at some stage in the prehistoric past – to realise that coherent narratives in sound that unfold over time could be formed through one simple principle: imitation. How did this come about? Perhaps as an initially unintended (and almost certainly unrecognised) consequence of the wider importance of sameness and similarity in our understanding of the world. If so, then it may be that by gaining a better understanding of how we create and perceive music, we will be able to come a little closer to fathoming how we function mentally as human beings. As Leonard Bernstein once said, music offers 'a striking model of the human brain in action and as such, a model of how we think';[28] to comprehend music is to know ourselves.

In particular, an understanding of how music works offers a fresh perspective on the other defining characteristic of humans with which this chapter has been concerned: language. There are a number of commonalities, but some key differences too. For example, proficiency in both music and language is typically acquired implicitly through exposure and interaction in the early years, when all children improvise songs and speech in day-to-day contexts to express their feelings and to communicate with others. However, as far as adults in Western societies are concerned, music is regarded as an art form that is the province of the few – primarily produced by a handful of performers as recordings, who recreate the work of an even tinier number of composers for consumption by all the rest of us (who very rarely attend live performances). In terms of *content*, language ultimately comprises words, which tend to have strong 'absolute' meanings that convey more or less specific information; conversely, the musical message largely resides in the differences between notes, which have the capacity to induce a series of emotional responses. With regard to *structure*, repetition is the exception in language, but the rule in music. As far as function is concerned, 'real-life' consequences often follow from language, whereas the ideas expressed through music exist only in the imagination. Finally, music precedes language in early development – indeed, without the former, the latter would struggle to get off the ground.

Function	Language	Music
Universal characteristics	Highly evolved and complex communication through sound	
	A feature of all societies	
	Understanding typically acquired implicitly through exposure and interaction	
Engagement	Most people engage with language reactively, proactively and interactively as children and adults	In the West, most people engage with music reactively, proactively and interactively as children, but only reactively as adults
	Primarily improvised by everyone in day-to-day contexts to express feelings and communicate	In the West, primarily produced by a handful of performers as recordings, in re-creating the work of a tiny number of composers for large audiences (who generally aren't present at the performance)

Function	Language	Music
Elements	Largely comprises words, whose core meanings are symbolic, representing different aspects of human experience; refers to things 'beyond itself' – hence cross-modal relationships are essential	Largely comprises notes, which exist in their own right as non-symbolic perceptual entities; refers primarily to itself – hence unimodal relationships (existing only in the domain of sound) are sufficient
	There are a large number of basic units of meaning (hundreds of thousands of words are available in English, for example)	There are a small number of basic units of meaning: for the majority of listeners, most music comprises melodies made up of 12 potential small intervals of pitch, and six low whole-number ratios of duration (taken as the gap between the onsets of notes)
	Words tend to have strong 'absolute' meanings, which can be qualified through relationships with other words	For most people, notes tend to have weak 'absolute' meanings: it is the relationships between them that bear the burden of the message
Structure	Words (in English) can be categorised as fulfilling one of eight different basic 'functions' (parts of speech), with many subcategories, that work together in 10 different ways to form meaning: through semantics, syntax, simile and metaphor, standpoint, source, sequence, sound, spoken quality, shared knowledge and social context (see pp. 130 and 131).	In tonal music, notes can fulfil one of 12 functions with regard to pitch and usually up to one of four different functions in relation to metre (the pattern of accented and unaccented beats)
	Structure (syntax) depends on the function of words, which rely on semantics; hence many forms of structural relationship are possible	Musical structure ultimately depends on one type of relationship – 'zygonic' – through which imitation is perceived between any features of notes or the connections that may be perceived between them
	Repetition is the exception	Repetition is the rule
	Maximum level of semantic abstraction is relationships between relationships (second-order relationships) – as in analogies ('blue is to sky, as green is to grass')	Maximum level of abstraction is relationships between relationships between relationships (third-order) – as in a beat that regularly speeds up
	The sequence of words is important, though there can be some flexibility, which can lead to different shades of emphasis	Sequence is of primary importance in the identity of a melody: change the order of events and you will have a different tune

Function	Language	Music
	Tends to convey specific information	Tends to convey general feelings
Meaning	Demands shared understanding of concepts that are conveyed symbolically; understanding of everyday language tends to be '(virtually) all or nothing' – though with literature there is more room for the imagination	Only limited shared understanding is required: pieces of music can be understood satisfactorily at different levels, from complex emotional narratives in sound, to series of simple patterns
	Meaning often arises over time through concatenations of ideas that are abstracted; omissions and errors can cause difficulties in understanding	For most listeners, music exists more or less 'in the moment'; errors or gaps in transmission or reception tend not to be critical for basic levels of engagement
	Meaning is highly contextually dependent	Associative meaning is contextually dependent; intrinsic musical meaning is much less so
Consequences	'Real-life' consequences often follow from what is said (although language can convey imaginary ideas)	Music exists outside 'real-life', conveying ideas that exist only in the realm of the imagination
Development	Language follows early musical development	At its simplest, engagement with music occurs early in development – as a primary means of communicating with others

Table 4 The nature and function of language and music: similarities and differences

Complexity and the Problem of 'Greatness'

Are some pieces of music better than others? Or of greater value? Questions like these have engaged philosophers, thinking musicians and consumers of music – adults, adolescents and children alike – from time immemorial. If you ask toddlers which song they think is better, *Twinkle, Twinkle, Little Star* or *The Wheels on the Bus*, they will tell you without a second thought (perhaps by performing the appropriate actions); if you consult the views of theorists such as Heinrich Schenker and Rudolph Reti as to how to gauge the artistic merit of pieces from the Western classical canon, they are likely to allude to discovering the music's deeper unity beneath a surface diversity; if you ask psychologists about judgements of 'greatness' in music, they may well put the question to a (more or less) representative sample of the population to ascertain what people tend to think;[29] and if you ask philosophers which has greater value, Schubert's lied *An die Musik* or Schumann's *Ich Grolle Nicht*, they will probably furrow their brows and mutter something about insuperable epistemological difficulties. It seems that the more you know, the harder the question becomes. But, as Leonard Meyer says:

> Whatever the difficulties, uncertainties, and the hazards may be, the question 'What makes music great?' is one that anyone deeply concerned with his art must attempt at least to answer. We cannot … escape from the problem of value.[30]

So what criteria should we use? Let us turn to Meyer again, who notes that there are established technical criteria for judging whether a piece is good or not. For example, it must have

> consistency of style: that is, it must employ a unified system of expectations and probabilities; it should possess clarity of basic intent; it should have variety, unity, and all the other categories which are so easy to find after the fact.[31]

But, as he points out, these qualities are necessary but not sufficient to determine *greatness*.

> Indeed the tune 'Twinkle, twinkle little star' possesses style, unity, variety, and so forth. And if we then ask is Bach's B Minor Mass better than 'Twinkle, twinkle' – using *only* these technical categories – we shall, I am afraid, be obliged to answer that they are equally good, adding perhaps, 'each in its own way.'[32]

To address this issue, Meyer seeks recourse in a recurrent theme of his music-philosophical thinking: that of uncertainty. If a tune charts a course that is immediate and obvious, then it is unlikely to be 'great'. Rather it is in the circuitousness of melodic design, whereby the ear is led first in one direction and then the other, delaying the gratification of returning 'home' to the tonic, that distinguishes 'high art' from the musical vernacular. On first inspection, this account seems reasonable enough, in that it accords with some everyday musical experiences. Compare, for example, *Twinkle, Twinkle*, as harmonised by Mozart in his set of piano variations K. 265, with the opening of his Piano Sonata,

K. 333 (see Figure 66). Both use a similar part of the major scale; both comprise a series of short phrases of equal length; both make use of leaps up in pitch followed by descents in steps, including, notably, $\hat{6}, \hat{5}, \hat{4}, \hat{3},$ $\hat{2}, \hat{1}$; and harmonically both start from the chord on the first degree of the scale, 'I', before moving to the chord on the fifth degree, 'V', and then returning to the tonic ('I'). *But*, as we should expect from Meyer's definition, K. 333 does indeed take a more circuitous route, with the chord on the second degree – ii – being intercalated between I and V. As we noted in relation to Bach's first prelude from *The Well-Tempered Clavier*, this minor harmony can evoke a particular feeling of yearning in the context of a piece in the major mode, and so it is in K. 333.

So much for circuitousness at the macro-level – but the melody of K. 333 is characterised by 'delayed gratification' on a moment-to-moment basis too: whereas in *Twinkle* the notes of the melody each fit precisely and immediately with their harmonies, in K. 333, the ear is often made to wait for this satisfaction through the pervasive use of appoggiaturas – discordant pitches that, as we have seen, are adjacent to harmony notes and resolve by moving up or down a step to them. Although each of these instances of tension and resolution lasts for only a fraction of a second, taken as a whole they have a cumulative effect: the listener comes to expect that although the piece is in the major key and therefore ostensibly cheerful, things in reality aren't that straightforward; shadows are constantly flickering across the light (see Figure 66). Arguably, this is what gives Mozart's music its depth and interest. An unremitting cheeriness that is insensible to life's tribulations can be as wearing in music as it is in people.

Yet we shouldn't forget that since Mozart used the tune of *Twinkle, Twinkle* (*Ah! Vous dirai-je, Maman*) as the inspiration for a set of variations, presumably the uncomplicated, not to say rather obvious, melody must, in his view, have had at least some artistic merit or potential. But in K. 265, the art is not so much in the innocence of the theme as in material that Mozart derives from it. He was merely adopting the tried and tested approach of drawing ideas from the musical vernacular of his day to create something of higher aesthetic value. By beginning a piece with an undemanding, familiar tune, and leading the ear through an increasingly complex series of melodic perambulations around essentially the same harmonic circuit, composers could satisfy both their own desire for musical sophistication while pleasing an audience who needed to sense how the music works and enjoy it during a first hearing (since rapid appreciation was a prerequisite for future commissions). Besides this, by incorporating everyday pieces such as children's songs, folk melodies and hymn tunes into their works, composers ensured that the flowering of their high art was rooted in a musical language that everyone could understand – something made possible since the music of the nursery, the inn and the street shared the same background organisation – the same musical 'DNA' – as that performed at the palace, the concert hall and the opera house.

* * *

Perhaps, though, comparing *Ah! Vous dirai-je, Maman* with the opening of K. 333 is insufficiently stern a test of Meyer's criterion of musical greatness, since the former was, after all, only ever intended to be a children's song, and therefore straightforward in design, whereas the latter was conceived as art, with the greater complexity that this almost inevitably entails. A fairer test would be to compare K. 333 with a more directly comparable work, perhaps by a 'lesser' composer, and see in that case how well Meyer's notion of value being linked to the inhibited resolution of musical expectations stands up. As it happens, there is a piece that fits the bill perfectly: J. C. Bach's Sonata for Piano (or Harpsichord), Op. 5, No. 3 (see Figure 66). This sonata is particularly apposite, since it forms one of a set with which Mozart is known to have been acquainted, and many features in the musical 'background' and 'foreground' are similar.

For example, in the 'background', both pieces share a uniformity of timbre, and dynamics prescribed within a small range, from *piano* to *forte* (*p* to *f*). Aesthetically, this means that there is little overt expressiveness that *originates* in relation to these aspects of sound. In this regard, it is interesting to note that timbre and loudness are important features of the affective vocalising that preverbal infants and their carers use to share their feelings (see pp. 189–190). Hence these qualities of sound have a more immediate impact on listeners than music-specific attributes such as tonality, which demand a higher level of structural processing. This, then, is one explanation of the emotional restraint that is generally held to characterise pieces such as Mozart's K. 333, J. C. Bach's Op. 5, No. 3 and others in similar style, particularly for listeners newly approaching the works. The music's expressive qualities are principally bound up in the integrated structuring of pitch and rhythm, which requires familiarity with the piece to process fully. It is also in these two domains that the great majority of 'background' organisation, and by far the most musically significant and sophisticated, occurs.

For example, both pieces have a regular beat (with some minor flexibility in performance) and both use the same 'common time' metre (four crotchet beats in the bar). Inter-onset intervals (IOIs) and the durations of notes (which usually amount to the same thing) fall within a limited range, the longest in each case being a minim (which would last about a second in performance), the shortest for the most part being a semiquaver (an eighth of a minim), with the notes of trills being somewhat shorter than that. In terms of the relationships between successive IOIs, by far and away the most common ratio is 1 : 1 (see Figure 49). This means that the likeliest thing to happen is that a given note will be followed by another of the same length. Similarly, the distribution of intervals between adjacent notes in the melody of both K. 333 and Op. 5, No. 3 is highly constrained, with the preponderance being small (three scale steps or less). Harmonically, both movements are dominated by major and minor triads and 7th chords and their inversions,[33] with around two thirds being constructed on the tonic and dominant (I and V) and around 90 per cent on I, ii, IV and V. The great majority of harmonic transitions are +4 scale degrees (for example, changes from I to IV, ii to V, or V to I) or +5 (for instance, I to V, or IV to I). Both sonata movements use an essentially two-part texture – typical of keyboard music of this genre – in which right hand and left hand parts fulfil respectively the roles of melody and accompaniment, the latter offering harmonic and rhythmic support to the former, which tends to be the ear's primary focus of attention.

Taking all these factors together, it is evident that, at any given time, over a dozen different forms of 'background' organisation are at work in the sonatas. It is not clear how the brain handles so much simultaneous information, though, presumably, the high level of repetition enables the listener to make a number of assumptions, thereby reducing the moment-to-moment processing load, and ensuring that there is sufficient mental capacity available to focus on the 'foreground', where the main musical narrative plays out. The extraordinary thing is how Mozart (or, indeed, any other composer) could possibly devise pieces of any originality when working within such tight stylistic constraints – where so much of the musical organisation is predetermined. However, the structure-bearing capacity of pitch and rhythm appears to be immense, giving composers effectively limitless scope for creating new abstract patterns in sound (the first five or six pitches of a tune are all that is typically required to identify it as unique – see p. 35).

Moving now to the 'foregrounds' of the sonatas, a number of distinct features of K. 333 appear to be attributable to Op. 5, No. 3. For example, there is a close resemblance between the opening melodies, in terms of pitch, rhythm and harmonic structure, and the 'Alberti'-style left hand parts, with their repeated patterns of broken chords, are also very much alike. Particularly striking is the similarity of the four-note motif that opens K. 333 to a fragment of melody embedded near the beginning of Op. 5, No. 3, and the use of appoggiaturas that is evident in these two short figures continues to be an important feature of both melodies as they unfold (Figure 66).

On the face of it, then, the two movements share a good deal in common, and the two openings, in particular, are very similar. To listeners familiar with the Western classical style, they both make complete musical sense. Yet K. 333 and Op. 5, No. 3 are *not* the same, and, argu-ably, do not constitute equally fine works of art. To my ear, K. 333 offers a more fulfilling aesthetic experience – it is a 'greater' work of art – a judgement that others have made over time, for the Mozart sonata has long featured in the standard piano repertoire, while the Bach is seldom heard. So where does the difference lie? Is Meyer's definition of musical value right?

Let us consider where Op. 5, No. 3 stands in relation to K. 333 with regard to its capacity for implying certain continuations and then

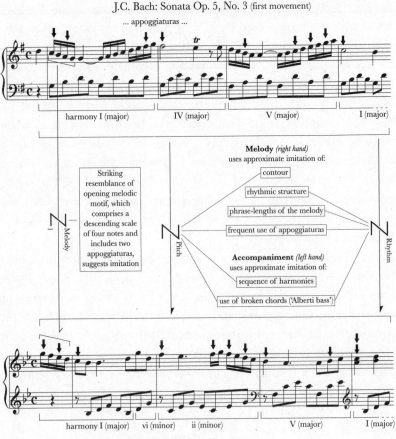

Figure 66 *Similarities between J.C. Bach, Sonata Op. 5, No. 3 and Mozart, Sonata K. 333, and probable elements of derivation.*

delaying them, and for setting up patterns of tension and resolution, thereby making listeners wait for consonance – for a feeling of repose. In this respect both movements are very much the same: the function of chord ii in K. 333 as the route to chord V is taken by chord IV in Op. 5, No. 3. And, like K. 333, Op. 5, No. 3 makes extensive use of appoggiaturas. Therefore, Meyer's criterion of greatness seems to fall down. So let us consider the two pieces, instead, from the perspective of zygonic theory, and see whether that sheds more light on the problem – for if the theory is correct, and can satisfactorily explain how music works and how abstract patterns of sound are able to create meaning, then it should be able to point up the essential differences between the two movements. In particular, it will enable us to weigh up the balance between structure (patterns of imitation) and content (pitches, intervals, durations, IOIs and so on), and account for the emotional responses they evoke.

In both opening melodies, the appoggiaturas provide important affective triggers, set off by the sense of movement from tension to resolution that each evokes. In Bach's Op. 5, No. 3, this effect is felt most powerfully in bars 2 and 4 where the discords that are created extend for two complete beats. However, while these and the other appoggiaturas – key aspects of the music's expressive 'content' – are integrated into the structure of the passage, the connection between the two is not rigorously worked through (see Figure 67). So, for example, though the initial figure includes two appoggiaturas, enriching the simple scalar descent, these are lost in the subsequent ascending scale, although a further appoggiatura appears incidentally at its climax (at the end of bar 1). And while the two-beat appoggiatura in bar 2, the first main expressive gesture of the piece, is conceivably, though at most weakly, linked through imitation to the three that precede, there is no real sense that it grows organically from them. Bars 3 and 4 proceed along similar lines, whereby despite their pattern of intervals in structural terms deriving from bars 1 and 2, the asymmetrical nature of the transposition means that the appoggiaturas do not read across.

In the melody that opens K. 333, however, the position is rather different (see Figure 68). Structure and content are systematically yet unobtrusively integrated, so that the logic of the music and its expressive character are fused in an abstract discourse that is wholly persuasive. Listeners are propelled straight into the action by the initial descending figure, comprising two appoggiaturas which lead the ear naturally to a third that is augmented (doubled in length) and unambiguously establishes the first degree of the scale – the tonic – on the downbeat of the first complete bar. However, this proves to be just a stepping stone to a fourth appoggiatura, which, augmented again, bears even greater expressive emphasis. Significantly, this falls on chord ii, which is a minor harmony and provides the

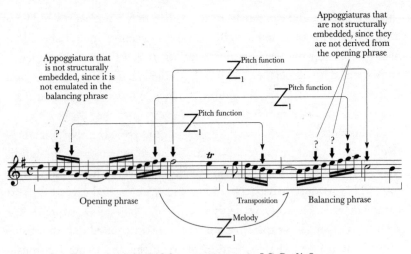

Figure 67 *A third of the appoggiaturas in J.C. Bach's Sonata,*
Op. 5, No. 3 are not structurally embedded.

first hint of the emotional depths lying beneath the surface elegance of the music that find fuller expression later, particularly in the 'development section' (the central part of the movement in which material presented in the 'exposition' is transformed, and so cast in a new light). What makes the appoggiatura on chord ii all the more telling, is that both structure and content are locked in to what has gone before, deriving from the preceding material through transposition and rhythmic augmentation.

In terms of content, this fourth appoggiatura in K. 333, heard structurally as a product of the first three, does more than *replace* in current consciousness their affective qualities: it *transforms* them. The major harmonic context of the earlier appoggiaturas becomes minor, which, given the prevailing major mode, evokes a sense of yearning, highlighted by the dissonance of the fourth appoggiatura, which seeks to be resolved. Intuitively, such resolution demands a further appearance of the appoggiatura over tonic harmony and, again, Mozart achieves this through compelling though unobtrusive structural logic. An elaborated and transposed version of the opening descent (which extends the initial pattern of appoggiaturas) leads to a transposed version of the fourth appoggiatura over a dominant chord (V), and from there – harmonically continuing the movement through chord ii – to an inverted form over the tonic (I),

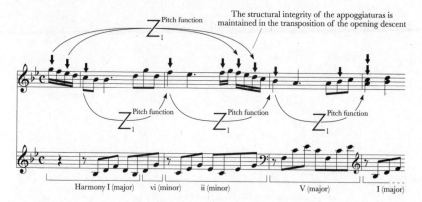

The changes of harmony give each of the appoggiaturas at the end of phrases a unique expressive effect
Beyond this, by deriving from the one that precedes, each appoggiatura is structurally integrated into the narrative
That is, each appoggiatura transforms the last, imbuing it with an expressivity that is *functional* as well as *ornamental*

Narrative effect of appoggiaturas

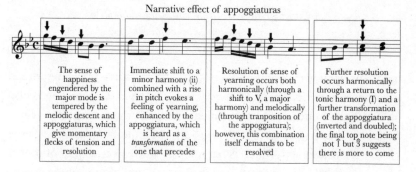

The sense of happiness engendered by the major mode is tempered by the melodic descent and appoggiatura, which give momentary flecks of tension and resolution	Immediate shift to a minor harmony (ii) combined with a rise in pitch evokes a feeling of yearning, enhanced by the appoggiatura, which is heard as a *transformation* of the one that precedes	Resolution of sense of yearning occurs both harmonically (through a shift to V, a major harmony) and melodically (through tranposition of the appoggiatura); however, this combination itself demands to be resolved	Further resolution occurs harmonically through a return to the tonic harmony (I) and a further transformation of the appoggiatura (inverted and doubled); the final top note being not 1̂ but 3̂ suggests there is more to come

Figure 68 *The integration of structure and content in K. 333 means that the appoggiaturas function expressively both 'in the moment' and to articulate the emotional undulations of the broader musical narrative.*

reinforced in parallel thirds. This doubling emphasises the sense of resolution, while the melodic ascent to the third degree of the scale (rather than resting on the tonic) implies that there is more to come.

Next, we compare the ways in which melody and accompaniment are integrated in terms of structure and content in the two sonata movements. In Op. 5, No. 3, an opening connection is made through retrogression, but the largely simultaneous ascent and descent of the two parts has a neutralising effect, and the music has a somewhat 'four-square' feel about it. Following this opening relationship, there are no further significant links between motifs, and the Alberti bass fails to rise above the

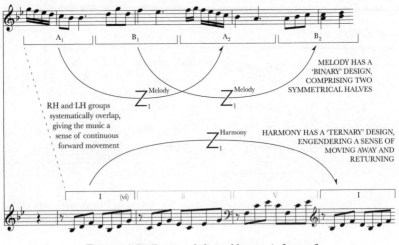

Figure 69 *Different melodic and harmonic forms of symmetry are integrated in the classical style.*

mundane, merely supplying the melody with a succession of rhythmised harmonies (see Figure 66). In K. 333, though, while retrogression is also used initially to tie in the left hand part with the right, since the accompaniment follows the lead of the melody, the imitation delivers a sense of forward movement, which is maintained as the overlapping of motifs between treble and bass continues. The effect is emphasised, moreover, by the off-beat start to the figuration, which puts a spring in the step of the music, and, subsequently, through repetition of the opening quaver rest, allows it to 'breathe'. In the second half of the first complete bar of K. 333, there is further imitation as the left hand echoes the rising arpeggio of G minor in close imitation. In the second bar a further connection emerges as the descending semiquavers in the right hand (principally derived from the opening gesture) can also be heard as an elaborated version of the preceding C minor broken chord in the left. Hence, in addition to its own, internal logic, the accompaniment shares a mutual sense of agency with the melody. Aesthetically, this imbues the music with a particularly strong sense of coherence and purpose.

Finally, note that other subtle details of design exist on a formal level too. For example, the two-part structure of the melody, in which the second half is generated from the first through transposition, complements the sense of return engendered by the accompaniment, in which the opening harmony and figuration are repeated (with slight variation) at the end of the four bars (see Figure 69). These two forms of symmetry interact to produce the poise so typical of the classical style.

***

What does this analysis, framed by zygonic theory, of the openings of K. 333 and Op. 5, No. 3 tell us? First, that before J.C. Bach and Mozart even started work on their sonatas, they were destined to operate within a tight framework of 'background' organisation, determined, in particular, by the composers' (doubtless subconscious) decisions to respect the parameters that defined the style of classical keyboard music in the mid to late eighteenth century. As a result, the movements are replete with many forms of structure that are variously common to some, many or virtually all other pieces. Yet, the capacity for potential combinations of pitch and rhythm to exist is such that this degree of control was probably necessary for their audiences to be able to make sense of them – particularly at a first hearing; and, as we have hinted, it was essential for J.C. Bach and Mozart's survival as composers that their new compositions were instantly accessible. Mozart's genius (as opposed to Bach's talent) lay in the ability to craft something original and of lasting value within such tight constraints, and K. 333 has foreground qualities that Op. 5, No. 3 does not. What are these? Our analysis suggests that the aesthetic worth of the sonata – or at least the opening of its first movement of it – is ultimately attributable to the consummate fusion of structure and content.

Of course, it is not possible, on the basis of this one brief account, to produce a theory that would enable us to *predict* the prospective aesthetic value of a piece on the basis of certain patterns of relationships. But zygonic theory gives us a tool with which at least a partial interrogation of this thorny issue may be possible. It is clear, however, on the basis of the evidence presented here, that the mere presence of unity – whether to the deep tonal forms unearthed by Schenker, or of the motific type identified by Schoenberg – does not in itself ensure musical worth. Nor, as Leonard Meyer would have it, does it appear that a composer's capacity for thwarting, manipulating and eventually realising the expectations that are aroused in listeners by sophisticated musical patterning is sufficient. Rather, it is my contention that what makes K. 333 great music is the manner in which the expressive qualities of its notes and intervals, its 'content', are integrated with structure. Not a single note is redundant: all are locked together in a multidimensional imitative framework that, by utilising each note in several different ways, maximises their expressive capacity. Yet all that listeners hear is the illusion of effortless beauty.

Other Forms of Musical Meaning

Our discussion up to this point has focussed on what Meyer would have called 'absolutist' accounts of musical meaning, which pertain to the fabric of music itself, seeking to explain how patterns of sound can engage the emotions in a kind of abstract narrative. Now we turn to what Meyer terms 'referentialist' explanations of meaning in music, which arise through association with the 'external world'.

Building on the work of the American psychologist John Watson in the early part of the twentieth century, behaviourists showed that humans can learn (implicitly) or be taught (explicitly) to respond to almost any object or event in the environment in a positive or negative way.[34] In our evolutionary past, such 'conditioning' clearly had huge survival value, saving the vital time and mental energy that evaluating each new circumstance from scratch would have demanded. This propensity lives on in us today, and individual pieces of music – or even just fragments or features of them (such as genre and style) – share the capacity with other stimuli to become emotionally 'tagged'. In fact, music seems to be particularly susceptible to acquiring this kind of (arbitrary) meaning: people's associations of certain works with incidents in real life or with individuals to whom they are close or places that hold a special connection for them can be so powerful that they become indelibly etched in memory. Hence, when people talk about 'meaning' in music, they are quite likely to be referring to the emotions aroused by particular pieces that have a special place in their personal history.

Why should music be particularly prone to 'catching' the emotions that are stimulated in listeners by other features of the environment in which it is heard? Maybe it is because music is both non-representational yet has the capacity to evoke an emotional response. In this respect, each piece is a 'tabula rasa', waiting for an affective state to be etched upon it in the mind. But whatever the reason, it means that 'pure' musical meaning can be overlaid (or even confounded) by the vicissitudes of personal experience. For example, after she was widowed, my mother would experience emotional anguish upon hearing the *Hornpipe* from Handel's *Water Music*, since it was the music to which she and my father had elatedly walked down the aisle following their marriage some thirty years earlier. Yet the piece, particularly the opening, could hardly be more cheerful: that, of course, is why it was originally chosen as a wedding march! And had I asked my mother, she would doubtless have acknowledged that the music was intrinsically joyous in tone (she knew that others still found it so); it was *she* who had changed. The musical code had not altered, nor her ability to interpret it. What had happened was that the effect of this particular musical narrative had become overwhelmed by circumstance.

On a lighter note, the British psychologist John Booth Davies gives the following wry account of what he terms the 'DTPOT' phenomenon ('Darling, they're playing our tune').[35]

> The lady from whose mouth this apocryphal saying is supposed to have emanated has acquired a specific emotional response to a specific tune simply because she heard it at a time when some other pleasurable business was taking place, at some time in the past. ... Even the most unmusical people usually have an associative response of this type to at least one or two tunes. (A man might therefore justifiably feel some alarm if his unmusical wife suddenly develops an apparently spontaneous liking for a new tune.)

* * *

The fact that music is so susceptible to acquiring external meanings has had a wide range of consequences, variously positive and negative, according to one's point of view, throughout history. In particular, it has been a source of concern to those who seek authority over others because of its unique capacity, through association, to stir the emotions in relation to culture, nationhood and religion, reinforcing political affiliations or fomenting revolution, reifying the sacred or elevating the profane. Yet music is intrinsically *abstract*, and it is its power to convey so much while saying nothing tangible at all that makes its message difficult to control and therefore (some have believed) dangerous in the wrong hands.

For example, Plato thought that the State should control all aspects of musical practice, including the choice of instruments, with only the lyre and the harp being used in cities (although shepherds could play pipes in the country).[36] Subsequently, the Christian church found music particularly problematic at various stages of its evolution. In the mid-sixteenth century, for instance, the Council of Trent set out a number of edicts, which included strongly discouraging composers from using 'secular' melodies in ecclesiastical contexts.[37] Yet what is 'secular' (and what 'sacred') is purely a cultural construct that can be visited on music willy-nilly, as intrinsically it bears no meaning of this kind. Incredibly, almost five hundred years later, a similar concern is alive and kicking – hard – in the land of the free, with American Pastors railing against rock 'n' roll, the 'Devil's music', whose pumping beat is the sound of 'Satan's lawlessness':[38] a very human conceit of which Old Nick himself would no doubt be proud.

The church is not alone in attempting musical censorship, of course; certain (authoritarian) political regimes have expressed concern about the power of particular pieces or styles too. In the 1930s, for example, Stalinist Russia's notoriously brutal efforts to control the arts were epitomised in their cruel and unpredictable treatment of the composer Dmitri Shosta-kovich. His opera *Lady Macbeth of Mtsensk* was first greeted as evidence of the success of 'Socialist construction', exemplifying the 'correct policy of the party'. The entirely arbitrary nature of such a connection soon became apparent, however, when, following Stalin's attendance at a performance in 1936 at which he made his displeasure at Shostakovich's score evident, the infamous article 'Muddle instead of Music' appeared in *Pravda*. Shos-takovich's music was thenceforth denounced as 'formalist', and at times he feared that he would meet the same barbarous end as many of his friends and associates.

At the other end of the social (and political) spectrum, the music that is played in shops today is likely to be calculated with clinical – not to say cynical – precision, not only to increase sales, but also to affect purchasing in particular ways. For instance, work by psychologist Adrian North and my colleague at the University of Roehampton, David Hargreaves, in the 1990s, showed that the country of origin of music being played in the background of off-licences influences the type of wine that customers buy.[39] Just a hint of the French accordion, and the Chardonnays are likely to give the Astis and the Liebfraumilchs a run for their money – even if shoppers aren't aware of the music being played.

* * *

A fundamental difference between language and music is that the former largely functions symbolically (with its primary meaning arising from the capacity of words to point to things beyond themselves and secondary meanings accruing to sounding qualities such as rhyme, assonance and metre), while music's meaning stems largely from the capacity of individual sounds and the relationships that are perceived between them to evoke emotional responses in their own right, and for these responses to be transformed over time through imitation, enabling abstract narratives in sound to be constructed. However, while additional musical meanings are possible 'through association' (described, for example, in the DTPOT scenario) other, *symbolic*, connections are possible too, through which a piece of music – or even a few distinctive notes – can come to have a truly semantic meaning, similar to language (or even substituting for it). These may be entirely arbitrary, as for example, in ring tones, advertising jingles and some door chimes. In more musical contexts, examples include the 'leitmotif' – a characteristic melodic, harmonic or rhythmic idea that is associated with a particular person, place, emotion or idea. Richard Wagner famously uses leitmotifs systematically in his mammoth cycle of four operas, *The Ring*, adding an additional symbolic strand in an already complex multimodal texture of music, words and theatrical action. Sergei Prokofiev provides a more modest example, expressly designed for children, in *Peter and the Wolf*. Here, people and animals are represented using melodies whose identities are reinforced by appearing consistently on particular instruments, including the bird (on the flute), the cat (clarinet), the duck (oboe), the grandfather (bassoon), and Peter (the strings). On a less specific level, the theme tunes of films and television programmes are designed to function symbolically too – seeking to attract listeners' attention immediately and to be instantly memorable, so that on future occasions only a snippet is necessary to bring the movie or TV show to mind. Indeed, directors sometimes reinforce a programme's unity and identity by using excerpts from the theme as background music in the course of the action, as in the 1995 BBC production of Jane Austen's *Pride and Prejudice*, with its faux-Mozartian signature tune by Carl Davis that recurs throughout.

As well as potentially being arbitrary, the connection between a fragment of music and its meaning may occur through the imitation of sounds in the environment (with varying degrees of verisimilitude), such as the growling of the big cat in *Tiger Rag*, which was first recorded by the Original Dixieland Jass Band in 1917, or the rhythmic chugging of the steam train in *Pacific 231* (see Figure 54). The extent to which such sounds are in any case intrinsically 'musical' (before being introduced into a composition) is discussed later.

Imitation of *other* sensory modalities – visual images, for example – may also arise, in one of two ways. First, as humans, we seem to have a sense of where a quality of sound or light exists on a possible continuum of variation, which means that it is possible for an association to exist between the two; loud sounds more naturally equate to bright lights than dim ones, for example, and *vice versa*.[40] More surprisingly, perhaps, listeners – including those who have never used music notation – generally seem to identify a rise in pitch with a change in position of a dot, diagonally upwards and to the right on a page (or computer screen).[41]

Second, precise connections between sensory modalities are possible at a more abstract level, when one perceived quality can be regarded to exist as a *ratio* of another. In the second half of the twentieth century, composers such as Karlheinz Stockhausen took advantage of this fact to produce notation through which music could be made to symbolise other things. For example, in *Sternklang* of 1971, representations of twenty-eight constellations provide visual imagery for performers to interpret. Here, the sense of derivation works from image to sound, in that the relative positions of dots on the page are used to determine the relationships between intervals and so, ultimately, pitches. Two horizontal guide lines, each deemed to represent a pitch from a given set based on the overtone series, provide the necessary points of reference to enable every dot to stand for a further pitch in its own right, since in the vertical dimension two different distances exist between each dot and the lines, between which a ratio can be gauged and transferred cross-modally through a *tertiary zygonic relationship*. Once the sounds are produced by the performer, they can be said to represent a given cluster of stars, and therefore function symbolically. For most listeners, one suspects that the convoluted symbolism will be more conceptual than auditory, however.

Finally, we should acknowledge that for some people a direct connection exists between aspects of musical sounds and phenomena in other sensory domains, through *synaesthesia* – a neurological disposition in which the stimulation of one sense leads to involuntary experiences in another.[42] A number of well-known musicians, working in a variety of cultures, eras and genres, including Duke Ellington, Billy Joel, Nikolai Rimsky-Korsakov and Olivier Messiaen, reported seeing different colours in response to particular pitches, harmonies, tonalities or timbres, for example. However, synaesthesia is not confined to elite composers and performers, nor is the response to sound restricted to simple patches of colour. For instance, in a study that I undertook with Christina Matawa[43] of the musicality of children who had been born extremely prematurely, and who had lost some or all of their sight as a result of their time spent in an incubator, a nine-year-old boy, Joshua, describes how minor keys produce the sensation of a 'bluey-grey tunnel', which he is 'rushing down', while major keys are perceived as an 'orangey-red room' in which there are 'darker, shallow holes on the floor'. Individual notes conjure up powerful associations for Joshua too. The note B flat elicits the image of a light blue room with large windows in the distance, for example, whereas B is simply green. Like many other premature babies with severe sight loss, Joshua has AP (absolute pitch), which is often implicated in synaesthesia involving musical sounds.

It is important to appreciate that synaesthetic relationships are not intrinsically imitative in nature, since they stem directly from idiosyncratic neural circuitry. But they can form the basis of cross-modal structures where connections between sounds and other types of perceptual input are repeated, as in Scriabin's 5th Symphony, *Prometheus: The Poem of Fire* of 1910, which includes a part for a machine known as a 'clavier à lumières' or 'colour organ', designed specifically for the piece. Its contribution is notated on a staff of its own, at the top of the score and using a treble clef. It has two parts, one of which changes consistently with the harmony (always going to the prevailing 'root').[44] *Prometheus* was performed with coloured lighting for the first time in 1915 in the Carnegie Hall, and has been reproduced in multimedia form occasionally since. Judging from video recordings, the effects are spectacular, though the systematic relationships between harmony and colour are difficult to detect.

* * *

The meanings that music can acquire through association, symbolism or direct imitation form part of the 'cognitive environment', within which its perceived content and structure, and the aesthetic response they evoke, reside – and in part determine. The meaning of a piece on any given occasion is also influenced to a greater or lesser extent by forces beyond music, pertaining both to *intrinsic* factors (the inner world of the person concerned) and to *extrinsic* ones (his or her reaction to the immediate circumstances in which a performance is being heard). Among the intrinsic elements are the emotional and aesthetic range of experiences that listeners bring to bear; their knowledge of music, gained through previous hearings of the performance in question (where it is recorded) and other renditions of this and other pieces; their music-processing abilities; attitudinal issues, such as values, beliefs, preferences and propensities; and their prevailing mood, which will provide the affective backdrop against which any emotions aroused by the music will be superimposed as phasic perturbations. Components in the extrinsic equation include listeners' reactions to the immediate circumstances in which a performance is being heard, including the behaviour of the performer and the reactions of other people who are present, through empathy and 'emotional contagion'; the social context; and the nature of its location.

Defining Music

Having put forward an explanation of how music works, and – in this chapter – how it creates meaning, we are now in a position to offer a definition of 'music', and, by extension, establish what it is *not*. There are those that contend that, since music has varied (and continues to vary) so much with time, place and culture, it would be impossible to arrive at a single, fully-inclusive definition of music.[45] As Jean-Jacques Nattiez says: 'By all accounts there is no single and intercultural universal concept defining what music might be.'[46] However, that is not the same as arguing for a more limited form of universality, whereby there may be *aspects* of music that are necessary to its existence, even if they are not sufficient to offer a comprehensive definition in all contexts. Clearly, one contender here is the notion set out in zygonic theory of abstract patterns of sounds being structured through imitation. But before examining this possibility in detail, let us consider what others have said.

One of the most common definitions of music that one encounters is Edgar Varèse's all-embracing notion of 'organised sound', which the com-poser coined in the 1920s in an attempt to broaden the generally-accepted concept of 'music' that was prevalent in the West at the time, to include his own, experimental work. The controversy this caused had less to do with the idea of musical elements needing to be 'organised' than Varèse's inclusive definition of 'sound' in a musical context, which encompassed what many people took to be 'noise': that is, sounds they did not like and which therefore could not, in their view, constitute 'music' – the art of the beautiful.[47]

Almost one hundred years later, the universe of sounds that people regard as potentially 'musical' has widened considerably, and it is easier to focus on the real problem with Varèse's definition: that organised sound does not have to be 'musical'. In his ecological approach to the perception of auditory events, William Gaver identifies two different ways in which we hear sounds: through 'musical listening', which focuses on perceptual qualities such as pitch and loudness, and via 'everyday listening', which is more concerned with function[48] – for example, the chink of cutlery in the kitchen may indicate that dinner is about to be served. To these two categories, we should add the organisation of sound as verbal language.

Hence Varèse's definition of 'organised sound' can be seen to suffer from what a developmental linguist would call 'overextension', in that it does not apply exclusively to music.

A further step is taken by the philosopher Roger Scruton, who makes it clear that music 'relies neither on linguistic order nor on physical context, but on organization that can be perceived in sound itself, without reference to context or to semantic conventions'.[49] But by resolving one issue, Scruton raises another: that of 'perception'. Whose perception? As Fred Lerdahl points out,[50] the organisation that composers utilise in their work need not be detectable by listeners. Thus what is music to one person's ears need not be music to another's. Indeed, it is conceivable that material that was never intended to be construed as music (ranging from the sounds of nature to the noise of machines) could be heard as such. Hence we appear to have argued our way back to the relativist position that what constitutes music is purely in the ear of the beholder, and that so-called 'universals' are necessarily illusory constructs pertaining to the prevailing culture of discourse. But this feels counterintuitive. The very fact that the great majority of people apparently engage with what they think of as 'music' every day of their lives implies that there is a single concept, or, at least, a bundle of concepts, to which most of us, in part or as a whole, can subscribe. So let us see if we can escape the circularity of the arguments that have been advanced by analysing what makes music 'music' using zygonic theory. Such thinking can be summarised as follows.

1. The essence of music is that one sound or group of sounds is heard (typically subconsciously) as deriving as a whole or in part from another or others through imitation of one or more of its features.

2. Hence music is a *purely cognitive phenomenon* (existing only in the mind), and while there may (but need not) be physical correlates of our internal audition, these do not constitute 'music'.

3. A sense of derivation through imitation enables us to hear a series of discrete sonic events as a coherent stream of abstract sounds – as 'music': and just as each event has the capacity to induce an emotional response, so the contingencies we hear in a

series of musical sounds can evoke an emotional narrative that unfolds over time.

4. This is distinct from meanings that derive, in one way or another, from extra-musical connections. Sounds do not become 'music' purely on the basis of such associations, though external links may form a key part of the musical message on either an individual basis or one that is more general (such as a national anthem).

5. Almost without exception, it appears that mature, 'neurotypical' humans intuitively understand music: that is, almost all of us have the capacity to hear sounds and the relationships between them as being derived from one another through imitation; this requires no formal education (and occurs in the early years).

By extension, these assertions give rise to five further thoughts.

6. A sense of derivation through imitation is a *necessary* feature of all structures that we perceive as musical; however, it is not *sufficient* to guarantee aesthetic merit, which is attributable to the way in which 'content' and 'structure' interact.

7. Since derivation through imitation is a necessary feature of musical coherence; pieces are inevitably infused with repetition in all perceptual domains and at all hierarchical levels, from individual sounds to complete sections of movements.

8. In fact, music is typically supersaturated with far more repetition than is required for it to be intelligible, and this has two consequences: (a) listeners do not need to hear all the available structure for a given musical message to make sense, and (b) different listeners (or even the same listener on different occasions) can apprehend different structural elements, yet each can still have a coherent musical experience.

9. Moreover, it is possible that a sense of derivation through imitation that was conceived by a composer will not be detected by listeners, and *vice versa*. Nonetheless, there is normally enough common perceptual ground for pieces of music to exist as shared and meaningful cognitive enterprises.

10. Music can and may well be associated with other social and communicative activity (such as dance and verbal language), which may interact with the cognition of purely musical structures and contribute additional layers of meaning. In some cultures, the notion of 'music' embraces more than just abstract patterns of sound (and includes dance and other movement). Nonetheless, streams of sound, structured through a sense of derivation through imitation, are a feature of all musical experience. In essence, music is the same the world over; the differences are to do with surface detail rather than fundamental principles.

So in answer to the two questions, 'How does music work?' and 'How does it create meaning?': it can be said that **the structure of music stems from its elements being heard as deriving from one another through imitation, thereby creating a sense of contingency between notes that extends to the emotional responses that each can evoke, forming an abstract, affective narrative that unfolds over time.**

What *isn't* Music?

Having arrived at a definition of music, we are now in a position to ascertain where the boundaries between what music *is* and what it *isn't* lie – a particular issue with certain styles of twentieth-century Western classical music, which some still regard as little more than noise.

To put this into context: there is generally no controversy around the idea that the pieces people download onto their iPods, listen to on the radio or go to hear at concerts – from Bach to Count Basie, Ravel to Radiohead – constitute 'music'. The debate is around the 'edges'. For instance, there are those who believe certain everyday sounds – particularly sounds of nature – should be classed as music, such as Tennyson's 'babbling brook'.[51] Now, this may be regarded as music to the poet's ear, but zygonic theory would contend that it can be so only in a metaphorical sense, since there is no imitation present; no coherent narrative in which sounds are deemed to derive from one another through imitation. Hence rushing water (or similar features of a naturally occurring soundscape, such as pattering rain or the wind sighing through the trees) fail the 'musical' test.

With another natural sound – birdsong – the position is more complicated. Birds typically use short, distinct motifs that, generally speaking, they learnt as youngsters from adults of the same species. They often repeat their calls to form chains of avian 'melody'. As Browning famously observed:[52]

> That's the wise thrush; he sings each song twice over,
> Lest you should think he never could recapture
> The first fine careless rapture!

But do such concatenations constitute music? Imagine, for example, a male cuckoo singing to defend his territory, with a series of the familiar two-note calls.

It is, of course, impossible to say for sure whether the bird acts with any sense of self-imitation as he sings to warn off others, or whether the repetition that occurred was merely a by-product of his communicative instincts. There is evidence that cuckoos have some awareness of their vocal products, since they can distinguish their own songs from those of other species. However, since research has shown that the development of their singing need not have been influenced by adult cuckoos, and as their calls are very similar across a wide geographic range, it appears that they are innate rather than learnt, and therefore *not* deliberately imitative.[53] It is perfectly conceivable, though, that humans may hear successive 'cuckoos' as being derived through imitation, implying that the series of calls constitutes, in their minds, music.

So is a sequence of cuckoo calls music or not? The repetitive nature of the pairs of sounds means that they *have the capacity to be heard as music*, even though they were produced (we assume) with other-than-musical intent. Hence, the classification of the sequence as music will depend on the knowledge and beliefs of the listener. Let us try changing elements of the four 'cuckoo' calls to see where the threshold occurs (see Figure 70).

First, we will lower them a little in pitch (down four semitones) and even up their spacing in time, so each 'cuckoo' has an identical rhythm. Does this make them music? No: the change in pitch should make no difference as to whether one hears imitation or not, though the equal spacing would tend to support that interpretation.

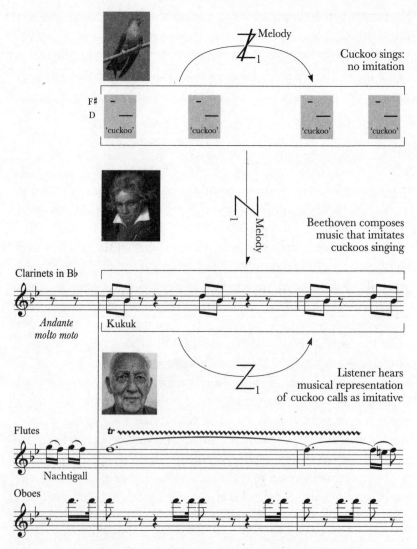

Figure 70 *The three stages through which birdsong becomes perceived as music in Beethoven's* Pastoral *Symphony.*

Let's try something else: change the sound to that of a clarinet. This tone colour is indicative of a musical instrument and therefore, very likely, a sense of human agency. The chances of the motifs being heard as deriving through imitation – of the passage being heard as music – increase markedly.

Finally, imagine a context in which the transformed cuckoo calls are heard in combination with a stylised nightingale's song (played on the flute) and a depiction of the quail's repeated calls (on the oboe), and appear in the context of the slow movement of a Western classical symphony. To the culturally attuned ear, the implication of imitation is now irresistible, and representations of the sounds of nature are definitively 'music'.

So the answer to our original question, 'Is birdsong music?', is 'no' as far as the bird is concerned, but 'potentially yes' to the human listener, and 'certainly' when the song is itself imitated in a musical context.

* * *

We now return to the question of music and language, this time to investigate some of the challenges of seeking to establish a clear-cut boundary between them. In general, language generally fails the 'musical' test, since it is driven by semantics rather than the imitation of the sounding qualities of words. However, exceptions do exist: rhyme, assonance and alliteration, for instance, provide examples where musical logic has arguably encroached upon the realm of verbal language. The regularity of metre in poetry can also be interpreted as imitation in sound and so be construed musically. Whether or not listeners *do* hear phonetic and metric repetition in a musical way remains to be determined. Some indirect evidence does exist, however. For example, recent work of the neuroscientist Aniruddh Patel indicates that elements of linguistic and musical processing may share resources in the brain,[54] and empirical research over several decades has suggested that in songs, music and language may be encoded together,[55] although expert singers may have the capacity to decouple the two forms of auditory communication in neurological terms.[56] Then, the presence of a melody can increase phonetic recognition, and a tune can facilitate the learning and recall of attendant words, *provided that the music repeats.*[57]

Given this, if aspects of language alone were being processed musically, we could reasonably assume that strings of words that were structured 'musically' (for example, through the imitation of words' sounding qualities, as in poetry) would be learnt and recalled more easily than in the inherently 'non-musical' prose. And there is indeed evidence (assembled by the psychologist David Rubin)[58] that poetic forms support memory. Furthermore, it appears that the cognitive advantages of 'word-music' may not be confined to learning and recall: alliteration has been shown to aid verbal comprehension,[59] for example, and children find it easier to learn words when their form and meaning are related (as in onomatopoeia).[60]

But what about manifestations of language in which the sounds of speech are absent? Morse code is the classic example, in which rhyme, assonance, alliteration and metre are, of course, eliminated, and with them, any phonetic and metric similarities that could potentially be heard in a musical way. However, as the system uses only one (constant) pitch and two different lengths of sound (the short 'dits' and the longer 'dahs'), there is an immense amount of repetition. Could this be construed as music?

To those using Morse code as a form of communication, the answer is usually 'no', since any replication is driven either by the design of the code (for example, the three dits, represented as dots, that make up the letter 'S' and the three dahs, shown as dashes, that make up the letter 'O'), or by semantics (as in the repeated 'S' – 'dit-dit-dit' – in 'SOS', for instance).

For those who do *not* recognise the code as a representation of verbal language, it is conceivable that it may be interpreted in a musical way, though the irregular additive nature of its structure in time (in which the duration of a 'dah' is three 'dits', the interval between sounds that make up the same letter is equivalent to one 'dit', and the time *between* letters is three 'dits') makes it difficult for most Western ears (used to processing the beat through regular division) to hear it rhythmically.

However, the fact that Morse uses materials that resemble the notes that are the building blocks of much music means that it has been relatively easy for composers to incorporate the code – or, at least, readily recognisable transformations of it – into pieces. Such modifications enable the syntactic demands of music for repetition and the semantic requirements of Morse to correspond to a series of letters that make up a word to be reconciled.

Take, for example, the theme from a UK television series featuring the aloof Oxfordshire detective Inspector Morse, which originally aired from

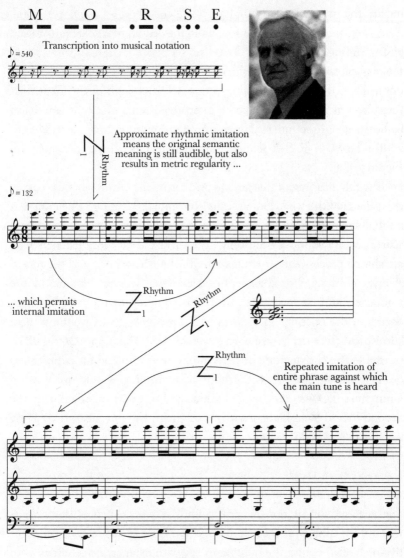

Pheloung: *Theme from Inspector Morse*

Figure 71 *In the right context, Morse code can be heard as music but still retain something of its original identity.*

1987–2000. The composer, Barrington Pheloung, captured something of the enigma of the central character by incorporating his name into the music. This was achieved by playing the code around a quarter speed, changing some lengths of the sounds so they could fit into a regular beat, and sounding the entire M-O-R-S-E sequence repeatedly, high up in the musical texture, against which the main tune weaves sinuously much lower down. These strategies mean that, while enough of the identity of the code was retained for it to be interpreted semantically, it could also be heard as pure sound, structured through imitation that occurred both within the M-O-R-S-E sequence and between its many appearances (in Figure 71).

The full meaning of this new, hybrid form arises from what the cognitive scientist Gilles Fauconnier calls 'conceptual blending': Pheloung has created something that is more than Morse code + music; it is 'Morse-music', whose subtleties can only be appreciated by those listeners who are able to process the structures of both the Morse code and the music. A reverse example, of a conceptual blend that was *not* planned by the composer, but that was subsequently foisted upon the music by listeners, occurs in the opening four notes of Beethoven's 5th Symphony. These correspond to 'V' in Morse code ('di-di-dit-dah'), and, in 1941, the BBC started to use the opening of the symphony as a theme for radio shows beamed across Europe, in the hope of reminding people of Winston Churchill's famous two-fingered salute, and so boost morale during the Second World War. Here, what was originally pure music, subsequently acquired a semantic overlay.

* * *

The introduction of 'non-musical' sounds in works such as Beethoven's *Pastoral* Symphony and Pheloung's *Theme from Inspector Morse* is effective precisely because the quotations toy with listeners' sensibilities as to what constitutes music and what does not, but ultimately don't challenge accepted Western definitions. However, in the twentieth century, composers deliberately created pieces that were intended to test audiences' preconceptions – that set out to break the boundaries of what is typically regarded as 'music'. John Cage's notorious *4'33"* of 1952 is perhaps best known among these 'experimental' works: written for any instrument or combination of instruments, which are not actually played. So what does the music consist of? According to Cage, the sounds of the environment that listeners hear while it is performed. Clearly, *4'33"* fails the criterion for 'music' that derives from zygonic theory, since while there will almost inevitably be sounds present during a performance, none of them is likely to be structured through imitation (unless there happened to be another piece that was audible at the time – in which case, would *4'33"* still be *4'33"*? This is the kind of ontological question that Cage would no doubt have enjoyed grappling with.)

No less provocative were some of La Monte Young's early works, which, like much of Cage's oeuvre, sought to question the nature and accepted definitions of 'music'. For example, each of his *Compositions 1960* examines a particular preconception about the nature of the art form and, to make the point, carries ideas to their extreme. For instance, *#2* is called 'Build a fire'. The instructions are as follows:

> Build a fire in front of the audience. Preferably, use wood although other combustibles may be used as necessary for starting the fire or controlling the kind of smoke. The fire may be of any size, but it should not be the kind which is associated with another object, such as a candle or a cigarette lighter. The lights may be turned out.
>
> After the fire is burning, the builder(s) may sit by and watch it for the duration of the composition; however, he (they) should not sit between the fire and the audience in order that its members will be able to see and enjoy the fire.
>
> The performance may be of any duration.
>
> In the event that the performance is broadcast, the microphone may be brought up close to the fire.

So in addition to the visual, and presumably olfactory, elements of the performance, sound evidently retains a little importance, at least. Its place in proceedings is even more negligible in *Composition #5*, where Young writes:

> Turn a butterfly (or any number of butterflies) loose in the performance area.
>
> When the composition is over, be sure to allow the butterfly to fly away outside.

The composition may be any length but if an unlimited amount of time is available, the doors and windows may be opened before the butterfly is turned loose and the composition may be considered finished when the butterfly flies away.

In relation to this piece, Young claims that it draws people's attention to the fact that even a butterfly – which people would normally think of in purely visual terms – also makes the tiniest of sounds. Again, though, neither these auditory wisps nor the crackling of the fire would constitute 'music' as it is defined in zygonic theory.

Irrespective of this, the works of Cage and Young and others belonging to their relativist family of thinkers do raise an intriguing point in relation to how meaning in art – painting, drawing and sculpture – in some ways resembles and in other ways differs from meaning in music. Traditionally, the primary import of pictures and three-dimensional forms such as statues derives from their capacity to *represent* the visual and tangible in the 'real world', with subsidiary connotations arising from the work of art itself, through stylistic conventions such as compositional symmetry, the depiction of perspective, and preferences for certain types of textures, lines, shapes and particular shades of colour. This is the opposite of music, whose principal significance lies in the power of its constituent sounds to evoke an emotional response, supplemented by secondary meanings resulting from connections with the wider world.

However, *abstract* art (in which no external representation can be discerned) behaves in aesthetic terms more like music. For example, the content and structure of the images used in an abstract painting are determined wholly by the artist's aesthetic sensibilities, through which the relative sizes and proportions of lines and shapes are weighed, the impact of contrasting colour juxtapositions are assessed, and the effects of larger-scale symmetries are appraised. Moreover, as in music, external (and arbitrary) mental associations can accrue to abstract designs – a capacity that is exploited by some commercial companies in their (non-representational) logos.

What of styles of art – such as Cubism – that seem to lie mid-way between the representational and the abstract? Take, for example, Georges Braque's masterpiece, *L'Homme à la Guitare* ('Man with Guitar'), completed in 1912, which seems to owe as much to the repetition of geometric shapes as to the imitation of features of a human being and his musical instrument. Here, an equivalent piece of music would be one in which the demands of internal, imitative structure were balanced with external forces of representation. Arguably, this equilibrium is achieved in pieces such as Paul Hindemith's *Mathis der Maler* symphony of 1934, whose three movements relate to the Isenheim Altarpiece painted in the early sixteenth century by Matthias Grünewald, which juxtaposes religious serenity with depictions of suffering – contrasts that are mirrored in the three movements of the music. So in *L'Homme à la Guitare* we have a semi-representational, semi-abstract painting that depicts a musician, while *Mathis der Maler* offers the listener a semi-abstract, semi-representational piece of music that symbolises a work of art.

With some *conceptual* art – which, in the hands of people like Joseph Kosuth, Damien Hirst and Spencer Tunick often involves everyday objects, animals and people appearing not as representations but *as themselves* in unexpected contexts – the distinction with music of the type created by La Monte Young disappears completely. Compare, for example, his *Composition #5* with Hirst's *In and Out of Love* of 1991, in which hundreds of butterflies swirl around two windowless rooms. The concept may have been different from that of Young's piece, but the physical reality (apart from the fate of the butterflies) is very much the same.

Coda

In the course of this chapter it has become evident that, in a literal sense, music means nothing at all. It is no more than abstract patterns in sound. But unlike language, whose words are in hock to the things that they represent, notes are free to convey pure emotion, unfettered by the need for semantic understanding. As my colleague Ian Cross from Cambridge University puts it, music has a 'floating intentionality'.[61] And whereas language can be acquired only through experiences beyond the words themselves (otherwise the necessary symbolic connections could never be made), music only requires ... music. Its structure, its content, its *meaning*, are designed for humans to grasp through pure exposure. They are self-evident. To those with open ears, this gives music the capacity to span the chasms that otherwise divide epochs, cultures and continents. Music may not be uniform, but it is universal.

This very ubiquity can lead to the erroneous notion that the human 'need' for musicality as we perceive it today drove our evolution in a teleological sense, as though a retrospective sense of destiny could somehow propel natural selection towards a particular end. The reality, of course, is somewhat different. Many of the core cognitive abilities required for musical understanding are not in themselves 'musical', but stem from more general – in evolutionary terms, more primitive – mental attributes; they are necessary *precursors* of musicality, without which it could not have subsequently evolved, and which reach right back to our pre-*Homininae* past.

First among these is the fact that sound has the capacity to evoke a range of emotional responses, and *different* sounds tend to trigger *different* responses that are consistent. Second is the perception of cause and effect – an awareness that one thing can act on another to effect change. Where this happens reliably, we (and many other animals) have the capacity to learn that one thing may be contingent on another. Third, the survival of living organisms often relies on their ability to detect, at some level, that one thing is the same as another: without it the world would be incomprehensible, since what looks the same, sounds the same, and smells and tastes and feels the same, *is* in some sense the same, despite the fact that it's a different physical entity. So we can interact with it in the same way (for example, by choosing to eat it) and the result will (hopefully) be similar to outcomes experienced previously.

Into this primitive mix we can add higher orders of thought that appear to be uniquely human: *belief* and *imagination*. In an environment characterised by difference and complexity, any things that are the same or similar, are probably so for a reason: either through a common cause (a God or a person made them that way), or because one begat the other (through procreation). Explanations such as this are important because they enable us to discern a deeper underlying simplicity beneath surface complexity. And finally, through imagination, we can suspend disbelief: in our minds, we can see images and hear sounds that don't exist; we can pretend that one thing (or person) is another; and we can ascribe living qualities and capacities – sentience – to inanimate objects.

All of these capacities and tendencies are essential to our understanding and appreciation of music, but none of them was impelled in evolutionary terms by music-developmental ends. However, it may be, as the modern human brain evolved, that other, purely musical, abilities that build on these cognitive foundations – above all, the wherewithal to express oneself emotionally, and to understand others, through abstract narratives in sound – became important for survival. Why? Current thinking stresses the importance of music in early bonding between parents and infants, and the sense of cohesion within wider social groups that participation in musical activities can afford.[62] There is an increasing recognition too of the potential role of music in the development of empathy – the faculty that enables us to recognise the thoughts and feelings of others.[63] If I can copy the sounds you make, then I must in some respects be like you;[64] the emotions that I experience as I make sounds like yours may be the same as the emotions that you experience. And the process is reciprocal. If you imitate me, then to a degree you must understand me, must know how I feel, must even have a sense what it is like to be me. My music, your music, *our* music can bind us together as families, as tribes and as societies in a way that nothing else can.

4

We Are All Musical

NOTWITHSTANDING THE SEEMINGLY INTERMINABLE worldwide hype around talent shows and the largely ephemeral celebrities they spawn, the human race cannot really be divided into two groups: a very small, elite cadre of 'musicians' and the *hoi polloi* – the so-called 'non-musicians'. If this were actually the case, then there would be no audiences for the stars to perform to, since to understand and enjoy the songs they sing and the pieces they play requires an active 'musical mind', with the propensity to respond to the different qualities of the sounds that are produced, and the capacity to perceive intentionality in the many forms of repetition that bind them together. The truth is that almost everyone has the ability to make sense of music as we have defined it: an abstract narrative in sound, whose elements are heard as deriving from one another through imitation. The pioneering ethnomusicologist John Blacking's assertion that musicality may be 'a universal, species-specific characteristic' is surely right.[1] That is to say, being musical is part of being human. Perhaps even a defining trait.

At what stage, though, does musicality emerge in our development as individuals? At what point can we say that a child is 'musical'? When, at eighteen months or so, little Tom can't resist dancing and clapping along to his favourite TV theme tune? Or, at three-and-a-half, when Ellie can sing her first nursery rhyme more-or-less in tune all the way through? Actually, these questions miss a crucial point in what it is to be 'musical'. For sure, an important element of musicality is being able to reproduce patterns in sound and even entire pieces drawn from our cultural heritage. But that isn't the whole story, and to understand why, let us revisit what competence in using *language* means, and how it is acquired.

Long before children are able to express themselves in words, their brains learn to process a good deal of what other people say. To an extent, this imbalance continues throughout life. As adults, our *receptive* vocabularies (words that we can recognise and understand should we hear them) are larger than our *expressive* vocabularies (words that we use ourselves when we speak). In Western cultures, music offers a more extreme case of the same phenomenon. We can all recognise (if not necessarily name) many pieces of music – typically hundreds if not thousands of songs and instrumental pieces, ranging from pop songs to advertising jingles, from Christmas carols to Mahler symphonies, from soccer chants to national anthems. Evidently, then, we each have a great deal of musical information stashed away in our brains. And it's not just a case of recognition. We tend to have clear musical preferences, and sometimes react powerfully – even ardently – to our favourite pieces.

But what about *expressing* ourselves musically? In private situations (singing in the bath or shower) and in some public contexts (karaoke nights, football matches), typically bolstered by alcohol, we can effortlessly access our database of melodies, acquired just by listening, and metamorphose into more or less willing performers. For most of us, though, the majority of the time, such situations are the exception rather than the rule. In the West, the binary division of roles into those who produce and those who consume music means that we tend to be chronically inhibited from performing in front of others. I think of it as the 'curse of The X-Factor' (and other talent shows), which, as we intimated above, publicly and unforgivingly reinforce the notion that, as far as making music is concerned, there are a tiny minority who *can* while the vast majority *can't*. And for those who are brave enough to try, derision is a likely consequence. Safer to remain quiet!

This unfortunate polarity is purely a social construct, however, and doesn't exist in communities where music is more generally participatory – often woven into the rituals of daily life, ranging, as we saw in Chapter 1, from the *iorram* or rowing songs of the Isle of Mull to the rhythms which Northern Ewe children in Eastern Ghana create as they pound dried cassava in mortars. So are the oarsmen of Mull or the Ghanaian girls by their nature more musical than typical urban Westerners? There is no reason to think so. It's just that the former feel comfortable expressing themselves through music in the presence of others. However, there is no evidence either that Western concertgoers appreciate the music any less than the performers on stage. There is no evidence that audience members' intuitive understanding of the pieces that they hear is of a lower calibre than that of the musicians. And there is no evidence that listeners' emotional responses to music are less deep, less vivid than those of the singers or instrumentalists. So what is the difference between performing musicians and others?

Quite simply, what make performers special are the thousands, even tens of thousands, of hours that they have spent practising to develop their technical proficiency. And inevitably there are neurological and physical changes that occur collaterally as part of this daunting journey to accomplishment. But if performing musicians 'turn off' the intellectual component of their music making – the part of their brain that consciously attends to what they are doing – it seems that their intuitive responses to music are the same as everyone else's. Some Western classical musicians can happily lose themselves dancing to the relentless repetitive rhythms of technopop. And at the same time, we can all enjoy a great performance of classical music without necessarily being able to emulate it ourselves.

The truly amazing thing is that, by and large, this intuitive understanding of music is already in place by the time children begin their formal education at the age of four or five, *provided that* they have been offered a rich, diverse and interactive set of musical experiences. Without any conscious effort on their part (although the adults around them will have to have worked hard), most of the musical processing power that will serve them for the rest of their lives will be in place, and they will already be experts in making sense of music. Admittedly, as we mature emotionally through adolescence and adulthood, we will come to appreciate music (and all art) at deeper levels. But typical five-year-olds have all the elements of musicality that they need to understand and enjoy the music of their culture.

If we are already musical experts so young, then it begs the question, when do these abilities start to develop? What path do they take?

From Music Theory to Developmental Psychology

In seeking to answer these questions, I'm going to report on a new approach that I developed over the last few years in a research project called *Sounds of Intent*: a joint initiative of the Applied Music Research Centre at the University of Roehampton, the International Music Education Research Centre at University College London, and the Royal National Institute of Blind People. Shortly after the turn of the century, the first phase of *Sounds of Intent* set out to discover something that no one had ever investigated before: how children with learning difficulties, including those with autism and sensory impairment, develop musically. Is it in the same way as everyone else, or does their musical development occur more slowly or even, in some cases, more quickly? Or do children with intellectual disabilities engage with music in a fundamentally different way from the so-called 'neurotypical' population? The latter question was central to the second phase of the *Sounds of Intent* study, which investigated the musicality of a cross-section of *all* children in the early years – disabled and able-bodied alike.

The main question posed by Phase 2 of *Sounds of Intent* proved surprisingly challenging to answer – not least since, despite fifty years of research[2] into the musical development of young children, the pathway from the earliest auditory experiences to mature musical engagement was still not properly defined. Prior to *Sounds of Intent*, psychologists and music educators could only hazard a guess as to what a six-month-old baby takes from exposure to a classical symphony, for example, or how a one-year-old hears ragtime – let alone what a teenager with profound and multiple learning difficulties is likely to make of, say, reggae. But, arguably, this ignorance was inevitable since there was no generally accepted, overarching theory of how music makes sense. Hence it simply wasn't possible to say what form the journey towards musical understanding might take.

Work on the *Sounds of Intent* project, like virtually all previous research into young children's musical interests and abilities, started by adopting an *inductive*, or 'bottom up', approach – amassing hundreds of video-recorded observations of pupils in action from schools from all over the UK, and, through analysing these, trying to identify patterns in their behaviours and interactions, and sequences in the way skills are acquired. The problem with this *modus operandi* was the sheer complexity of the picture that started to emerge. Without knowing what we were looking for, with so many variables, it was virtually impossible for the research team to make any headway. Where did the capacity to sing a nursery rhyme fit developmentally with the ability to copy a short rhythm on the drum, for example? Or if a child seemed to prefer one person's singing voice over another, was that a more (or less) advanced behaviour than responding to sounds that got gradually louder?

We needed to identify some overarching principles to guide our thinking, and quite by chance, at the same time as leading the *Sounds of Intent* research, I was also developing the zygonic theory of musical understanding. Since this theory suggests that music makes sense through the brain's capacity to identify and process different manifestations of intentional repetition in the context of a variety of sounds, it follows that at some point children must learn how to do that, without needing to be explicitly taught.

So, in considering how, as youngsters, we develop musically, I decided to look down the other end of the telescope, as it were, and switch to using a 'top-down' or *deductive* method of research. That is, instead of working from specific examples to try to construct a general model of how music development occurs, I resolved to formulate a theory of how this might happen, based on the zygonic conjecture, and thereafter to look for corroboration (or contradiction) in the data offered by the young children whom the *Sounds of Intent* research team were observing.

Those of us working on the *Sounds of Intent* project now had a way forward: we knew that at some stage during the first four or five years of life, including the last three months *in utero*,[3] children typically make the transition from being unable to make sense of music to having a good grasp of the way it functions, at an intuitive level. And plainly, the manner in which the developing brain gets to grips with the way music works is not an overnight affair. Rather, musical abilities must *evolve*, continuously or in defined stages, or possibly a combination of the two.

Having in mind broadly comparable developmental areas, it seemed that an incremental path was the most likely. For example, as far as language is concerned, children start to speak by acquiring a few key words (for example, 'cat'), which they subsequently learn to juxtapose in pairs ('cat up') and then short phrases ('Cat up tree'). Eventually, these become amalgamated into longer and more complex sentences ('The cat's up the tree and he can't get down), which are generated through an intuitive understanding of the syntax of the language (or languages) to which a child is exposed.[4] With regard to the transitions between these three stages, it seems that successive levels of linguistic ability do not *replace* those that precede. Rather, they build on them, since, for example, an understanding of how individual words work is needed before children can grasp how they can relate to one another.

If music-processing abilities are like those pertaining to language, and do indeed develop in identifiable stages, then it may be that these are somehow reflected in the way that music is structured. That is to say, it may be that the increasingly advanced cognitive skills that children bring to bear as their capacity for making sense of music evolves are reflected in its design. If this is the case, then it should be possible to analyse a piece of music and identify types of structure of differing levels of complexity that correspond to a hierarchy of music-processing abilities.

Such a hierarchy was implied in the observations made in Chapter 2. First, at its simplest, musical structure involves imitative relationships between single notes – logical connections between individual *events*. In some ways, as we saw in Chapter 3, such events are comparable to words, in that they typically function as the smallest units in an auditory narrative, though their capacity to evoke a response – their musical meaning – is largely determined through their relationships with other notes. In contrast, words, despite having a certain contextual dependency too, have strong 'absolute' meanings. The word 'cat' is sufficient to elicit an image of

Imitation of pitch

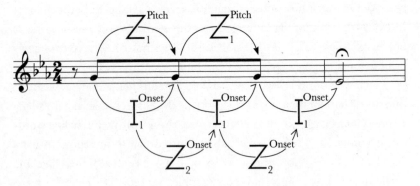

Imitation of inter-onset intervals

Figure 72 *The simple structure comprising four zygonic relationships that underlies the opening motif of Beethoven's 5th Symphony.*

a furry mammalian quadruped that meows, whereas a single note played in the mid-range of the piano (for example) is, if anything, rather neutral in effect.

Beyond this, *groups* of musical events that are proximate in time and similar in sound can cohere in the mind to form motifs: a second structural level that has a linguistic parallel in two- and three-word combinations that constitute short, more or less self-contained phrases. Third, there are *frame-works*, imaginary matrices of pitch and time, whose elements have different perceived probabilities of occurrence according to a listener's previous exposure to pieces in a particular style or genre. These are in some ways equivalent to the generative grammars that enable us to form new and potentially complex (though immediately comprehensible) utterances using words. These three structural levels are hierarchical in the sense that 'higher' (more advanced) levels *necessarily* build on 'lower' (more elementary) ones.

To hear the three structural levels in action, let us turn once more to the opening of Beethoven's 5th Symphony. To the ear that makes sense of bars 1 and 2, we can surmise that imitative relationships must be constructed in the mind between the repeated pitches and IOIs (inter-onset intervals) that are heard to form the 'fate knocking on the door' motif (see Figure 72).

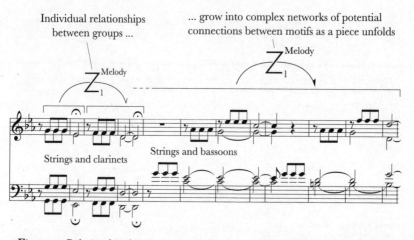

Figure 73 *Relationships between groups of notes are cognitively more demanding, as they involve greater numbers of musical events occurring over longer periods of time.*

It seems reasonable to assume that recognising such imitation between individual musical *events* (or pairs of them) takes the least mental processing power of all forms of structure, since it requires at most two or three items of musical information, in the form of notes or chords or the intervals between them, to be held in working memory and compared. The temporal envelope within which such structures occur is constrained – sometimes, as in the case of the opening of the symphony, extending to little more than the perceived present.[5]

A cognitively more demanding type of musical structure occurs between *groups* of notes, which usually take the form of motifs (as in the Beethoven example, see Figure 73). Organisation of this kind necessarily involves four events or more, since at least two are required to create a group (and, clearly, a minimum of two groups is required).

The timespans of such structures are potentially greater than those involving events alone, and may even implicate long-term memory. There is likely to be a greater degree of abstraction from the perceptual 'surface' too, since the imitation of rhythms that are internally irregular may be acknowledged through *tertiary* level relationships (connections between connections *between connections*).

There is a third structural level: imitative links between *frameworks* of

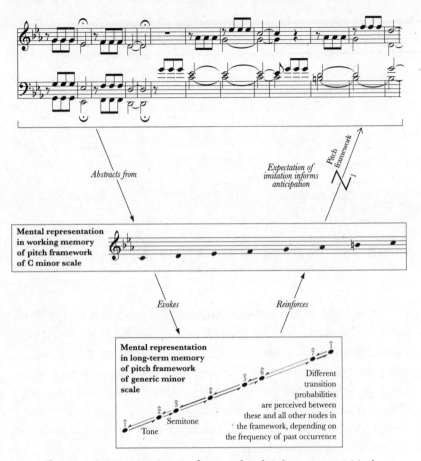

Figure 74 *Relationships between* frameworks *of pitch are more cognitively demanding still, involving the consolidation of large quantities of data over long periods of time to produce highly abstract mental representations.*

pitch and onset times, which appear to be the most cognitively demanding of all (see Figure 74). As we observed, they depend on the existence of long-term 'schematic' memories – in the case of a listener stylistically attuned to the Beethoven symphony, built up from substantial exposure to other pieces in the minor mode and set in a duple metre. Here, as we remarked in Chapter 2, it is assumed that the details of the perceptual surface and individual connections perceived between musical events are not encoded in long-term memory discretely or independently, but are combined with many thousands of other similar data to create probabilistic networks of relationships between notional representations of pitch and perceived time. That is, large amounts of perceptual information are merged to enable the deep level of cognitive abstraction to occur.

In summary, then, it is hypothesised that the cognitive correlates of musical structure grow in complexity as one moves from *events* to *groups* and then *frameworks*, reflecting an increasing amount of perceptual input, experienced over longer periods of time, and processed and stored using progressively more abstract forms of mental representation. Moreover, the logic of the music-theoretical model suggests that the cognitive operations pertaining to higher levels of structure must build on and incorporate those required to process lower levels, since connections between groups comprise series of relationships between events, and links between frameworks are established by acknowledging the correspondences that exist between groups.

In the light of this information, it appeared to the *Sounds of Intent* research team that there was indeed a threefold hierarchy of forms of musical structure – *events*, *groups* and *frameworks* – that could potentially tie in with the pattern of musical development in the early years. There were two sources of evidence against which this proposition could be tested: the literature on young children's engagement with music and sound, and the observations emerging from the second phase of the *Sounds of Intent* project.

Turning first to the literature – comprising accounts of research characterised by the special ingenuity demanded of those who wish to work with babies, toddlers and infants – this contained many examples that appeared to support the 'three stage' hypothesis through which an understanding of musical structure is acquired. For example, the American psychologist Andrew Meltzoff's work over many years shows that young children have a built-in propensity to imitate others, and that this plays a part in early interactive sound-making using individual musical sounds.[6] Similarly, Mechthild Papoušek, a developmental psychologist based at the University of Munich (who with her Czech husband Hanuš formed a renowned early years research partnership in the second part of the twentieth century), in analysing preverbal communication in babies from just two to seven months old, found that up to half of these infants' vocal sounds are part of reciprocal matching sequences that the children engage in with their mothers.[7] Papoušek's findings complement work by other researchers showing that babies less than five months of age can replicate individual pitches,[8] copy changes in pitch,[9] and emulate vowel-like sounds made by others. Each of these forms of interaction involves imitation at the level of *events* – showing engagement with musical sounds at the first level of the structural hierarchy.[10]

Engagement at the next level first appears from seven to eleven months, when babies repeat and vary *groups* of sounds, using them as the basic units of structure, through babbling that, according to Papoušek, involves producing 'short musical patterns or phrases that soon become the core units for a new level of vocal practising and play'.[11] Gradually, groups of sounds may be linked through repetition or transposition to form chains, and the first self-sufficient improvised pieces emerge. My colleague Graham Welch, Professor of Music Education at UCL, notes that between the ages of one and two, 'a typically spontaneous infant song consists of repetitions of one brief melodic phrase at different pitch centres'.[12] These are unlike adult singing, however, because 'they lack a framework of stable pitches (a scale) and use a very limited set of contours in one song'.[13] From the age of two-and-a-half, so-called 'potpourri' melodies may appear,[14] which borrow and may transform features and fragments from other, standard songs that have been assimilated into the child's own spontaneous singing.[15] These self-generated melodies, which use materials derived from a repertoire that is familiar from a child's musical culture, are fittingly termed 'referent-guided improvisation' by the Hong Kong-based early years music education specialist, Esther Mang.[16]

Finally, from around the age of four, or thereabouts (the age can vary considerably), two advances occur, which pertain to the third level of the music-structural hierarchy: *frameworks*. First, children develop the capacity to abstract an underlying pulse from the surface rhythm of songs and other pieces (meaning that he or she can perform 'in time' to a regular beat that is provided). Second, according to David Hargreaves, children's singing acquires 'tonal stability', with the clear projection of a key centre across all the phrases of a piece.[17] These abilities imply a cognisance of repetition at a deeper structural level in the 'background' organisation of music.

While the *Sounds of Intent* research team found the music in the early years literature encouraging in terms of supporting the notion of three phases of development in music-structural cognition, it didn't specify how each kind of mental processing arises and how the different stages are connected. For this, the observations of children in action, engaging with music in many different ways, which were gathered during the second phase of the *Sounds of Intent* project, proved to be crucial.

The *Sounds of Intent* Project

Research in the second phase of the *Sounds of Intent* project was undertaken at Eastwood Nursery School: Centre for Children and Families – an integrated provision in south-west London that offers early years education and care to local families. The facility is inclusive, providing services to children irrespective of any special educational needs or disabilities they may have, and reflects a wide social and cultural demographic characteristic of many urban settings in the UK. As a consequence, the children's experiences and expectations of life at home are very diverse, and for many, English is an additional language.

The children were observed by Angela Voyajolu, who had also been Research Officer for Phase 1 of the *Sounds of Intent* project. She attempted to capture, through video recording, a broadly representative sample of the forms of children's musical engagement that occurred during their days spent at Eastwood, for subsequent analysis by the research team as a whole. Children were observed in a range of contexts, and it was found that the majority of musical activities happen frequently and spontaneously throughout the day, including not only adult-led activities in which music was the primary focus of attention, but also free-flowing musical interactions with peers and self-directed play in which music was sometimes incidental.

Here is a small sample of Voyajolu's observations:

'Little Ellen, just four months old, lying in her cot, makes vocal sounds as she stares at the mobile slowly rotating above her.'

'Marcus, eleven months old, explores the small keyboard in different ways, playing clusters of sounds with his right hand and individual notes using his index finger.'

'Imani, eighteen months, loves copying the sounds his child-minder makes by scraping one piece of Lego against another.'

'Kai, aged two, plays the snare drum in the garden, alternating with two sticks, creating different beats.'

'Cindy and September, both three, take it in turns to sing siren noises down cardboard tubes, copying each other's patterns.'

'Róża, three-and-a-half, improvises a song made up of bits and pieces of nursery rhymes that she knows, as she rocks to and fro on the rocking horse.'

'Suravi, four years old, sings *Happy Birthday* as part of a game after making a cake with candles out of clay. His singing is in time and largely in tune.'

'Akio, aged four-and-a-half, joins in *The Wheels on the Bus* with his class, singing in tune with the teacher's guitar accompaniment and tapping a drum in time to the beat.'

Of these, Imani and Kai were apparently creating simple musical structures by imitating *events*; the efforts of Cindy, September and Róża were organised using *groups* of notes; and Suravi and Akio were utilising *frameworks* (in the domains of pitch and time) to guide their efforts. The sounds that Ellen and Marcus made seemed to be 'pre-structural', characterised by sensory exploration in which imitation did not play a part.

Significantly, Voyajolu found that it was quite common for a child to engage with different levels of musical structure within a single observation period – even within the same activity. For example, three-year-old Anushka, playing outside with James (who was a few months younger, on the autism spectrum and in the very early stages of language development), demonstrated a burst of regular bangs on the drum that she intended her companion to emulate, subsequently using their playing as an accompaniment to a vocal rendition of *Twinkle, Twinkle* (music-making utilising *frameworks*). James copied the beat, though not in time with

Anushka, (thereby showing an understanding of structure at the level of *events*), and attempted to imitate the song as well, managing to vocalise the contour of the descending pitches of the fourth line, 'Like a diamond in the sky', using the consonant 'd' and different vowel sounds (indicating that he could process the organisation of *groups* of sounds).[18]

From Voyajolu's observations of the children at Eastwood, it was also evident that there were no particular ages at which different levels of musical ability emerged. For example, one eighteen-month-old boy, Declan, could sing nursery rhymes largely in time and in tune with his mother, whereas four-and-a-half-year-old Becky was still struggling to imitate single pitches accurately. So this suggested that the rate at which music-structural understanding develops in children varies greatly. And although there was insufficient evidence to be sure, from talking to parents and carers and the children's keyworkers it seemed likely that the biggest single factor causing the diversity was the musical environment of the children at home. Those who were consistently encouraged to engage in musical activities by the adults around them almost invariably seemed to thrive musically, whereas others, for whom music was confined to auditory clutter emanating mainly from the television – one stream of sound among many others in background of day-to-day life – tended to fare less well.

Setting these observations alongside the findings from the literature on music in the early years strengthened the research team's view that the three levels of musical structure identified by zygonic theory (pertaining to events, groups and frameworks) are indeed reflected in the development of children's understanding of musical structure, as shown in the varying degrees of sophistication of the music that they make on their own and with others. However, it was evident too that there is a 'pre-structural' stage in the evolution of musical understanding, in which sounds are relished and produced purely for the sensory pleasure that they bring, without being consciously organised. And before *that*, the findings of the first phase of the *Sounds of Intent* research suggested that some children with profound and multiple difficulties are not yet at the stage of being able to process sound cognitively at all – or only to a very limited degree (equivalent in 'neurotypical' development to a scenario that occurs *in utero* more than three months before birth).

Hence the *Sounds of Intent* team concluded that there must be at least five, overlapping levels of musical development that have only a loose correspondence with age. Of these, the first is typically over before birth, the second begins prenatally and continues thereafter, followed by levels three, four and five, which commence in the early years and remain with us all our lives. For example, the visceral impact of hearing a symphony orchestra in full flow never leaves us (Level 2); adults derive just as much joy as their children from parent-baby interactions in which one party copies the vocal sounds made by the other (Level 3); and football fans of all ages relish joining in with call and response chants on the football terraces (Level 4). As we shall see, an additional, sixth level exists, which typically commences in adolescence.

Level 1 'Being oblivious'

Level 1 describes a state in which hearing is not working. This would normally be found in a foetus before the last trimester of pregnancy, in which the auditory system becomes fully functional. It is important to recognise that being unable to process sound is not the same as being deaf or hard of hearing but cognitively intact, since in such circumstances it may nonetheless be possible to perceive pitch through vibration, as the virtuoso percussionist Evelyn Glennie has shown.[19] Others may have learning difficulties of such profundity that their brains learn to process sound at some point in childhood (rather than *in utero*) or even not at all. In other cases, cognitive impairment may result from trauma or illness later in life. In either scenario, the brain's responses to sound need not produce an observable, physical reaction: recent electroencephalographic (EEG) research undertaken at the Royal Hospital for Neurodisability in Putney, London, shows that some patients who were diagnosed as being in vegetative states – who, it may have been assumed, would be unresponsive to music – reacted measurably at a neurological level to music-therapeutic input.[20] And people in the later stages of dementia have been shown to respond positively to music when all else appears to be lost.[21] So, being completely oblivious to sound – failing to engage with music at all – whether as a child or an adult, is very unusual.

Level 2 'Sounds interesting'

Level 2 is about our first, basic reactions to sound. This stage of hearing is typically functional from around the twenty-sixth week of gestation, from when, as every mother knows, her unborn child may start to respond vigorously to what he or she hears! By the time they are born, babies can recognise different sounds and remember them: they are likely prefer the sound of their mother's voice to others, for example, and react differentially to the qualities of pieces of music to which they were exposed in the womb.[22] In the first few weeks and months of post-natal life, babies react to an increasing variety of sounds – loud or quiet, high or low, mellow or harsh, long or short, moving or still – and develop preferences. They learn to make sounds for themselves, first using their voices, then their bodies and objects in the environment. Above all, they come to enjoy interacting with other people by using sound, in the beginnings of what Colwyn Trevarthen, writing from the perspective of developmental psychology, has called 'communicative musicality': the early intimate interchanges of vocal give and take that babies share with their parents and other carers.[23]

Level 3 'Copy me, copy you'

Level 3 is about grasping simple pattern and predictability in music: in terms of zygonic theory, the acknowledgement of structure at the level of *events*. Typically, towards the end of the first year of life, it appears that the human brain starts to process music *as music* – distinct from language and everyday sounds. This can be understood by reference to my 'ecological' model of the development of auditory processing that builds on the work of William Gaver. This identifies the three different ways in which, neurotypically, we hear sounds: through 'musical listening', which focuses on perceptual qualities such as pitch and loudness; 'everyday listening', which is concerned with attending to events such as a door slamming or a microwave humming; and 'linguistic listening', which is ultimately based on the perception and cognition of speech sounds. The 'ecological' model ties in with evidence from neuroscience, which, as we observed in Chapter 3, suggests that, while music and language share some neurological resources, they also have dedicated processing pathways.

It is not known, though, precisely how the three types of auditory

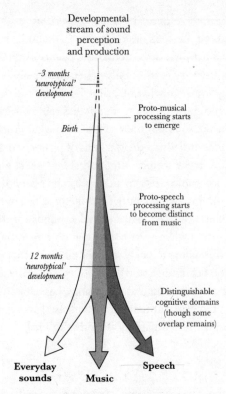

Developmental
stream of sound
perception
and production

-3 months
'neurotypical'
development

Proto-musical
processing starts
to emerge

Birth

Proto-speech
processing starts
to become distinct
from music

12 months
'neurotypical'
development

Distinguishable
cognitive domains
(though some
overlap remains)

Everyday
sounds

Music

Speech

Figure 75 *The emerging streams of music and language
processing in auditory development.*

processing – relating to everyday sounds, music and speech – become
defined in the brain's architecture following the initial development of
hearing around four to three months before birth (although research is
underway),[24] and there is currently some debate as to which develops
first.[25] This uncertainty may in part be due to the fact that researchers
haven't been working with a clear definition of 'music' to inform their
assumptions, and may regard any kind of vocal exchange that lacks
semantic meaning as musical (since it is not linguistic). But this is not
the case. To be music, there must be perceived imitation – otherwise
what we would have is auditory content without structure. However,
the fact that, from an early age, babies *do* copy vocal sounds and relish
being copied long before they can use or understand words suggests
that music is indeed a precursor of language. In any case, singing and

speech appear to follow discrete developmental paths from around the beginning of the second year of life.[26]

That still leaves 'everyday sounds', which, it seems, must perceptually be the most primitive of all, since they require less cognitive processing than either music or speech. So we can presume that, early on in development, the brain treats all sound in the same way, and that music processing starts to emerge first, followed by language. The residue that is left remains as 'everyday sounds'. Hence the ecological model of auditory perception can be represented as shown in Figure 75, in which it is assumed that, typically, music and language come to have gradually more distinct neural correlates during the first post-natal year.

From the point of view of musical understanding, children not only intuitively learn to compare one sound with another, but also get the sense that the human repetition of sounds can embody the notion of *intentionality*. It is interesting to speculate whether a baby's awareness of imitation in sound – that is, the idea of *derivation*, which makes music what it is – stems from early interactions with parents and carers, through which the notion of self and other, and the realisation that one person has the capacity to *influence* another's sounds, is acquired. That is, if it weren't for the 'copy' games that adults play with their children, would a sense of *agency* in patterns of sound ever develop?

Level 4 'Bits of pieces'

Level 4 is about our growing understanding of musical motifs – *groups* of sounds. Virtually all pieces are constructed through the repetition and transformation of motifs in one form or another. Through many hours of exposure to music, children grasp this form of structure with no conscious effort, and, without the need for instruction, they start to experiment with motifs themselves, and, quite intuitively, work out how they can be satisfactorily juxtaposed. One of the results of this early, self-initiated musical creativity is the emergence of 'potpourri' songs, which usurp musical shreds and patches from pieces the child has heard, and stitch them together into novel combinations.[27] For example, here is the song that Róża, aged three-and-a-half, was observed singing on a rocking horse:

Figure 76 *A transcription of Róża's 'potpourri' song.*

The ancestry of most of the motifs is clear – they derive with varying degrees of fidelity from fragments of children's songs with which Róża was familiar. The intervals between pitches are often only approximately reproduced and their rhythms are changed as necessary to fit with the modifications that she makes to the sounds of the words, which seem to be treated largely as an additional strand of musical information that functions, timbre-like, alongside pitch and rhythm. The motifs follow one another in a line of music that meanders like a rivulet of water charting a new course down a slope, which flows briefly in one direction before being deflected by a pebble or twig and starts to trickle in another. Streams of sound and water both happen 'in the moment': one cannot predict with any certainty what will happen next, nor how things will end.

Where coherent connections do exist between Róża's motifs – aside from those that already existed in the tunes that she borrowed, such as the approximate repetition of motif 1 ('See saw') to form motif 2 ('Marjorie Daw') – these use the most basic form of linkage that is available, which is for the second motif to pick up from the pitch with which the first ended. An example occurs between motifs 2 and 3, 'Majorie Daw' and 'Have a new master'. Since Róża omits two words from the original song ('Jack shall'), a change in the melody is in any case necessary, but she ensures musical coherence, at least, by singing 'Have' to the same pitch as 'Daw'. As this type of relationship between motifs involves the storage, retrieval and manipulation of less musical material than one in which the entire contents of each are repeated or transformed, it is less cognitively demanding. It remains an essential item in the composer's toolkit, however, far beyond the creation of potpourri songs in early childhood: there is a beautiful example in the second movement of Bartók's 3rd Piano Concerto, when the 'cellos descent points to the first entry of the soloist (see Figure 60).

Level 5 'Whole songs in time and in tune'

Level 5 is about grasping the imaginary *frameworks* of pitch and time that characterise virtually all music. This occurs through exposure to tens, hundreds or even thousands of songs and other pieces, through which children learn (without being consciously aware of it) that the music of their culture tends to use the same underlying patterns of notes over and over again. As this pattern becomes more strongly fixed in children's minds, and they get better at controlling their voices, they sing noticeably more in tune. And as we saw in relation to *Twinkle, Twinkle*, some combinations of notes occur more often than others, particularly at the ends of pieces, adding to children's sense of a deeper structure in music – telling them when the melody is about to finish, for example. At the same time, they get a feeling for the regular beat that is found in most music, to which they can clap their hands or tap their feet. As early years practitioners know all too well, these things make it much easier for young children to sing and play music together! Most of the youngsters that Voyajolu observed had reached this stage by the age of four, although, as with other musical milestones, there was huge variation.

At this point in their developmental journey, children really are musical experts. In the same way that almost all of us acquire verbal language naturally, just through exposure and interaction with supportive adults, so it is with music, as the pioneering Japanese violin teacher, Shinichi Suzuki realised, when he invented his pedagogical approach for young children that relies in the first instance on listening, copying and playing by ear.[28] Certainly, the children at Level 5 who were studied by the *Sounds of Intent* research team profited from trying out a range of instruments that they could physically manage, including the keyboard, the recorder and the ukulele. The important thing appeared to be for adults to adopt a child-centred approach, encouraging youngsters at first to play the tunes that they can already sing, and, above all, instilling a love of music strong enough to see them through the hours of practice that will later be needed if they are to develop technical expertise, and (if necessary) to keep them going through the challenges of acquiring musical literacy that is the norm with some genres.

Level 6: 'Musical Maturity'

Level 6 is about reaching 'musical maturity', which occurs when young people, typically in adolescence, come to understand the social and emotional impact of the music they listen to and, as performers, intuitively know how to convey their feelings through devices such as 'rubato' (speeding up and slowly down for expressive effect), vibrato, and the use of dynamics. It is very rare for young children to display prodigious, adult-like talent, though not entirely unheard of, as stars like Yehudi Menuhin and Shirley Temple show. But the important thing to remember is *all* children have the capacity to develop a natural understanding and appreciation of music at this level. Music is at once an art for all while capable of sustaining an elite.

***

The skills that emerge in the course of these six stages of music-cognitive development are *cumulative* in nature, something that has profound implications, both for the way that music makes sense to adults and to young children. As mature listeners, it means that music can be appreciated not only with the full force of one's concentration over an extended period, when deeper structural relationships may become apparent, but also 'in the moment',[29] by focussing on structures that are nearer to the 'perceptual surface' – which may occur, for example, when one's concentration wanders during a performance. It seems reasonable to assume, as one's ear starts to attend to the music once more, that it will be 'local' relationships, initially between events and then involving adjacent groups, that will be formulated first. This would explain why, when turning on the radio in the course of the performance of an unfamiliar piece, for instance, it still seems to make perfect sense, albeit in a more superficial way than hearing the entire work from the start.

Even more significantly, perhaps, the fact that most music is structured in three different ways (involving *events*, *groups* and *frameworks*), means that babies and other young children can enjoy the same pieces as their elders, but in a way that matches their perceptual and cognitive abilities. So in the case of the first movement of Beethoven's 5th Symphony, for instance, a child who is still functioning at the pre-structural ('sensory') stage may simply relish the qualities of the sounds passing by; a toddler who can discern structure at the level of events may pick up on moment-to-moment regularities such as the many repeated notes; a youngster who can process groups of notes as self-sufficient entities may recognise the 'fate knocking on the door' motif as it reappears in different guises; and his older sister may grasp something of the movement's tonal framework, and feel a sense of return when the opening of the movement is repeated in the 'recapitulation'.

I think of playing or singing to a mixed group of children in the early years as rather like supplying the power for a number of light bulbs of different wattages, wired up in a single circuit. The person generating the music supplies the same stream of sounds – an identical 'musical current' – to everyone present, who will draw from a single input whatever they need in order to make sense of what is going on. This means that the children, despite being at different music-developmental levels, may all be 'lit up' musically at the same time, since they can each take different things from a single musical experience.

Clearly, in terms of scaffolding young children's musical development, it will be important for adults to expose them not only to 'stage-appropriate' music but also to more advanced material – otherwise how would the child ever gain the experiences necessary to move on? The beauty of musical design for brains that are still maturing, is that by being able to encapsulate different structural levels at the same time, a child who is listening may be able to appreciate one level fully while still learning to process another, deeper form of structure that is also present. And, as we have seen, one level of structure feeds into another: the organisation of groups relies on the orderly arrangement of events, and frameworks depend on groups. Music really is a brilliant piece of human-developmental engineering – and, despite its complexity, one that is designed to be learnt implicitly. By virtue of its integrated nature, musical structure leads the ear naturally from the simple to the more complex.

The notion that we are all 'musical by design' is supported by John Sloboda's research that indicates that, as young children, four out of five of us probably had the potential to become performers at a professional level:[30] all that was needed was sustained application throughout childhood and adolescence – adherence to Malcolm Gladwell's '10,000 Hour Rule'.[31] Yet how many adults in advanced societies, if asked, would say that they were 'musical'? Very few. And time and again, when working with children, their parents ruefully confide in me 'I started to learn the piano, but gave up when I was 11' (or thereabouts). They all express the regret that they did not persist. So what is going wrong?

Partly, the failure of most people to engage in active music making beyond childhood is a consequence of the expectations of a society that reveres a small musical elite and in so doing subjugates the musical potential and more modest aspirations of the majority. They are consigned for ever to be second-class musical citizens, 'listeners' rather than 'composers' or 'performers', passive recipients rather than active participants, consumers rather than producers. Yet this dichotomy is by no means universal: while many societies in the developing world acknowledge the importance of musical leadership, participation by all is the norm.

It may be the case that many adolescents stop developing their practical music-making skills since they find what is on offer through formal educational channels – to use their language – a 'turn off'. Despite projects such as *Musical Futures*, a programme that is rooted in pupils' own musical interests and ambitions,[32] 'school music' can all too often bear little relation to the popular culture in which young people are typically deeply immersed (as listeners) in their leisure hours. Those who go on to succeed as performers of popular music in one form or another are usually self-taught, feeding off the recognition of their peers rather than teachers or parents.[33] Some youngsters do follow a conventional 'classical' music education all the way through from early childhood, on into the teenage years and subsequently through music college or university and out into the world of the professional classical performer – a journey demanding exceptional levels of tenacity and self-belief. It goes without saying that the necessary dedication and sacrifice will only ever appeal to a very few. But the important point is this: in my view, if more teachers – and parents – were to adopt a more child-centred approach to music education, which genuinely built on individual's interests and motivations rather than (in many cases) predetermined social expectations, which fostered and celebrated musical achievement in a range of spheres and genres, then a greater number of people could (and, I believe, would) attain far higher levels of practical musical expertise and engagement that would be sustained throughout their lives.

* * *

Having established that the overwhelming majority of us are far more musical than we think we are, there is no doubt that a very few do have exceptional talent at which the rest of us can only marvel. And genius is never as striking as when it manifests itself early on. The oft-quoted example is that of Wolfgang Amadeus Mozart, who was born in Salzburg in 1756, when the transition from the Baroque to the Classical period of Western music was already well under way. A truly remarkable prodigy, the infant Mozart was taught to play the harpsichord, violin and organ by his father, Leopold, and began composing before he was five years old. From the age of six, Wolfgang and his older sister, Nannerl, went on tour with Leopold, and were acclaimed across Europe. Throughout all this upheaval, Mozart continued to develop musically, and by the time he was thirteen he had already written sonatas, concertos, symphonies and even two short operas.

There is no better example than Mozart's to fuel both sides of the 'nature/nurture' debate of musical talent. Since Mozart's father, Leopold, was himself a professional musician, the possibility of a genetic predisposition towards exceptional music making is evident. Equally, though, we know that the Mozart children were brought up in an environment suffused with music, and that Leopold was a great teacher (in the year that Wolfgang was born he published a major treatise on how to play the violin, the importance of which is still recognised today). Mozart's example, while exceptional in terms of the level of his achievement and the age at which this was reached, is broadly typical of many musicians, who tend to be born into 'musical' families that encourage them from an early age. Johann Sebastian Bach, for example, born in 1685, represented the fifth generation of musicians in his family, which, over two centuries, went on to have over seventy musical members of professional standing. Hence both genetic and environmental factors, it seems, are likely to play a necessary role in the formation of musical genius. A brain with the potential to be wired up for exceptional musicality is required, but this is no more important than an environment – particularly in the early years – that will stimulate the production of the necessary connections.

How do prodigies arise? Clearly, something unusual must happen very early on in musical development. And yet it is not anything that ultimately affects our capacity to make sense of music, or to be emotionally engaged with it, since we all have the intuitive capacity to understand and appreciate the music of Mozart and other exceptional young talents. So what was it that made him special?

It seems that absolute pitch ('AP') is a *necessary* though not a *sufficient* factor in the development of all prodigies. Leading music education researcher Gary McPherson's book devoted to the topic[34] includes accounts of classical composers and performers such as Ludwig van Beethoven, Mozart, Fanny Mendelssohn and her brother Felix, Clara Schumann, Franz Liszt, Pablo Casals, Jascha Heifetz, Ervin Nyiregyházi (who was studied as a child by the Hungarian psychologist Géza Révész), Olivier Messiaen, Glenn Gould and Yo-Yo Ma; popular musicians of the twentieth century such as Michael Jackson and Stevie Wonder; and my pupil, Derek Paravicini – all of whom had or have AP. There seems to be something about the perceptual immediacy and power that this rare ability[35] bestows, which, time and again, draws toddlers who are possessors irresistibly towards music, and it confers a huge advantage, particularly in the early stages, upon those seeking to learn to play an instrument.

Incredibly, there are two special groups of children with learning difficulties who behave in many ways as though they were prodigies (although by no means all of them go on to develop outstanding musical skills as performers) with whom I have worked for much of my professional life, following my early experiences with Anthony at Linden Lodge School. These are so-called 'savants'.[36] Despite their disabilities, these young people have exceptional musical skills, which invariably include AP. As we shall see, they present a number of challenges to teachers. But, as the account of my interactions with Derek in Chapter 2 showed, they also offer unique insights into the musical mind.

Musicality in Blind Children and Those on the Autism Spectrum

Around 45 per cent of children born blind or who lose their sight shortly after birth, and 8 per cent of those on the autism spectrum, have AP. This compares with an estimated 1 in 10,000 of the 'neurotypical' Western population. Why is there this extraordinary discrepancy? We will consider first the case of those without sight.

It seems that a high proportion of children who are severely visually impaired from the time they are born attach particular importance to everyday sounds, and, as a consequence, the trajectory of their auditory development may well differ from that taken by almost all fully-sighted, 'neurotypical' children. How do you we know this? The evidence is to be found in a series of three surveys of the parents of visually impaired children that I undertook over a period of ten years, with co-researchers including Wisconsin-based psychiatrist Darold Treffert, who has devoted his life to studying the epidemiology of what he terms 'savant syndrome', and Linda Pring, Professor of Psychology at Goldsmiths College in London, who has specialised in researching the effects of blindness and autism on human development.

The surveys contribute to a wider project called *Focus on Music*, which explores how visual impairment may impact on children's evolving musicality, and comprises a series of studies, each of which pertains to a particular eye condition that can cause different levels of visual impairment ranging from total blindness to partial sight, and that can have associated disorders, including learning difficulties and autism. Two of the conditions studied to date are genetic: 'septo-optic dysplasia' and 'Leber congenital amaurosis', and one affects some babies who are born too early: 'retinopathy of prematurity'. In each case, data were gathered from over thirty children, making a little under a hundred in all. A comparison with a fully-sighted group was also undertaken.

According to their parents, two thirds of the children who were categorised as being 'educationally blind' (which means either having no sight, just the perception of light, or some sense of movement and shape) showed a high level of interest in everyday sounds. This compares with just under a third of those who were described as being 'partially sighted', and only one in eight of those in the comparison group, who had no visual impairment. Accordingly, there appears to be an inverse relationship between children's level of vision and their interest in everyday sounds, those with the least vision being the most interested.

These findings support the common sense notion that, with little or no sight, sound has a greater appeal than would otherwise be the case, and offers a ready source of stimulation in the absence of visual input. For instance, the mother of a five-year-old boy noted that he 'loves repetitive sounds – [he] will press toys which make noises over and over to hear the sounds'.[37] Here, a simple auditory stimulus seems to have become something of a fixation, an idiosyncrasy that parents report time and again. For example, one mother wrote of her six-and-a-half-year-old blind son, Liam, being obsessed with the noise of the microwave, 'so much so that he becomes upset if he can't make it into the kitchen before it is finished. More recently he has become interested in the tumble drier. He lies on the floor and listens to it and gets upset when it stops. He also loves the noises of the vacuum cleaner, washing machine and dishwasher.'[38]

To appreciate the significance of these sorts of unusual interests, it is helpful to consider them in the context of William Gaver's 'ecological' analysis of hearing (see pp. 195 and 196), which privileges the *function* of sounds in auditory perception over their *form* – that is, their acoustic properties. Gaver writes as follows:[39]

> Imagine that you are walking along a road at night when you hear a sound. On the one hand, you might pay attention to its pitch and loudness and the ways they change with time. You might attend to the sound's timbre, whether it is rough or smooth, bright or dull ... These are all examples of *musical listening*, in which the perceptual dimensions and attributes of concern have to do with the sound itself, and are those used in the creation of music.
>
> On the other hand, as you stand there in the road, it is likely that you will not listen to the sound itself at all. Instead, you are likely to notice that the sound is made by an automobile with a large and powerful engine. Your attention is likely to be drawn to the fact that it is approaching quickly from behind. And you might even attend to the environment, hearing that the road you are on is actually a narrow alley, with echoing walls on each side.
>
> This is an example of *everyday listening*, the experience of listening to events rather than sounds. Most of our experience of hearing the day-to-day world is one of everyday listening: we are concerned with listening to the things going on around us, with hearing which are important to avoid and which might offer possibilities for action. The perceptual dimensions and attributes of concern correspond to those of the sound-producing event and its environment, not to those of the sound itself.

Yet that is precisely the opposite of what the young blind children were reported to be doing: rather, they were treating *everyday sounds* as though they were *musical* – a foible that was facilitated, no doubt, by the fact that tumble driers, washing machines, vacuum cleaners and dishwashers all emanate distinct pitches, extended in time and rich in harmonics. Before considering the consequences of this curious inversion of function and form on auditory development, we will examine the position of children on the autism spectrum.

Here, the difference in the way that the world is perceived forms part of what the leading autism researcher Francesca Happé calls the 'beautiful otherness' of the autistic mind, which hears and sees the surrounding environment with a startling, sometimes alarming, intensity. Children with 'classic' autism – the kind that the Austrian-American psychiatrist Leo Kanner first identified in 1943, who have problems with language as well as finding it difficult to relate to other people, and who exhibit obsessive patterns of behaviour – seem to engage with a different reality, a different sense of what counts as important, a different understanding of what is interesting. Not wrong, just *different*. Often vividly, viscerally different. A mode of perception shot through with perplexity at the way others think, feel, behave and communicate, yet one that is often infused with a genuine warmth and affection that are discernible if one can see beyond the disconcerting inflexions of a narrow range of speech, the awkward body language, and the strained sense of personal space that can characterise the autistic persona.

Young people with classic autism may interact with others in a way that is at once egocentric, yet free from disingenuousness and unkind irony. They may display a maddening adherence to routine, yet evince a loyalty that is rock solid among the shifting sands of human relationships. And they will certainly have a love of repetition, a yearning for repetition, an *insistence* on repetition, for which music, constructed entirely on the principle of imitation, could have been designed especially to assuage, and, as we'll discover, is unique in its capacity to satisfy.[40]

Music opens up a channel of communication that, unlike verbal language, lacks the capacity to command, to judge, to criticise ... and so to threaten. Rather, making music with others creates a safe interpersonal space in which thoughts and feelings can be expressed and shared: a window through which autistic and 'neurotypical' people can view each other's minds on equal terms – a unique antidote to the 'mindblindness',[41] which, as Simon Baron-Cohen, Professor of Developmental Psychopathology at the University of Cambridge, has shown, bedevils the lives of many people on the autism spectrum.

So what *is* autism? Whereas we can all imagine, at some, superficial level, what it must be like to be blind – intuitively feeling the need to warn a visually impaired person of an approaching step up or down, for example, and perhaps feeling the urge to describe the visual scene around – putting oneself in the shoes of someone who may be able to tell you what day of the week you were born, yet wouldn't know that two 50p pieces make £1, can be disconcerting, to say the least. And the difficulty that lay people may find in pinpointing what autism means is reflected in the lack of a medical definition of the condition. Autism is elusive. It is not *one* thing with a single physiological source: researchers have not been able to isolate a particular part of the brain that is wired up anomalously and say 'this is the cause' and 'this is its effect'.

There is, though, general agreement that autism is a lifelong, neurological condition that manifests itself early on; typically within the first two or three years of childhood.[42] And everyone acknowledges that its effects can be profound, pervading the whole of a child's development. However, its identification rests solely on the basis of *observed behaviours*, which can vary widely both between and within individuals in different contexts and at varying stages of their maturation. Diagnostically, the best that clinicians can currently do is to refer to a list of attributes, and say that if a child exhibits certain combinations of these, then he or she can be described as having an 'autism spectrum condition'. Hence, as our understanding of brain function improves, it seems likely that the notion of 'autism' will be resolved into a number of more specific forms of neurodiversity.

For now, though, the criteria for autism set out by the World Health Organisation ('WHO')[43] and the American Psychiatric Association ('APA')[44] are the most widely used. The latter define the condition in terms of two broad characteristics: qualitative impairment in social interaction and communication, and restricted, repetitive and stereotyped patterns of behaviour, interests and activities. An 'impairment in social interaction' is taken to mean, for example, little or no eye contact, difficulties in developing relationships with peers, and a perceived lack of social or emotional reciprocity. An 'impairment in communication' refers to a dearth of language, characterised by the inability or unwillingness to initiate or sustain a conversation, words or phrases used in apparently meaningless ways, and a lack of make-believe play. 'Restricted, repetitive and stereotyped patterns of behaviour, interests and activities' encompass preoccupations that are abnormal in intensity or focus, frequently with features of objects that seem to have no bearing on their usual day-to-day functions.

Towards the end of the twentieth century, three theories dominated academic thinking about the causes of autism, each associated in a different way with WHO/APA definitions. Defective 'theory of mind'[44] – the ability to attribute mental states to oneself and others, and to understand that others may have ideas that differ from one's own – was held to be responsible for 'impairment in social interaction'. 'Weak central coherence'[46] – the tendency to think about things in terms of their parts rather than as a whole – was linked to communication difficulties (as well, more positively, as accounting for enhanced perception of detail and some 'savant-like' abilities). 'Executive dysfunction'[47] – a problem with the domain of processing that regulates and controls other cognitive functions – was thought to lead to rigid and repetitive behaviours.

While these accounts make perfect sense, they do not appear to be able to explain all the characteristics of children on the autism spectrum, particularly those pertaining to sound and music. Consider the idiosyncratic behaviours and interests of some of the autistic children with whom I have worked over the years. Anna, aged four, for example, has 'echolalia', a form of speech that involves repeating much of what is said to her. For instance, if her mother says 'Hello, Anna' to her, she will respond with 'Hello, Anna'. Even the inflection of her voice is the same as her mother's, yet the words apparently convey no meaning. Ben, a teenager, constantly wants to listen to the jingles that he downloads from the internet – he would be on his iPad all his waking moments if he were allowed. He doesn't even play the clips all the way through: usually just three or four seconds of them, over and over again. He must have seen and heard these tiny fragments of sound thousands of times, but he never seems to get bored. Callum, aged 11, invariably puts his hands over his ears and starts rocking and humming to himself whenever the ringtone on his father's phone sounds, yet he totally ignores the sound of his mother's phone, which is much louder. Romy will introduce everyday sounds that she hears into her improvising. For example, she plays the complicated descending multi-layered drone of the aeroplanes coming into land at Heathrow as chords, and somehow integrates them into the music she is playing. Omur, aged three, repeatedly bangs away at one or two particular notes on his piano (mainly 'B' and 'F sharp', high up in the right hand), sometimes persisting until the string or the hammer breaks. Finally, Derek (who, as we have seen, is also blind), copies the sounds of the page turns in his own rendition of a Chopin waltz that his piano teacher played for him by tapping his fingers on the music rack above the keyboard. The main theories of autism are awkwardly mute on these topics. So what is the element missing from our understanding?

Observation of hundreds of children on the autism spectrum from across the UK, undertaken as part of Phase 1 of the *Sounds of Intent* project, suggests that many of them may share a similar fascination for everyday sounds. For example, Freddie, at the age of nine, would habitually flick any glasses, bowls or pots that were within reach. Once, he even removed the twenty or so flowerpots from the patio and brought them into the kitchen, arranging them like some earthenware gamelan. Then he ran around, playing his newly constructed instrument with characteristic finger-flicks, in a state of some excitement – on some occasions producing recognisable fragments of melodies and on others making up new motifs.

Why did Freddie do it? Why did he find the sounds of the flowerpots so attractive? Blind children, deprived of the visual input that would otherwise have been their principal source of information about the environment, often seem to be especially attracted to salient features in the *auditory* landscape. And we have also observed how, without the visual data to contextualise and make sense of environmental sounds (to know what is making a certain noise and why), some auditory information can remain at the *perceptual* level, rather than acquiring *functional* significance. Hence the hum of the microwave and the whirr of the washing machine are treated as abstract phenomena, rather than heralding a hot meal or clean laundry. But why should some children on the autism spectrum apparently process sound in a similar way to those who are blind?

A proportion of autistic youngsters have problems in processing visual information, and many more have problems with 'sensory integration': connecting incoming data from different sensory modalities.[48] That is to say, the process of 'binding', which, as we have noted (pp. 43–44), links incoming streams of perceptual information in different sensory domains in the mind to produce single, coherent experiences, appears not to be fully functional. As a consequence, such children have a tendency to process sounds as though they were visually impaired.

* * *

In my academic work as a music psychologist, I have suggested that the kinds of behaviours and ways of engaging with sound and music that parents report in their blind or autistic children exist as a consequence of the 'exceptional early cognitive environment' ('EECE') that arises from the unusual sensory processing abilities and propensities that either (or in some cases both) of the two conditions generate. EECEs can have a number of effects, including the possibility that certain sounds, especially those that are particularly salient or pleasing to an individual, acquire little or no functional significance. Instead, they tend to be treated as elements of music. The EECE conjecture also suggests that everyday sounds that involve repetition or regularity (such as the beeping of a microwave or the ticking of a clock) may be processed in music-*structural* terms. This would imply that the children hear the repetition that is actually generated mechanically or electronically as being imitative. So, for some blind or autistic children, the ecological model of auditory development (see Figure 75) needs to be modified as follows, with some everyday sounds being diverted into the stream of music (see Figure 77).

There is, of course, another possibility we should acknowledge: that the blind and autistic children who are preoccupied with the sounding qualities of certain everyday objects and the repetitive patterns that some of them make don't actually hear them in a *musical* way but purely as regularities in the environment. This may well be so, and, furthermore, it could be that those same children don't hear music as 'music' either, but merely as patterned sequences of sounds, to which no sense of human agency is transferred. Why should this be the case? Perhaps because such children were not naturally inclined to engage in early vocal interactions with carers, which I have suggested may embed a sense of imitation in sounds that are repeated. However, the accounts of Romy reproducing the whines of jet engines of aeroplanes coming in to land and integrating them into her improvisation at the piano, of Derek evidently regarding

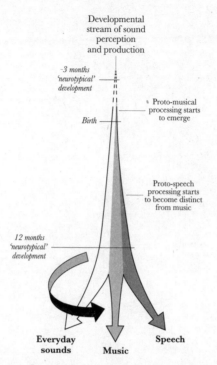

Figure 77 *Some everyday sounds may be processed as music by blind children and those on the autism spectrum.*

the rustle of a page turn as part of a Chopin waltz, and of Freddie appropriating everyday objects (flowerpots) to be used as musical instruments, suggest that some autistic children at least do perceive everyday sounds in a musical way.

It may well be that this tendency is reinforced by the prevalence of music in the lives of young children:[49] in the developed world, they are typically surrounded by electronic games and gadgets, toys, mobile phones, MP3 players, computers, iPads, TVs, radios and so on, all of which emanate music to a greater or lesser extent. In the wider environment too – in restaurants, cafés, shops, cinemas and waiting rooms, cars and aeroplanes, and at many religious gatherings and other public ceremonies – music is ubiquitous. So, given that children are inundated with non-functional (musical) sounds, designed, in one way or another, to influence emotional states and behaviour, perhaps we should not be

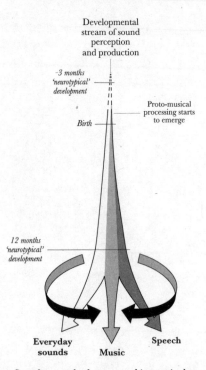

Figure 78 *Speech may also be processed in musical terms by some blind children and some of those on the autism spectrum.*

surprised that the functional sounds with which they are often co-occur should come to be processed in the same way.

EECEs have other potential consequences too. For example, the development of language can be affected, resulting in, among other things, 'echolalia' – a distinctive form of speech widely reported among blind and autistic children,[50] which was originally defined as the meaningless repetition of words or phrases.[51] American autism researcher and clinician Dr Barry Prizant was among the first to observe, however, that echolalia actually fulfils a range of functions in verbal interaction, including turn-taking and affirmation, and often finds a place in non-interactive contexts too, serving as a self-reflective commentary or rehearsal strategy.[52] Given the zygonic hypothesis that imitation lies at the heart of musical structure, it could be argued that one cause of echolalia is the organisation of language (in the absence of semantics and syntax) through the structure (repetition) that is present in all music. It is as though words become musical objects in their own right, to be manipulated not according to their meaning or grammatical function, but purely through their sounding qualities. Indeed, recent research has shown that repeating short series of words makes them sound musical for all of us.[53] This implies a further modification to the ecological model of auditory development (see Figure 78).

It is of interest to note that echolalia is not restricted to certain exceptional groups that exist on one extreme of the multidimensional continuum that makes up human neurodiversity: it is a feature of 'typical' language acquisition in young children,[54] when, it seems, the urge to imitate what they hear outstrips semantic understanding. This would accord with a stage in the ecological model of auditory development when the two strands of communication through sound – language and music – are not cognitively distinct, and would support the notion that musical development precedes the onset of language.

Abstract structures derived from the imitation of sounds continue to exist in language beyond echolalia. Hence, it is not possible to draw an absolute distinction between music and language, even when the latter is fully developed, in adults. In fact, the two exist on a continuum, like this:

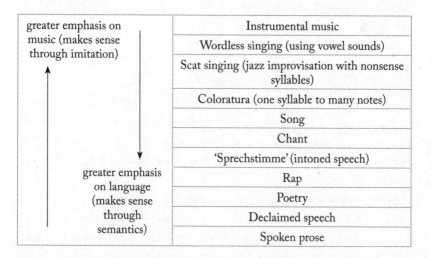

greater emphasis on music (makes sense through imitation) ↑	Instrumental music
	Wordless singing (using vowel sounds)
	Scat singing (jazz improvisation with nonsense syllables)
	Coloratura (one syllable to many notes)
	Song
	Chant
↓	'Sprechstimme' (intoned speech)
greater emphasis on language (makes sense through semantics)	Rap
	Poetry
	Declaimed speech
	Spoken prose

Table 6 Music and language overlap to varying degrees in different art forms.

For children growing up with an EECE, it is worth noting that music itself can become 'super-structured' with additional repetition, as the account, for example, of Ben (p. 210) shows: it is common for children on the autism spectrum to play snippets of music (or videos with music) over and over again. It is as though music's already high proportion of repetition, which, depending how you measure it, is at least 80 per cent,[55] is insufficient for the mind ravenous for structure, and so it creates even more! Speaking to autistic adults who are able to verbalise why (as children) they would repeat musical excerpts in this way, it appears that the main reason (apart from the sheer enjoyment of hearing a particularly fascinating series of sounds repeatedly) is that they could hear more and more in the sequence concerned as they listened to it again and again. Bearing in mind that most music is highly complex, with many events occurring simultaneously (and given that even single notes generally comprise many pitches in the form of harmonics), to the child with finely tuned auditory perception, there are in fact a plethora of different things to attend to in even a few seconds of music, and an even greater number of relationships between sounds to fathom. So, for example, while listening a hundred times to a passage for orchestra may be extremely tedious to the 'neurotypical' ear, which can detect only half a dozen composite events, each fused in perception, to the mind of the autistic child, which can break down the sequence into a dozen different melodic lines, the stimulus may be rich and riveting.

Exceptional Musical Ability: Savants

We now return to the question of absolute pitch, and consider its impact on early musical development. While it is thought to be a feature of all infant prodigies' profiles of abilities, it is an essential element in the evolution of exceptional musical skills in those with learning difficulties – so-called 'savants'.

It seems that blind and autistic children whose development is affected by an EECE, and who tend to hear sounds as phenomena in their own right, continue to have a strong focus on individual pitches for their own sake beyond the first year of life, when 'neurotypical' brains are moving away from this and learning to prioritise the relationships between them.[56] As we saw in Chapter 2, what gives a tune its unique identity is not its constituent notes, but how they compare with one another. That is not how the perception of melodies starts out, though, nor, in those with an EECE, is it how things continue, at least for a while longer than in children developing 'neurotypically' – perhaps up to the age of 24 months or so. The evidence for this is to be found in the astonishing prevalence of AP among children who are born blind or who lose their sight early on (which, as we have seen, is thought to be around 45 per cent),[57] those who are partially sighted (around 11 per cent)[58] and those on the autism spectrum (conservatively estimated at 8 per cent),[59] which tends to manifest itself around the age of two.[60] This compares with the distribution of AP in the Western population as a whole, which is thought to be around 0.01 per cent.[61]

It is very rare to find such high orders of difference in the incidence of a perceptual ability between different sub-groups of the human population – a ratio of some 4,500 : 1 in the case of blind children compared to those who are fully sighted. Evidently, there is something distinct in the way that parts of the brain responsible for pitch memory wire themselves up in many children who have never had sight.[62] But then, blindness is an extreme disability, given the central role that vision usually plays in providing the brain with information about the world, in integrating most other perceptual input, and in facilitating the development of many everyday concepts (from cause and effect to colour).

Leon Miller, now Emeritus Professor of Psychology at the University of Illinois, Chicago, first identified that AP is likely to be an essential factor in the development of musical savantism,[63] a conjecture supported by my own work with a number of savants over the last four decades. I think of AP rather like the starting pistol that, in the early years, signals the beginning of the marathon that those who have learning difficulties and are autistic and may also be blind have to run into order to develop exceptional music performance skills. Without AP, their journeys would never begin. And even the possession of AP is no guarantee that musical advancement will follow, since there are so many potential barriers to prodigious achievement among those with severe disabilities, both internal and external: many AP seeds have to be sown among the population of

Figure 79 *A typical taunting playground chant.*

those with learning difficulties for even one outstanding musical talent to grow in the challenging educational terrain that those who are 'twice exceptional'[64] have to face. But just why is AP so important?

In my experience it is this unusual ability that enables and motivates some young children with learning difficulties, blind or on the autism spectrum, from the age of 24 months or so, to pick out tunes and harmonies on instruments that they may encounter at home, in the nursery or at school – typically the keyboard or piano. This may well occur with no adult intervention (or, indeed, awareness). It seems that AP has this impact since each pitch sounds distinct, potentially eliciting a powerful emotional response; so being able to reproduce these at will must surely be an electrifying experience. But more than this, AP makes learning to play by ear manageable, in a way that 'relative pitch' – the capacity to process melodic and harmonic intervals – does not. To understand why, consider a typical playground chant.

The pitches of motifs like this are, in 'neurotypical' individuals, likely to be encoded in the mind, stored and retrieved principally as a series of differences between notes (although 'fuzzy' absolute memories will exist – a child would know if the chant were an octave too high, for example). However, for children with AP, the position is quite different, since they have the capacity to capture the pitch data from music directly, rather than as series of intervals. Hence in seeking to remember and repeat groups of notes over significant periods of time, they have certain processing advantages over their 'neurotypical' peers, who extract and store information at a higher level of abstraction, and thereby lose the 'surface detail'. Note that there are disadvantages to 'absolute' representations of pitch too, since on their own they cannot take advantage of the patterns that exist through the repetition of intervals, and make greater demands on memory. However, as there appears to be, to all intents and purposes, no limit on the brain's long-term storage capacity, this is not a serious problem; indeed, having an exceptional memory is something that is common to all savants.

I believe that it is this capacity for 'absolute pitch data capture' that explains why some children who are blind or on the autism spectrum and have learning difficulties are able to develop instrumental skills at an early age with no formal tuition, since reproducing groups of notes that they have heard is merely a question of remembering a series of one-to-one mappings between given pitches as they sound and (typically) the keys on a keyboard that produce them. These relationships are invariant: once learnt, they can service a lifetime of music making, through which they are constantly reinforced. On the other hand, were a child with 'relative pitch' to try to play by ear, he or she would have to become proficient in the far more complicated process of calculating how the intervals that are perceived map onto the distances between keys, which, due to the asymmetries of the keyboard, are likely to differ according to what would necessarily be an arbitrary starting point. For example, the interval that exists between the first two notes of the playground chant (a 'minor 3rd') shown in Figure 79 can be produced through no fewer than *twelve* distinct key combinations, comprising one of four underlying patterns. Moreover, the complexity of the situation is compounded by the fact that virtually the same physical leap between other keys may sound different (a '*major* 3rd') according to its position on the keyboard.

That is not to say that children with AP who learn to play by ear do not rapidly develop the skills to play melodies beginning on different notes too, and it is not unusual for them to learn to reproduce pieces fluently in every key (a capacity that, as a teacher, I strongly encourage). This may appear contradictory, in the light of the processing advantage conferred by being able to encode pitches as perceptual identities in their own right, each of which maps uniquely onto a particular note on the keyboard. However, as we saw in Chapter 2, the reality of almost all pieces of music is that melodic (and harmonic) motifs variously appear at different pitches through transposition, and so to make sense of music, young children with AP need to learn to process pitch relatively as well as absolutely.[65]

* * *

What is the day-to-day impact of exceptional musical ability on children with learning difficulties who are blind or on the autism spectrum likely to be? The answer is as varied as the children are themselves. Elsewhere, I have written at length about the extraordinary life of Derek Paravicini,[66] to whom the inspiration for much of the thinking in this book is owed. It is simply not possible to imagine Derek without his piano playing, in which the way he thinks, the way he feels, the way he relates to other people – his fizz, his fun, his fanaticism – are embodied. But there are many other children on the autism spectrum with whom I have had the privilege and pleasure of working too: no less exceptional in their different ways, and no less enlightening as to the nature of the relationship between us sapient primates and our music. I often think that the best way to understand a feature of a population is not, as mean-driven psychologists are wont, to look at the 'typical' (whatever that may mean), but at the exceptional. Since Derek and others with similar profiles of ability are, first and foremost, human beings, so a model of musical development that doesn't account for them is by definition an inadequate model. But more than that, the bright light of the extremes is uniquely placed to illuminate the average. Neurodiversity is not just a fascinating concept to which applied and social scientists should pay lip service; it should lie at the heart of our developing understanding of humankind.

In this philosophical context, I offer two accounts of children with whom I have worked every week for a number of years. They are taken from blogs that were designed to raise awareness of autism and musicality, and to stir the debate on the relationship between so-called 'disability' and ability.

The children – and their parents – come for sessions in a large practice room at the University of Roehampton. There are two pianos, so we don't have to scrap over ownership of the keyboard. A number of the children rarely say a word. Some, like fifteen-year-old Romy, don't speak at all. She communicates everything through her playing, indicating what piece she would like to choose next, and telling me when she's had enough. Sometimes, she teases me by seeming to suggest one thing when she means another. We share many jokes and the occasional sad moment too. For Romy, music is a fully-fledged proxy language.[67]

A session with Romy

On Sunday mornings, at 10.00 a.m., I steel myself for Romy's arrival. I know that the next two hours will be an exacting test of my musical mettle. Despite having severe learning difficulties, Romy is musical to the core: she lives and breathes music. With her passion comes a high degree of particularity: she knows *precisely* which piece she wants me to play, in which key and at what tempo. And woe betide me if I get any of the details wrong.

When we started working together, seven years ago, mistakes and misunderstandings occurred all too frequently, since (as it turned out), there were very few pieces that Romy would tolerate: the theme from *Für Elise* (never the middle section), for example, the Habanera from *Carmen*, and some snippets from 'Buckaroo Holiday' (the first movement of Aaron Copland's *Rodeo*). Romy's acute neophobia meant that even one note of a different piece would evoke shrieks of fear-cum-anger, and the session could easily grow into an emotional conflagration.

So gradually, gradually, over weeks, then months, and then years, I introduced new pieces – sometimes, quite literally, at the rate of one note per session. On occasion, if things were difficult, I would even take a step back before trying to move on again the next time. And, imperceptibly at first, Romy's fears started to melt away. The theme from Brahms's *Haydn Variations* became something of an obsession, followed by the slow movement of Beethoven's *Pathétique* Sonata. Then it was Joplin's *The Entertainer*, and *Rockin' All Over the World* by Status Quo.

Over the seven years, Romy's jigsaw box of musical pieces – fragments ranging from just a few seconds to a minute or so in length – has filled up at an ever-increasing rate. Now it's overflowing, and it's difficult to keep up with her mercurial musical mind: mixing and matching ideas in our improvised sessions, and even changing melodies and harmonies so they mesh together, or to ensure that my contributions don't!

As we play, new pictures in sound emerge and then retreat as a kaleidoscope of ideas whirls between us. Sometimes a single melody persists for fifteen minutes, even half an hour. For Romy, no matter how often it is repeated, a fragment of music seems to stay fresh and vibrant. At other times, it sounds as though she is trying to play several pieces at the same time – she just can't get them out quickly enough, and a veritable nest of earworms wriggle their way onto the piano keyboard. Vainly I attempt to herd them into a common direction of musical travel.

So here I am, sitting at the piano in Roehampton, on a Sunday morning in mid-November, waiting for Romy to join me (not to be there when she arrives is asking for trouble). I'm limbering up with a rather sedate rendition of the opening of Chopin's *Etude* in C major, Op. 10, No. 1, when I hear her coming down the corridor, vocalising with increasing fervour. I feel the tension rising, and as her father pushes open the door, she breaks away from him, rushes over to the piano and, with a shriek and an extraordinarily agile sweep of her arm, elbows my right hand out of the way at the precise moment that I was going to hit the D an octave above middle C. She usurps this note to her own ends, ushering in her favourite Brahms-Haydn theme. Instantly, Romy smiles, relaxes and gives me the choice of moving out of the way or having my lap appropriated as an unwilling cushion on the piano stool. I choose the former, sliding to my left onto a chair that I'd placed earlier in readiness for the move that I knew I would have to make.

I join in the Brahms, and encourage her to use her left hand to add a bass line. She tolerates this up to the end of the first section of the theme, but in her mind she's already moved on, and without a break in the sound, Romy steps onto the set of *A Little Night Music*, gently noodling around the introduction to *Send in the Clowns*. But it's in the wrong key – G instead of E flat – which I know from experience means that she doesn't *really* want us to go into the Sondheim classic, but instead wants me to play the first four bars (and only the first four bars) of Schumann's *Kleine Studie* Op. 68, No. 14. Trying to perform the fifth bar would in any case be futile since Romy's already started to play ... now, is it *I am Sailing* or *Oh Freedom*. The opening ascent from D through E to G could signal either of those possibilities. Almost tentatively, Romy presses those three notes down and then looks at me and smiles, waiting, and knowing that whichever option I choose will be the wrong one. I just shake my head at her and plump for *Oh Freedom*, but sure enough Rod Stewart shoves the Spiritual out of the way before it has time to draw a second breath.

From there, Romy shifts up a gear to the *Canon in D* – or is it really Pachelbel's masterpiece? With a deft flick of her little finger up to a high A, she seems to suggest that she would like *Streets of London* instead (which uses the same harmonies). I opt for Ralph McTell, but another flick, this time aimed partly at me as well as the keys, shows that Romy actually wants Beethoven's *Pathétique* theme – but again, in the wrong key (D). Obediently I start to play, but Romy takes us almost immediately to A flat (the tonality that Beethoven originally intended). As soon as I'm there, though, Romy races back up the keyboard again, returning to Pachelbel's domain. Before I've had time to catch up, she's transformed the music once more; now we're hearing the famous theme from Dvorak's *New World* Symphony.

I pause to recover my thoughts, but Romy is impatiently waiting for me to begin the accompaniment. Two or three minutes into the session, and we've already touched on twelve pieces spanning 300 years of Western music and an emotional range to match. Yet here is a girl who in everyday life is supposed to have no 'theory of mind' – the capacity to put yourself in other people's shoes and think what they are thinking. Here is someone who is supposed to lack the ability to communicate. Here is someone who functions, apparently, at an early years level. But I say here is a joyous musician who amazes all who hear her. Here is a girl in whom extreme ability and disability coexist in the most extraordinary way. Here is someone who can reach out through music and touch one's emotions in a profound way. If music is important to us all, for Romy it is truly her lifeblood.

How did Romy, a child with a severe learning disability, become such a talented – if more than a little eccentric – musician?

As the ecological model of auditory development in Figure 78 shows, I believe that it was her *inability* to process language in the early years, coupled with her *inability* to understand the significance of many every-day sounds, which led to her heightened *ability* to process sounds – *all* sounds – in a musical way. One traded off the other. In fact, without the former, it is almost certain that the latter would never have developed. Her disabilities and abilities are, I believe, different sides of the same coin.

Romy has AP, which, as we have seen, means that for her, every note on the piano sounds different, and is instantly recognisable as C, F sharp, B flat and so on. But there is more to it than this. For Romy, each pitch is like a familiar friend in an otherwise confusing world. And it's not just notes on the piano that Romy can recognise. To her, *any* note in *any* piece of music that she hears sounds distinct. If for most of us musical sounds pass by as a series of shades of grey, for Romy, harmonies seem to explode in her head in brilliant technicolour. A chord of E flat major is enough to make her literally tremble with excitement. And G7 can bring a tear to her eye – not in a negative way, but as a pure, deep, emotional response. But in itself absolute pitch does not an exceptional musician make: that takes around 10,000 hours of practice. So how did Romy come to be able to do what she does?

Like many children on the autism spectrum, she developed an early, obsessive interest in one thing – in her case a little keyboard, whose notes lit up in the sequence required to play a number of different children's songs. For Romy, this toy was one of the few things that made sense in the blooming, buzzing confusion of everyday life. And she would spend hundreds of hours engaging with it. It was reassuringly predictable compared with the loving humans around her, whose language and interactions subtly differed, as all interpersonal engagement does, from one occasion to another. The keyboard, though, *always* gave Romy the same response. When she pressed middle C it sounded the same as it did a few seconds ago, a minute ago, an hour ago – the same as it did yesterday, the same, even, as it did last year. Here was something that Romy could predict. Above all, here was something that she could control.

And so, through hours and hours and hours of playing and experimenting as a toddler, Romy taught herself where all the notes on the keyboard are. Today, for her, playing the piano is merely a matter of hearing a tune in her head (instantly available to her through the internal library of songs – her 'neural iPod' that she has wired deep into her brain) and playing along with it, pressing the right keys in turn as the required pitches pop into her consciousness. And it is not just music that Romy will play; as we have seen, she will also imitate the sounds of jet engines as planes fly overhead on their descent towards Heathrow, and she instinctively copies any doorbells or ringtones that have the presumption to puncture her otherwise indirigible piano lessons.

Absolute pitch can have other consequences for children on the autism spectrum. With such vivid aural imaginations, and heads full of tunes that seem to be constantly playing, external sounds can be at best superfluous and at worst an irritation, as the following account of a session with Freddie shows.[68]

Freddie – the silent musician

'Why's he doing that?' Freddie's father, Simon, sounded more than usually puzzled by the antics of his son.

After months of prevarication, Freddie, aged nine, was finally sitting next to me at the piano, and looked as though this time he really were about to play. A final fidget and then his right hand moved towards the keys. With infinite care, he placed his thumb on middle C as he had watched me do before – but without pressing it down. Silently, he moved to the next note (D), which he feathered in a similar way, using his index finger, then with the same precision he touched E, F and G, before coming back down the soundless scale to an inaudible C.

I couldn't help smiling.

'Fred, we need to hear the notes!'

My comment was rewarded with a deep stare, right into my eyes. Through them, almost. It was always hard to know what Freddie was thinking, but on this occasion he did seem to understand and was willing to respond to my request, since his thumb went back to C. Again, the key remained unpressed, but this time he *sang* the note (perfectly in tune), and then the next one, and the next, until the five-finger exercise was complete.

In most children (assuming that they had the necessary musical skills), such behaviour would probably be regarded as an idiosyncratic attempt at humour or even mild naughtiness. But Freddie was being absolutely serious and was pleased, I think, to achieve what he'd been asked to do, for he had indeed enabled me to hear the notes!

He stared at me again, evidently expecting something more, and without thinking I leant forward.

'Now on this one, Fred', I said, touching C sharp.

Freddie gave the tiniest blink and a twitch of his head, and I imagined him, in a fraction of a second, making the necessary kinaesthetic calculations. Without hesitation or error, he produced the five-finger exercise again, this time using a mixture of black and white notes. Each pressed silently. All sung flawlessly.

And then, spontaneously, he was off up the keyboard, beginning the same pentatonic pattern on each of the twelve available keys. At my prompting, Freddie re-ran the sequence with his left hand – his unbroken voice hoarsely whispering the low notes.

So logical. Why bother to play the notes if you know what they sound like already?

So apparently simple a task, and yet ... such a difficult feat to accomplish: the whole contradiction of autism crystallised in a few moments of music making.

As I later said to Freddie's parents, if I had to teach a 'neurotypical' child to do what his son had so effortlessly achieved, it would take years of effort and hundreds of hours of practice to get to grips with the asymmetries of the Western tonal system and their relationship to the quirky layout of the piano keyboard. Yet Freddie had done it unthinkingly, just by observing me play, hearing the streams of notes flowing by, and, just as Anthony and Derek had done before him, extracting the underlying rules of Western musical syntax, and subsequently using these to create patterns of sounds afresh. I had *never played* the full sequence of scales that Freddie produced. He had worked out the necessary deep structures intuitively, merely through exposure to the language of music.

* * *

We are now in a position to consolidate all this information and set out a model of how learning difficulties, blindness and autism impact on young children's musical development. The consequences of the EECE caused by the children's sensory processing differences are likely to include difficulties in processing language, and difficulties in understanding the functionality of everyday sounds. At the same time, the children are likely to have a fascination with auditory detail and a love of pattern. Now, if we plug into this cognitive scenario two external factors – music's self-referencing structure (as set out in zygonic theory), and its ubiquity in the lives of children in the early years – then there is a tendency for *all* sounds to be processed in musical terms. In a significant minority of cases, this leads to the development of AP. Given the opportunity, this may in turn lead to children teaching themselves to play a musical instrument (often the keyboard) at an early age. The self-directed attention they give to this task can relatively quickly result in advanced skills. For some, music may even come to function, to a greater or lesser extent, as a proxy language.

For Freddie, for Romy, and for many other children on the autism spectrum, music may be the key not only to aesthetic fulfilment, but also to communication, shared attention and emotional understanding. It can do this because it is a language built not on symbolic meaning but on repetition – on pattern, on order, on predictability in the domain of sound. Music may be important for all of us, but for those on the autism spectrum, it is nothing less than essential brain food.

Coda

This chapter was concerned with musical development in an 'ontogenetic' sense: how musical abilities, propensities and preferences evolve in each of us. In this regard, there are four things of which we can be more or less sure. First, four to three months prior to birth, before the auditory system is developed, we have *no* understanding or appreciation of music. Second, as adults, while the range of music *production* skills is very variable, the great majority of us – whether a modern-day Mozart or Fanny Mendelssohn, or the man or woman next door, even if they have learning difficulties – intuitively grasp the import of music in one form or another, if only unwittingly as a supplementary strand in films, TV programmes, advertisements and the like. Third, most musical development – like the acquisition of the skills needed to process language – occurs in the early years,[69] and it is probably the case (as with language) that an impoverished start in life, in which engagement with music is neither encouraged nor facilitated, will have a negative impact from which it is increasingly difficult for children to recover as they grow older. Fourth, there are identifiable stages in the development of musical understanding that correspond to the different ways in which music is structured at the level of events (notes), groups (motifs) and frameworks of pitch and time (modes and metres). These make increasing demands on cognition

– both processing power and memory – and the evidence from the *Sounds of Intent* project suggests that the abilities needed arise sequentially in development, through which one skill builds on another.

It is intriguing to speculate the extent to which this *ontogenetic* path is mirrored *phylogenetically* – in our evolution as a species. The last chapter concluded by speculating how primitive responses to sound combined with *belief* and *imagination* as the human brain developed brought about the creation of music. We can now add to this evolutionary perspective using the theories of music development set out in this chapter. We can be sure, as with the ontogenetic model, that first on the scene – long before humans became humans – was the capacity to process everyday sounds (*Sounds of Intent*, Level 2). From this, some species developed the ability to imitate sounds, and to recognise the imitation of their own sound-making, as found in human babies as they communicate with their caregivers (at *Sounds of Intent*, Level 3). It is interesting to compare these human skills with those of certain (non-human) animals, such as the calls of lar gibbons, in which each breeding pair exhibits unique variations on series of hooting sounds of different lengths that often culminate in dramatic vocal glides over a wide pitch range.

What happened next in the evolution of our musicality? With the exception of some contemporary styles that deliberately avoid them, it seems that all the world's musics use, and from time immemorial have used, motifs in one guise or another: whether melodic, harmonic or purely rhythmic. This is equivalent to *Sounds of Intent*, Level 4. However, not all kinds of music utilise advanced modal systems (frameworks of intervals in the domain of pitch) – *Sounds of Intent*, Level 5. So can we assume that the former preceded the latter phylogenetically? There is intriguing evidence from music historians that supports this notion. It seems that, in some ancient cultures, new works were created through piecing together fragments (now known as 'melodic formulae'), which were culled from aggregations that were judged to be compatible, termed 'melody types'.[70] One of the reasons for their compatibility appears to be the fact that these motifs shared the same underlying framework of intervals. A number of different cultures have used melody types as the basis for improvisation and composition. Examples range from the eight 'echoi' of ancient Byzantine chant (a classification that still applies in the Armenian, Russian and Serbian churches) to the ragas of Indian music, each of which may be defined as 'a fusion of scalar and melodic elements'.[71] In some cultures, however, the use of melodic formulae gradually became less pervasive, leaving only a framework of intervals in which some transitions were felt to be more likely than others based on patterns of use – that is, 'modes'. As music psychologist Gerald Balzano puts it:[72]

> Just as the desired movement of a melody over time shaped the character of these pitch set materials [melodic formulae], so it was found that the character of the pitch set in turn shaped the perceptible quality of its melodies.

In terms of the *Sounds of Intent* model, this represents a shift from Level 4 (motifs) to Level 5 (modes). It does indeed seem to be the case that the ontogenetic path of musical development that we all trod was an echo of our long-distant phylogenetic past.

5

Composing, Performing and Listening

In a concert hall, two thousand people settle in their seats, and an intense silence falls. A hundred musicians bring their instruments to the ready. The conductor raises his baton, and after a few moments the symphony begins. As the orchestra plays, each member of the audience sits alone, listening to the work of the great, dead, composer.

SO BEGINS THE BOOK, *Musicking: The Meanings of Performing and Listening*, that turned out to be the swan song of the twentieth-century New Zealand-born sociomusicologist Christopher Small. Following a series of other examples of people engaging with music in a wide range of contexts, Small reiterates his long-held conviction that the thing we call music is not a thing at all, but 'an activity, something that people do'.[1] Zygonic theory expresses a similar view, but with the refinement that pieces of music are purely *mental* activities, which may but need not have physical correlates in the world beyond the brain. Composers, for example, may imagine series of sounds before notating them for others to reproduce; performers may silently rehearse a difficult passage before playing or singing in a concert; and listeners may remember what a piece sounded like after having heard it.

This chapter tackles some of the questions that often arise in relation to these three roles: composing, performing and listening to music. Positioning this discussion in the context of zygonic theory enables us to shed new light on a range of issues that have exercised critics and musicologists for a number of years, as well as being of relevance to those with a general interest in how music works for the people who, in one way or another, create or consume it.

The Challenge of Understanding Composers' Work

Composing must surely be one of the most mysterious of human pursuits. It is notoriously difficult to study since, while elements of what is occurring can be externalised at the piano or on a computer, for example, all the key decisions are made silently, between the ears. And trying to reflect on the mental processes that are in train when devising a new piece is fraught with difficulty: for if absorption in creative activity is about letting go of external concerns – being in what Hungarian-American psychologist Mihaly Csikszentmihalyi calls a state of 'flow' – then to have to keep stepping back from that stream of intuition as one seeks to crystallise thoughts in words is surely a recipe for stopping the act of composition dead in its tracks. Maybe some future technology that scans the *mind*, enabling neuroscientists to access thinking directly, rather than, as at present, only permitting them to survey the *brain* by imaging cerebral blood flow or monitoring electrical activity, will allow psychologists in years to come to understand how musical works are generated in real time. But until then, with only physiological measures available to us as pale proxies of the cognitive experience, we have little choice but to rely on the tangible evidence of the compositional process that is currently accessible: scores – visual representations of music – in printed or digital form. However, even in the case of detailed sketches such as the ones that Beethoven left (unwittingly) for posterity, dots and lines and scrawls on the page are rather like fossils: mere impressions of life, each captured at a particular moment and petrified for ever – but the only evidence available to palaeontologists from which to piece together their retrospective narratives of events long past.

And therein lies the problem for music analysis. Just as fossils aren't dinosaurs, neither are scores music. But the temptation to treat them as such appears to be irresistible. Whereas music is intangible, ephemeral and, arguably, ineffable, scores are concrete, enduring and relatively easy to describe. But scores are nothing more than the silent residue that remains when the sounds of music have died away; they are merely imperfect – though perfectly serviceable – sets of instructions for players and singers, which assume a shared knowledge of the mores of performance within a given genre. However, for a certain breed of intellectual musician, scores are curiously intoxicating: they enable complex musical textures to be broken down visually and elements extracted that the ear alone could never have detected. They emancipate the analyst from being able to hear music only through the narrow chink of time afforded by the perceived present: notes from the past and the future can appear side-by-side at a single glance; passages can be played and replayed in the mind as often as desired; and events that last only a fraction of a second can be prolonged without limit. In short, scores enable the eye to subsidise the analytical income of the ear.

Why is this a problem? Because repetition in music is ubiquitous in all domains – pitch, timbre, loudness and time – and through studying scores *visually*, sufficient regularity becomes apparent for almost any tale to be concocted as to a composer's structural intentions (or intuitions): as we saw in the case of Heinrich Schenker, Rudolph Reti and Allen Forte, music analysts seem to have an uncontrollable urge to hunt down relationships in support of theories that have little or nothing to do with how music is actually heard, nor, as far as we can tell, how it was constructed in the first place. Like creation myths, one suspects that these accounts of music are more fanciful than wilfully false; and as twenty-first-century thinking develops a stronger identity of its own, it may be that these ideas will be seen as a foible of the mid to late 1900s and will be consigned to the 'historically interesting' category of musicological literature.

Take, for example, David Lewin's analysis of the famous passage from the opening of the development section of the last movement of Mozart's late G minor symphony (No. 40, K. 550). One of the composer's enduring masterpieces, it is generally agreed that the symphony as a whole is tragic in tone, and, at the point where Lewin's analysis begins, in the

Violin

Figure 80 *Apparent melodic disintegration in the development section of the last movement of Mozart's Symphony No. 40, K. 550.*

very heart of the movement, the depth of emotion is such that the music seems to be straining at the metaphorical leash of the classical tonal and rhythmic frameworks within which Mozart was working. The continuity of the musical texture suddenly fragments into individual jabs of sound – *staccato* notes in octaves, separated by large, tonally ambiguous melodic intervals and irregular periods of silence, played *forte* by the whole orchestra (excluding the horns, which would have been incapable of playing the passage in Mozart's day).

However, to create that sense of turbulent, raging grief, artistic finesse of the highest order was required; if Mozart had truly broken the musical mould, he would have evoked not a feeling of intense sadness, but merely a sense of chaos – of emotional 'white noise'. Listeners' willing suspension of disbelief would have snapped, and the musical narrative replaced with a meaningless string of unconnected sounds. So how did Mozart do it – how did he make orderliness sound disruptive?

According to Lewin,[2] Mozart pulled off the compositional feat through using the technique of 'retrograde inversion' in the domains of both pitch and rhythm. To see what he means, consider initially the pitches of the notes, which Lewin divides notionally into overlapping groups of three. The first of these is characterised by an ascending interval of four semitones, followed by a descent of seven. The next of Lewin's groups (which begins with the second note of the sequence) starts with a leap downwards of seven semitones, and then an ascent of four (he chooses to ignore the semiquaver triplet). The third group uses the same intervals as the first, the fourth repeats those of the second, and so on. Hence we have a succession of overlapping motifs like this (see Figure 81).

Lewin claims that each motif is related to the next by 'retrograde inversion': that is, by reversing it and turning it upside down. So, for

Figure 81 *Lewin's analysis of the melody as a series of overlapping motifs.*

example, playing the first pair of intervals backwards changes both their order of occurrence and their polarity (whether they rise or fall): that is, a transformation from +4 −7 to +7 −4. Inversion (changing polarity again) yields −7 +4, which is the pattern of intervals used in the second motif.

So Lewin's algorithm works, successfully mapping the first motif onto the second, the second onto the third, and so on. But what is the status of the relationships that are formulated? There is no suggestion in anything that Mozart wrote in the score, or described in correspondence, or is reported to have said, that indicates he constructed the passage using retrograde inversions of pitch. Nor is there any empirical evidence that listeners *do* or, indeed, *could* hear it in this way. Even using the score and replaying the music slowly in one's head, there is an immediate difficulty in that each pitch (following the first) has to fulfil two or three functions. So the third note, B, for example, needs to be heard as the last note in the first motif, the middle note in the second, and the initial note in the third, all at the same time − by any standards, a considerable feat of auditory gymnastics. And with the passage typically lasting only six seconds or so in performance, the ear has on average a little over half a second between notes in which to make these judgements. This is beyond our perceptual capacity.

This lack of realism in relation to the structure of pitch extends to Lewin's consideration of how the inter-onset intervals (IOIs) are organised too. His contention is that the series of IOIs between notes 6, 7, 8 and 9 in the passage (again, without the semiquaver triplet), which, measured in crotchets, is +4 +4 +2, is a retrograde inversion of the sequence of IOIs between the notes 7, 8, 9 and the onset of the chord that follows, which is +4, +2, +2.

Here, retrogression is relatively easy to understand: +4, +4, +2 becomes +2, +4, +4. But what of inversion? How can an inter-onset interval be turned 'upside down'? Lewin suggests two ways of achieving this: by dividing each IOI into 8, whereby

$$8 \div 2 = 4$$
$$8 \div 4 = 2$$
$$8 \div 4 = 2$$

or by subtracting each IOI from 6, so

$$6 - 2 = 4$$
$$6 - 4 = 2$$
$$6 - 4 = 2.$$

Again, the maths is impeccable, but what do the equations mean in auditory terms? To all intents and purposes, nothing. And once more, there is no evidence that Lewin's formulae played any part in Mozart's thinking as he composed the symphony. Yet, the argument goes, the patterns are incontrovertibly there: Lewin is only pointing out structural relationships that can be considered to exist between the notes in Mozart's score, and surely it's inconceivable that they just arose by chance?

Actually, it is entirely possible for Lewin's discoveries to be nothing more than artefacts of his logic.[3] For example, in terms of pitch, most people are surely more likely to hear the passage as a series of four equal descents, which are themselves equidistantly spaced. Although the leaps are larger and sound more dramatic than in many other passages, this is a common structural principle, which is used, for instance, in the bass line of Pachelbel's canon, which starts the piece and continues throughout (see Figure 82).

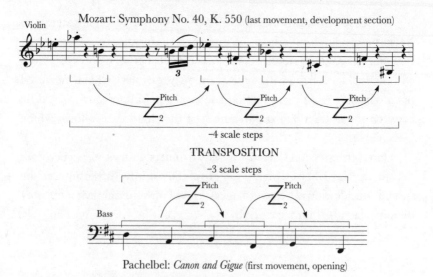

Figure 82 *Series of equally spaced melodic leaps are commonplace in music.*

In terms of zygonic theory, this simply means that imitation occurs every *other* interval. And it is not the case, as Lewin's analysis implies, that there is something special about Mozart's sequence that involved retrograde inversion, since *any* two interlocking chains of intervals that are the same can be understood in this way – it is just a mathematical by-product of a regular series of transpositions. One might as well say (as Lewin does in relation to the IOIs) that each interval that Mozart uses can be derived from the one preceding by subtracting it from a descent of three semitones, since

$$-3 - (-7) = 4$$

and

$$-3 - 4 = -7.$$

But what would be the point? There is plenty of evidence that the principle of parsimony set out by the fourteenth-century English theologian and philosopher William of Occam – his so-called 'razor' – applies in the domains of human perception and cognition: the brain's default approach is to seek the simplest explanation for incoming sensory data.[4]

This is particularly important as far as shared experiences of music are concerned since, as our discussion of Lewin's analysis suggests, the structure (and therefore the meaning) of any piece of music – even a fragment such as the passage by Mozart that we have been analysing here – has the potential to be understood in many different ways.

This latent ambiguity, illustrated here in relation to an extreme example of music analysis, actually goes to the heart of the more general relationship between composers and listeners – of how music can make sense in different ways to different people – which we will now explore in more detail. Recall that what sets musical structure apart from other patterned sequences of sound (that may occur in nature or mechanically, through human design) is a sense of *derivation through imitation* that resides – albeit intuitively – in the minds of listeners: physically there need be no difference between a beat provided by a percussionist and that supplied by a metronome, though we wouldn't normally regard the second as being 'music' because of our (usually unthinking) beliefs about the way that the sounds were being generated. But what if a composer's judgement as to the structural status of a relationship differs from that of an analyst or an 'everyday' listener? Clearly, there will be a mismatch, and it seems reasonable to assume, as composers (and analysts) spend a good deal of time contemplating music in a conscious way, in contrast to the majority of listeners, who don't, that such disparities are a common occurrence. So how can music survive – indeed, thrive – as a means of human communication in the face of widespread incongruence of this nature?

To answer this question, consider first the universe of relationships that *potentially* connect all the notes within a piece of music. Let us assume that sounds can be related through *any* function, and that relationships of *any* level are possible (for example, *quaternary* connections that link tertiaries). Evidently the number of relationships is theoretically infinite. Moreover, due to the regularities of music at the perceptual surface, many of these (again, a hypothetically limitless number) will express repetition. All but a very few, however, are imperceptible – though, somewhat surprisingly, this has not stopped composers making use of such relationships, as we shall see.

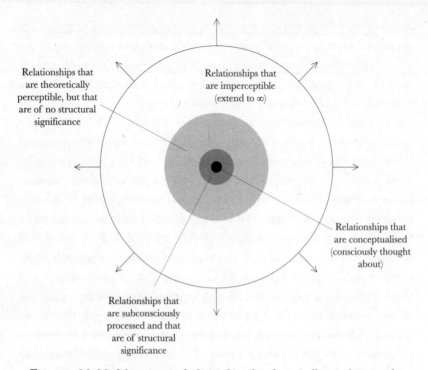

Figure 83 *Model of the universe of relationships that theoretically exist between the musical events that make up a piece, and their likely significance in human terms.*

A subset of all the relationships that conceivably exist between the notes of a piece comprises those that connect two identical (or similar) things and are potentially *perceptible* and *structural* – that could be heard as conveying a sense of imitation. Within this group, a further, much smaller subset will exist containing those structural relationships that actually *are* intuitively perceived by a listener when hearing a particular performance of a piece. This is likely to vary slightly from one occasion to another, due to the different patterns of attention that the listener will inevitably bring to bear. Finally, there is one further – even smaller – subset of relationships comprising those that are *consciously* acknowledged as performing a structural function; for example, by composers them-selves, analysts, or listeners attending, perhaps, with programme notes to hand, which point them in the direction of particular features of a piece. We would expect such relationships to be conceptualised from among those that are potentially perceptible, though they needn't be, as we shall see. So, the relationships between the musical events that make up a piece can be modelled as shown in Figure 83.

We can use this model to illustrate and compare different scenarios of composers, analysts and listeners engaging with a piece of music. For example, in the case of someone listening purely intuitively to a piece with which he or she is relatively familiar, the position can be represented as follows (Figure 84, Scenario A). No relationships attain a conceptual status, and we can assume that a moderate number of potential connections come to be activated in the involuntary processing of musical structure. Scenario B shows how this proportion is likely to increase in the situation where the listener knows the piece (and, perhaps, others in a similar style) very well. Here, we can surmise that the structural significance of a greater number of relationships that connect events in the music that are the same or similar will be registered subconsciously. Scenario C illustrates the opposite position, where a listener attends to a piece in an unfamiliar style for the first time. Here, we can presume that only a small part of the underlying structure is detected through the unwitting formulation of zygonic relationships: sufficient for the composition to 'make sense' as music at a basic level, but insufficient, we may surmise, for many of its organisational subtleties to be detected. Hence, we can further assume that, to this listener's ears, the capacity of the piece to convey *meaning* in the form of an abstract narrative in sound is limited. We can imagine that a similar position must exist for very young children who are still in the Level 3 or 4 of the *Sounds of Intent* music-developmental framework. Those at Level 2 wouldn't hear structural relationships at all – as in Scenario D.

Turning to composers, the situation is surprisingly variable. It is, of course, possible for a piece to be improvised with little or no conscious thought, in which case, a situation similar to that illustrated in Scenario A may pertain. However, composition is generally a more time-consuming and intellectually arduous process than this, in which it seems reasonable to assume that the number of subconsciously processed relationships that are of structural significance will be relatively large. Moreover, in such circumstances where the act of creation is an extended, thought-through

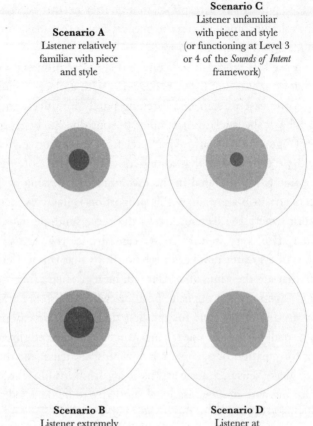

Scenario A
Listener relatively
familiar with piece
and style

Scenario C
Listener unfamiliar
with piece and style
(or functioning at Level 3
or 4 of the *Sounds of Intent*
framework)

Scenario B
Listener extremely
familiar with piece
and style

Scenario D
Listener at
Level 2 of the
Sounds of Intent
framework

Figure 84 *Listeners' grasp of the relationships that potentially exist between musical events will vary according to their level of musical development and their degree of familiarity with a piece and its style.*

process, it is very likely that the composer will have structured the new piece potentially by conceptualising relationships that, for the typical listener at least, are insignificant or are even imperceptible.

An example of conceptualised structural relationships that are perceptible is to be found in Bach's chorale prelude *Dies Sind die Heiligen Zehn Gebot* ('These are the ten Holy Commandments'), BWV 635, which according to the venerable Bach scholar, Albert Schweitzer, are symbolised by the tenfold repetition of the first phrase of the chorale played rapidly (in 'diminution') as a counterpoint to the tune[5] (see Figure 85, Scenario E). According to Peter Kivy, Professor of Philosophy at Rutgers University, who has written extensively on the aesthetics of music, the symbolism would have been 'unmistakeably clear to Bach's audience'.[6] However, his argument is somewhat weakened by the fact that he and Schweitzer pick out different points of imitation to be counted among the ten, indicating that, to contemporary ears at least (and sophisticated ones at that), there is clearly room for doubt!

Instances of conceptualised structural relationships that are imperceptible are to be found in pieces such as those by Stockhausen from the middle of the twentieth century, including *Klavierstück V* (1954–1955), *Gruppen* (1955–1957), and the revised version of *Punkte* (1962). Here the composer makes use of a series of tempos that emulate the frequencies necessary to produce an 'equally tempered' chromatic scale (one in which the intervals between successive notes are all identical) – a wholly inaudible link.[7]

Performers appear to bring varying amounts of conscious thought to bear on the interpretation of structural features, depending on the tradition in which they are working. For those playing or singing Western classical music, for example, a good deal of explicit planning may have occurred before a performance takes place, with the aim of drawing listeners' attention to particular elements in the musical texture as it passes by. This is more evident with some performers than others. Take, for example, the idiosyncratic recordings of the keyboard music of Bach made by the Canadian pianist Glenn Gould, in which the connections between different 'voices' in the contrapuntal music are meticulously articulated, often using changes in dynamics that weren't available to the composer himself on the harpsichord. So it could be argued that Gould was making structures that were planned by Bach easier for listeners to hear, although it would be equally reasonable to assert that the often quirky emphasis he places on particular features masks other elements that would normally have formed part of the intuitive listening experience.

Finally, the model may be used to interrogate the activity of music analysts. Some are content consciously to reflect on intuition. Take, for example, Donald Tovey, whose work was mentioned briefly in Chapter 1. The introduction to his six volumes of *Essays in Musical Analysis* (1935–1937) concludes:

> I once more beg to reassert my first article of musical faith: that, while the listener must not expect to hear the whole contents of a piece of music at once, nothing concerns him that will not ultimately reach his ear ... these essays ... do not contain speculative and fanciful thematic derivations which exist only to the eye.[8]

Contrast this with Allen Forte's approach to the analysis of atonal music using set theory (also mentioned in Chapter 1; see p. 20), with the stated aim of revealing 'concealed' structural components: by definition, then, these are likely to escape the attention of the typical listener – indeed, rather like the relationships identified by Lewin in the last movement of Mozart's Symphony No. 40, it is debatable whether some are actually perceptible, even to the score-assisted ear. Further along this path lie analyses such as that by composer György Ligeti of Pierre Boulez's *Structure Ia* (1951–1952),[9] for piano, which uses the technique of 'integral serialism', whereby pitches, durations, dynamics and 'modes of attack' are all rigorously controlled through being derived from predetermined series that are variously repeated or transformed throughout the piece. Boulez's stated aim was to eradicate from his musical vocabulary 'absolutely every trace of the conventional, whether it concerned figures and phrases, or development and form ... to win back the various stages of the compositional process, in such a manner that a perfectly new synthesis might arise, a synthesis that would not be corrupted from the very outset by foreign bodies – stylistic reminiscences in particular'.[10] However, the high degree of structural determinism is beyond the auditory processing capacity of listeners, and rather than hearing an integrated network of regularities, somewhat counterintuitively, the effect is the opposite – of randomness, which Ligeti describes as being comparable to the way the network of neon lights flashes on and off in a main street; the individual lamps are indeed exactly controlled by a mechanism, but as the separate lights flash on and off, they combine to form a statistical complex.[11] The different approaches taken by Tovey, Forte and Ligeti are modelled in Figure 85 (Scenario E) – see Figure 86.

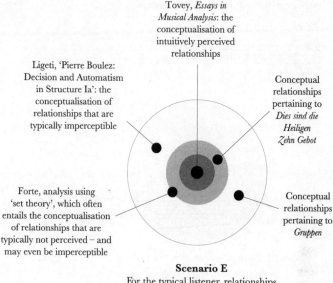

Tovey, *Essays in Musical Analysis*: the conceptualisation of intuitively perceived relationships

Ligeti, 'Pierre Boulez: Decision and Automatism in Structure Ia': the conceptualisation of relationships that are typically imperceptible

Conceptual relationships pertaining to *Dies sind die Heiligen Zehn Gebot*

Forte, analysis using 'set theory', which often entails the conceptualisation of relationships that are typically not perceived – and may even be imperceptible

Conceptual relationships pertaining to *Gruppen*

Scenario E
For the typical listener, relationships conceptualised by composers and analysts may be of little or no structural significance

Figure 85 *Different approaches to composition and analysis utilise relationships between musical events of differing perceptual and conceptual status.*

Taking Scenarios A–E together, it is evident that the same piece may yield a very different profile of perceived or conceptualised, structural or non-structural relationships, depending on the nature of the composer's, performer's, analyst's or listener's engagement with the music. A difficulty for composers who choose to create structures in sound that are incomprehensible to most listeners or even imperceptible, while consciously avoiding forms of organisation that were familiar from other pieces, is that there is likely to be a complete mismatch between the message sent and the message received. A challenge for analysts, score in hand, is to point up features that the majority of listeners, attending to music aurally, *could* potentially hear and that would enrich their listening experience. As the psychologist Burt Rosner and musicologist Eugene Narmour say, 'music theory in its analytic explanation of music should never ignore empirical perceptual data, since ordinary listeners are indispensable to the art of music and thus must ultimately figure in the theoretical disciplines

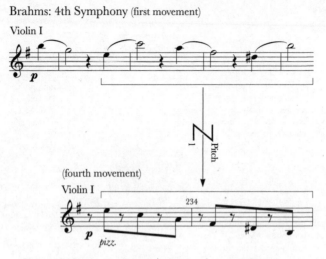

Figure 86 *Example of conceptualised imitation that has become embedded in the day-to-day listening experience.*

of both style analysis and analytical criticism.'[12] Similarly, Nicholas Cook expresses the view that most contemporary theorists 'feel uncomfortable about ascribing significance to inaudible relationships ... one of the most crucial questions we can ask about any theory of music – one which bears directly on the validity which we can ascribe to it – is how it relates to the perceptual experience of the listener'.[13]

How, then, can one justify analysis that reaches out beyond Tovey's precept, which is 'speculative' or even 'fanciful'? It may be, to quote Cook again, 'that music theory acquires validity not, like scientific knowledge, from being verifiable, but from serving some useful purpose – in enabling an analyst to arrive at an interpretation, communicate an insight, or resolve a problem.'[14] That is, relationships identified conceptually may inform perception – extending a listener's appreciation of structure, and therefore ultimately, perhaps, enhancing his or her aesthetic response. I can recall such an experience, when, having become acquainted with Schoenberg's analysis of Brahms' 4th Symphony,[15] connections between motifs from the main theme of the first movement and the last, which were based on a descending chain of 'thirds' (intervals that skip one scale step – see Figure 17), became apparent that were subsequently embedded in my day-to-day, intuitive mode of listening (although the nature of the connections I hear differs somewhat from those originally identified by Schoenberg).

In this case, Schoenberg's insight has permanently illuminated my view of Brahms' final symphonic masterpiece.

Defining Originality in Music

Notwithstanding Boulez's aspiration in his *Structures* to create works that bore no resemblance to anything that had gone before, in reality, no piece of music is an island: even the unorthodox *Structures*, in using the pitches that are available on the piano, belong to a centuries-old musical tradition. In fact, as we saw in relation to the first movements of the piano sonatas by J.C. Bach, Op. 5, No. 3 and Mozart, K. 333, compositions usually share a great deal of material, rather like the DNA that lies at the core of every living thing; and even pieces that sound very different will actually have a lot in common. The music of Bach and Boulez is not as different as people may commonly suppose. But how does the transfer of material between pieces occur? Are motifs like memes – Richard Dawkins' cultural units of transmission? And given that discrete works actually share many similarities, what is it that makes a piece unique? More prosaically, in an age when the intellectual ownership of ideas can be of huge monetary value, how are musical property rights assessed?

The reality of creating a new piece of music is not one of sitting at a desk with a blank sheet of paper and an empty mind. Composers cannot wilfully disconnect their auditory imaginations from their store of musical memories and suddenly become deaf to all that they have heard in the past, any more than artists can blind themselves to the visual imagery of drawing, painting and sculpture that they have previously seen, or writers ignore their knowledge of existing prose, poetry and plays. No. All literature, all art, all music, is influenced, in one way or another, by what has gone before.

In music, a crucial distinction needs to be drawn between material that conveys sufficient information to be salient in the context in which it is heard, and that which does not. In cognitive terms, the difference is one that exists between more substantial chunks of music that form distinct, self-contained traces in memory, as opposed to shorter, more generic, features that belong to a 'general store' of musical attributes. Another way of understanding the distinction is to contrast motifs that are characteristic enough to be associated in the mind with a given piece of music – that exist in its 'foreground' (such as those shown in Figure 12) – with those that figure anonymously in the 'background' of many works.

A similar situation is to be found in language, and it is helpful to draw an analogy. Take, for example, the word 'it'. Because this is so commonplace, 'it' has insufficient identity to function as a chunk of language that defines a literary work. 'It' is rather like an individual, mid-range pitch of short duration (and unspecified timbre) in music; even for those with AP, this would not be associated uniquely with a particular piece. Both note and word function 'deictically' – seeking to derive their meaning from the notes or words around, in the absence of which they convey very little.

What happens if we double the amount of information by adding a second word or note: let us say, 'It *was*' in language, and simple repetition (of pitch, duration and loudness) in music? In either case, this is still insufficient material to confer individuality; even if we restrict ourselves to the *opening* of novels and the beginnings of well-known melodies, there are many possibilities. For example, in literature we could have 'It was dark by the time I reached Bonn' or 'It was 7 minutes after midnight',[16] while in music, the theme from the slow movement of Haydn's *Surprise Symphony* (see Figure 26) or the children's song *London's Burning* are candidates.

Let us try adding a third word, giving 'It was *a*', and a further note in music that is the same as the first two. In each case, this still leaves us with a number of alternatives. For instance, among the books that begin in this way are 'It was a dark and stormy night' and 'It was a bright cold day in April, and the clocks were striking thirteen',[17] while in music, among the options are Bach's Fugue in D major, BWV 874, from *The Well-Tempered Clavier*, Book II, and the nursery rhyme *Here We Go Round the Mulberry Bush* (see Figure 87).

However, the addition of a fourth word or note often makes all the difference. 'It was a *queer*' specifies Sylvia Plath's semi-autobiographical novel *The Bell Jar*, which begins, 'It was a queer, sultry summer, the summer they executed the Rosenbergs ...' Similarly, by following three

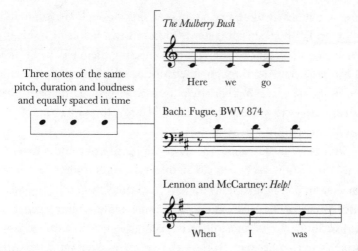

Figure 87 *A series of three identical notes in music is insufficient to define a piece.*

identical notes that occur in rapid succession with a longer one that is four semitones (a major 3rd) lower, a motif is produced that is exclusive to the opening of Beethoven's 5th Symphony (see Figure 74).

How typical is this? Are four notes sufficient to define all melodies? Glancing through Barlow and Morgenstern's venerable dictionary of musical themes,[18] whose categorisation ignores rhythm, it seems that five pitches are *necessary* and six pitches are typically *sufficient*, at least in traditional Western classical music, to specify a theme. Interestingly, this number falls within the range of George Miller's 'magical number seven, plus or minus two' (see p. 40), which as well as representing a perceptual limit, appears to correspond to the number of separate (uncompressed) items that can readily be held and manipulated in working memory.[19] This constraint must surely have played a part, albeit unwittingly, in the way that music evolved. Of course, the identity of melodies is not just about the disposition of pitch: rhythm is at least as important, and, as we saw in Chapter 2, by combining information from the two domains, four, three or even sometimes two notes are sufficient for a motif to exist as a standalone unit of music (see Figure 12).

What does all of this mean for listeners? From their point of view, the longer a musical segment that appears in two pieces is, the greater the chance that one will be perceived as arising through *direct* imitation of the other. With shorter fragments found in two works or more, it is more likely that any sense of imitation connecting them will be heard as being *indirect*, occurring through a network of relationships, as a feature of style. These low-level but pervasive similarities play an important part in enabling pieces to make sense at a first hearing, through ensuring that they are predictable in a general way.

I find it helpful to imagine the most diminutive of these snippets of musical information, such as melodic intervals, IOIs (inter-onset intervals) and harmonic progressions that are 'inherited' from other works, as functioning rather like DNA, and together making up a piece's 'genotype' – its set of fundamental musical constituents. To continue the analogy, the 'genetic overlap' between works – the degree of commonality – is far greater than one might imagine (as it is in living things). For example, my study of the first movements of six Mozart piano sonatas (including K. 333)[20] shows an 86 per cent level of similarity in the distributions of relative note-lengths, a figure that rises to 92 per cent in the case of IOIs. The sets of pitches used in the movements are 96 per cent the same, and the relative frequency with which melodic intervals occur has a 77 per cent match, while with harmonies it is 89 per cent. So, on average, an astonishing 88 per cent of the movements' 'musical DNA' is the same. However, the sonatas are distinct, and what makes them so is the way that their 'genetic material' is in each case arranged to express a musical 'phenotype' – a unique expression of elemental components (melodic intervals, IOIs and the like), characterised by distinct and memorable themes and their transformations.

A more extreme example of musical genetic similarity co-occurring with phenotypic contrast can be found in two pieces of music – one by Schoenberg, and one that I composed especially to be used in an experiment in learning and memory that was undertaken with Derek Paravicini.[21] I wanted to discover how Derek hears the 'atonal' works of what came to be known as the 'Second Viennese School': the music that Arnold Schoenberg, Alban Berg and Anton Webern composed in the first part of the twentieth century. This consciously sought to avoid the syntax of traditional Western classical music, with its constrained use of harmony and key. Rather, Schoenberg and his followers refrained from treating pitch hierarchically (whereby some notes are heard as being more settled than others through the extensive use of archetypal patterns of melodic and harmonic intervals), and all twelve members of the chromatic scale were allowed to function independently of one another.

Anecdotally, many listeners report that atonal pieces sound 'discordant' or 'wrong' and are difficult (if not impossible) to remember.[22] My hope was that a clearer light would be shed on what is occurring by having Derek attempt to learn a piece music of this type – the opening eleven bars of Schoenberg's Klavierstück, Op. 11, No. 1 – just by listening to it (the only means of accessing new material that is open to him), and systematically analysing his efforts to reproduce it.

The results – which were extraordinary – will be reported later in this chapter. For now, the important thing to note is that in order to gauge the impact of atonality on Derek's music-processing powers, it was necessary to compose a second, short piece, whose musical 'DNA' at the most elemental level (notes and intervals) was as similar as possible to the excerpt from Schoenberg's first Klavierstück, but which would conform to 'common practice' Western tonality. To this end it was decided to create material that was broadly Mozartian in style (see Figure 88). When working with Derek, it is important to give memorable names to the musical extracts that he will be asked to recall, so the passage from Schoenberg was referred to as the *Magical Kaleidoscope* (a label bestowed upon it by the analyst Allen Forte) and the faux-classical piece the *Kooky Minuet*, in deference to its somewhat quirky harmonies and triple metre. Inevitably, the two would differ 'phenotypically', but the extent of the 'genotypical' overlap (gauged through the distributions of relative pitches, melodic intervals, relative durations and IOIs) was 82 per cent – hardly less than in the six Mozart sonatas from my earlier study.

To give some sense of the difference in musical experience that the two pieces offered, read through this series of words: 'Single in good a wife be it want of in that a fortune is a possession man of universally a truth must acknowledged' (with apologies to Jane Austen) and then this one: 'It is a truth universally acknowledged that a single man in possession of a good fortune must be in want of a wife.'

Schoenberg: *Klavierstück*, Op. 11, No. 1, the *Magical Kaleidoscope*

Figure 88 *The opening of the* Magical Kaleidoscope *and the* Kooky Minuet, *with a high level of 'genotypical' overlap, but 'phenotypically' contrasting.*

It is evident that virtually the same musical 'DNA' (regarded as the highest form of resolution possible – notes and intervals) can give rise to strongly contrasting phenotypes, which the human brain appears to process in very different ways – as Derek's brain did. And the *Magical*

Kaleidoscope experiment shows how musical originality exists firmly at the 'phenotypical' rather than the 'genotypical' level.

The process through which the *Kooky Minuet* came to be created, with its high degree of pre-compositional constraint, was, of course, exceptional. How, then, do musical phenotypes and genotypes – and, therefore, originality and similarity – normally emerge and interact in the process of composition? From composers' own accounts of their work, it seems likely, as with the production of the *Kooky Minuet*, that this will involve conscious planning too, though blended with rather more intuitive 'flow'.[23] Preliminary, calculated decisions potentially include the choice of instrumentation and voices, the length and form of a work, which may have been commissioned for a particular occasion, and its 'feel'; there may be words to set or the narrative of a film or advertisement to follow. The subconscious choices that are taken in deciding structure and content on a moment-to-moment basis are more difficult to control and track, however, and while composers (in contemporary Western culture at least) wouldn't wish inadvertently to purloin a fellow musician's ideas, plagiarism – that is, imitation that can unambiguously be traced back to one other piece – may sometimes accidentally occur.

Alternatively, it is conceivable that motifs may materialise in a composer's musical imagination that are the same as others purely by chance. At least, this was George Harrison's claim in relation to his song *My Sweet Lord*, which bears a strong resemblance to *He's So Fine*, written by Ronald Mack in the early 1960s. Harrison was sued for breach of copyright, and the ensuing court case revolved around a musical analysis of the two songs – in particular, the two motifs that in both cases characterise the melodies.[24] The second of these patterns was deemed to be highly unusual, and the combination of the two was thought to have been unique to *He's So Fine* before the appearance of *My Sweet Lord*. However, Harrison's testimony of how his song was composed made it clear that there had been no intention to copy the earlier work. Nonetheless, he acknowledged that he had heard *He's So Fine* in the past, and the judge in the trial ruled that what must have occurred was 'subconscious plagiarism'. A good deal of money hinged on this judgement: it was decreed that a little over $1.5 million dollars of *My Sweet Lord*'s earnings were reasonably attributable to *He's So Fine*.

Things were rather different in Mozart's day. In Chapter 3, we saw how similar the opening of his Sonata, K. 333 is to J.C. Bach's Op. 5, No. 3, with which he was known to be familiar. However, the notion of the intellectual property rights pertaining to music was rather freer in the eighteenth century than it is in today's more commercially driven world. Indeed, the first international agreement involving copyright (initiated at the Berne Convention in Paris in 1886) was still a hundred years away. For composers prior to the nineteenth century, imitation was a way of learning one's art (as, for example, J.S. Bach as a young composer was famously wont to do): borrowing from and contributing to a shared library of musical resources that was then available for future generations.

If this approach seems quaint today, when a short musical motif can help consolidate a commercial brand in people's minds, whose identity may be worth billions of dollars, consider that in the mid-twentieth century, American musicologist Sigmund Spaeth forged an unlikely show business career by pointing out the similarities that exist between musical fragments that can be found in different pieces. Spaeth was especially adroit at showing how popular songs used material that could be found in older melodies, including those from the classical and folk traditions, and he became known as *The Tune Detective*, after the title of his radio show of the same name that aired on NBC in the early 1930s. Perhaps his most famous tongue-in-cheek discovery was the potential derivation of the novelty song *Yes! We Have No Bananas*, by Frank Silver and Irving Cohn, from a number of earlier works, including Handel's *Hallelujah Chorus* and the Scottish folksong *My Bonnie Lies Over the Ocean*. Spaeth didn't (seriously) attempt to claim that plagiarism – whether deliberate or subconscious – had occurred: 'Hallelujah Bananas' merely provided an example of the way that new pieces are constructed, which is largely by reconstituting extant materials (see Figure 89).

How does this process work? How can fragments from existing pieces be re-used to form a new narrative in sound that makes sense? As we saw in Chapter 4 (p. 197), virtually all children acquire the necessary skills, without formal instruction, in the early years, when they come to function at Level 4 of the *Sounds of Intent* framework of musical development. At this stage, they are able to take motifs from pieces of music with which

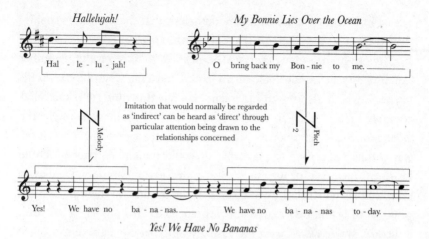

Figure 89 *Sigmund Spaeth's whimsical analysis of* Yes! We Have No Bananas *purporting to show its derivation from pieces such as the* Hallelujah Chorus *from Handel's* Messiah, *and* My Bonnie Lies Over the Ocean.

they are familiar, rearrange them, and potentially combine them with fresh ideas to form new melodies, as we heard in Róza's 'potpourri' song (Figure 76). And just as the coherence of charming inventions such as Róza's improvised tune often relies upon simple linkages between motifs, in which the beginning of one musical fragment takes off from where the last one ended, so the same principle applies to *Yes! We Have No Bananas* (irrespective of its analytical authenticity). The first motif connects to the second through the continuation of a descending scale, and the second is linked to the third through repetition of the note 'G'.

So much for the mechanics through which apparently disparate chunks of music can be connected in improvisation or composition. An important question remains, however: how does the mind select the motifs from long-term memory, and decide how each will be used, in combination with the others and, potentially, newly created material? This is by no means a straightforward task, since the musical fragments that are chosen or invented have to fit together in the moment, melodically and harmonically, as well as creating or reinforcing a broader tonal trajectory. And even given that motifs typically offer a range of alternatives for coherent juxtaposition, since they have a number of features that can be imitated, we can surmise, nonetheless, that there must be sophisticated mental processes at work to make the creation of music happen.

An insight into what occurs can be gleaned from the results of another experiment that I undertook with Derek Paravicini, when he was in his twenties, which also tested his memory – but this time for a specially-composed piece, some 20 bars long, that was in a gentle swing style: the *Chromatic Blues*.[25] Derek was asked to listen to the *Chromatic Blues* all the way through and then to play what he could remember, after which he heard the piece again, and the session ended. After two days, Derek was asked to play whatever he could recall of the music, and then the original protocol of listen, play and listen was repeated. This process was re-run a further twelve times, with increasingly long periods between sessions: extending from days to weeks and then months, a year, and finally two years.

The results were astonishing, though probably not in the way that most people would have predicted: the myth that musical savants have a kind of auditory eidetic memory – functioning rather like an internal iPod – is still widespread, despite three decades of my saying that it's not actually like that. The truth may be more complicated, but it is certainly no less interesting. Derek's mental images of sounds may be more vivid than most people's are, on account of his acute sense of AP (absolute pitch), but the *Chromatic Blues* experiment showed that he learns things in much the same way that all of us do, through an initial process of abstraction from the perceptual surface, in which underlying patterns and regularities are identified, as well as similarities with what is already known, before these representations are committed to memory. The subsequent process of recall is not one of replaying in a direct and linear way what has been 'recorded', but entails 'creative reconstruction': producing a new version of the original stimulus by piecing together whatever features and fragments can be remembered.

Because of the difficulties that most musicians have in reproducing the music to which they are exposed (beyond relatively simple melodies), the process of learning by ear hadn't been reported in detail before Derek's attempts to master *Chromatic Blues* were published in the research literature. The way in which people learn and recall text, though, was established many years ago through the pioneering work of Sir Frederic Bartlett, one of the founders of modern cognitive psychology, through a series of classic experiments that he undertook at Cambridge University in the 1920s. For example, some subjects were asked to read twice through an adaptation of a North American folk tale, and then told to write down whatever they could remember at various times afterwards.[26]

Here is the beginning of the story:

The War of the Ghosts

One night, **two young men from** Egulac **went** down to the river to hunt seals, and **while** they were there it became foggy and calm. Then **they heard war**-cries, and they thought: "Maybe this is a war party". They escaped to the shore, and hid behind a log. Now canoes came up, and they heard the noise of the paddles, and saw one canoe coming up to them. There were five men in the canoe, and they said: "What do you think? We wish to take you along. We are going **up the river** to make war on the people".

Eight days later, a subject referred to as 'H' recalled this part of the text as follows:

The War of the Ghosts

Two young men from Edulac **went** fishing. **While** thus engaged **they heard** a noise in the distance. "That sounds like a **war-cry**", said one, "there is going to be some fighting." Presently there appeared some warriors who invited them to join an expedition **up the river.**

This was typical of the data that Bartlett obtained. Most striking are the *differences* between the stimulus and H's response; few of the words, only 12 per cent, are the same (highlighted in bold), and the new text is less than half the length of the original. However, much of the sense of the story is retained. It seems that it was the *meaning* of the narrative, abstracted from the text, that was stored, rather than most of the words, and this was reconstructed into a flowing text that makes sense, both semantically and syntactically. Because some things were forgotten (*omissions*) and other things were changed (*transformations*) this meant that a third category of variation was inevitable: *additions*. These were often made through inference – through the inclusion of ideas that were not present in the original story, but which a suitably knowledgeable reader could reasonably assume from the imaginary context that it established. For example, the fact that the sounds of people's voices were heard 'in the distance' could reasonably be inferred from the assumption that the men making the noise could not yet be seen (and H appeared to have forgotten that it was night time and foggy). Other additions seem to have been made in the interests of keeping the narrative flowing: for instance, the words 'said one' were needed to contextualise the direct speech that had previously been described as just a thought. A number of such constructions, such as 'there is going to be', are in common usage, and appear to derive from the stock of linguistic expressions that we all retain in long-term memory.

These observations show that what H was doing went far beyond merely duplicating what he had heard; he was being truly creative. He was generating something with *original* features. Why did this occur in a memory test? We can assume, as H had been asked to reproduce what he had read as accurately as possible, that the reason for the changes was that the task exceeded the capacity of his working memory. The approximate narrative thread of the story was maintained, but little else, and the transformations and additions that he made each resulted in the generation of new material in ways that are typical of oral traditions. So let us now compare the position of H, trying to recall language, with Derek's efforts to remember and reproduce music. The melody in the first four bars of his rendition of *Chromatic Blues* – in comparison to the original – is shown in Figure 90.

We can be confident that Derek engaged with the task seriously and tried his best to accomplish what was asked of him. Like H, though, it is evident that he made considerable changes to the stimulus. In fact, my analysis of Derek's first rendition of the piece as a whole shows that he got a little over 40 per cent of the rhythm correct, and 20 per cent of the pitches – 30 per cent on average. While a remarkable achievement (far beyond what most professional musicians could achieve), that still leaves 70 per cent of *Chromatic Blues* unaccounted for. Hence, we can surmise that the piece exceeded the capacity of Derek's working memory. And

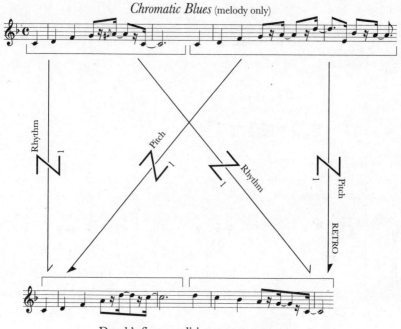

Figure 90 *Derek's process of creative remembering is evident in the first four bars of his rendition of* Chromatic Blues.

just as H produced a version of the story that made sense, so Derek intuitively created a stream of music that was coherent, and which, inevitably, entailed omitting, adding and transforming material.

An example of significant variation occurred straight away. Derek omitted the first motif and replaced it with a transformed version of the second. This may have been because in the original *Chromatic Blues* the second motif ends with a striking harmonic shift (to D major) that evidently lodged in Derek's mind, as he included it almost immediately in his rendition. His transformational efforts left him with a problem, however, in that it brought the music to a point that didn't occur in *Chromatic Blues* itself. So necessity became the mother of invention: he had to generate new material that would follow naturally from his initial gesture, offering balance yet a sense too that there was more to come. To this end, he opted to re-use ideas from his first motif by partially reversing the pattern

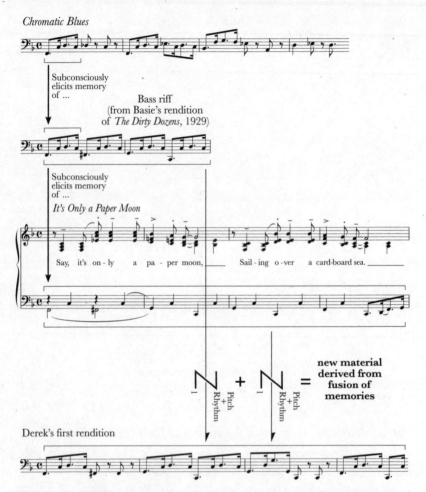

Figure 91 *Derek's use of new material deriving from the presumed fusion of memories of fragments and features of other pieces, stimulated by similarities with* Chromatic Blues.

of pitches while repeating the rhythm (a technique used, for instance, by George Gershwin in the opening two lines of *I Got Rhythm*).

At the same time Derek had to resolve the problem of what to do with the accompaniment. It seems that the opening rocking figure in the left hand part of *Chromatic Blues* brought to mind a common bass riff, used, for example, by Count Basie in his rendition of *The Dirty Dozens* (1929), with which Derek was familiar, and which fits with the beginning of his melody (see Figure 91). The four chords associated with the riff are also utilised by Harold Arlen in the first phrase of *It's Only a Paper Moon* – another favourite of Derek's – and the harmonic structure of the second phrase was pressed into service in his version of *Chromatic Blues* too.

Through Derek's process of invention, we can see how musical fragments from a diversity of sources can be made to fit together. Just 'copying and pasting' wouldn't work, since music can be performed in different keys and at different tempos, by different instruments or voices and at different levels of loudness. But the core of the musical message is conveyed by *differences* in pitch and *ratios* between inter-onset intervals: provided that these are maintained, the identity of the music will be preserved. This means, of course, that all other features can be varied to blend in with a given context. I call it the 'chameleon' effect.[27] The difference is rather like

<u>pasting</u> elements **of a text** FROM DIFFERENT SOURCES

without pressing the 'match destination formatting' button, whereupon

pasting elements of a text from different sources

becomes easier to read and more agreeable to the eye. So it is in auditory terms with motifs that can be transformed: by manipulating their 'surface appearance', but without changing key elements of their content or structure, they can be made to slot seamlessly into a single musical narrative, and the impression of a musical chimera is avoided.

It is evident that Derek's attempts to recall *Chromatic Blues* shed as much light on musical creativity as they do on memory, and it is possible to use his part-reproduction, part-improvisation to suggest how the intuitive element of composing may operate cognitively. Psychologist Alan Baddeley's model of working memory,[28] first set out with his colleague Graham Hitch in 1974, provides the starting point. Baddeley originally proposed a three-part cognitive system comprising a 'central executive', which coordinates and integrates information from two so-called 'slave' modules: the 'visuo-spatial sketch pad', which temporarily holds information about what we see, and the 'phonological loop', which provisionally stores words (by their sounds). These modules were necessary, since visual and auditory information is processed separately in working memory (shown by people's capacity to perform tasks that involve attending to visual images and sounds at the same time). Baddeley later added a fourth component to the model, the 'episodic buffer', which is thought to connect information gained from seeing and hearing concurrently, such as the memory of a story or scene from a film.[29] From his work with patients with short-term memory loss, who could nonetheless remember events that were long past, Baddeley surmised that the episodic buffer must also have links to long-term memory.

Although *musical* memory doesn't feature in Baddeley's proposal, it could be argued that the phonological loop, as well as having the capacity to process the sounds of words, may be able to handle music too. However, the fact that Derek's ability to understand and use language is limited seems to militate against this (at least in his case). As a child, when his prodigious musical skills were already much in evidence, echolalia dominated Derek's patterns of speech, and even today, in his late-thirties – and despite remarkable cognitive and social progress – the conversations that he now initiates and is comfortable to participate in tend to follow only a few well-trodden paths. One of my doctoral research students, Annamaria Mazzeschi, compared Derek's verbal memory to his capacity to learn music, by having him listen to a very short and simple biographical story, comprising only 80 words (of which 30 were repeated), and attempt to recall it, following the same schedule of sessions that the *Chromatic Blues* experiment used. Derek struggled with the task, and even having heard the story 26 times, Derek got only a little under 40 per cent of the story correct, as opposed to 83 per cent of *Chromatic Blues*.

This difference supports the idea, first mooted by the American musician and researcher William Berz in the 1990s, that working memory may contain a module devoted solely to music. Since creativity and memory overlap, this 'music processing module', or 'MPM', would be implicated in improvisation and other forms of composition that involve the spontaneous flow of ideas. Based on the way that Derek tackled *Chromatic Blues*, we can surmise that the key functions of the MPM in this context would be as follows. Initially, it needs to acquire from long-term memory, and temporarily store, in readiness for use, the information in the form of patterns of melodic or harmonic intervals and IOIs required to reconstruct musical fragments and features. As these abstract packets of data start to be reified in a stream of musical sounds, now in a defined key, at a particular tempo, with a certain loudness level and using a predetermined timbre, a new task emerges, which is to interrogate long-term memory to locate materials that will potentially fit with those already in service. This means that they will need to be both stylistically congruent (in terms of sharing similar micro-sequences of melodic intervals and IOIs and harmonic progressions with what has gone before) and capable of being logically attached to the end of the previous motif through repetition or regularity in some form. Again, the MPM needs to concretise these new sequences of musical code at the appropriate pitch and tempo, and may need to adjust them to match what has already occurred through adding, deleting or modifying notes. As the fragments are assembled, there may also be the need to create new material, to fill in potential gaps and secure the moment-to-moment coherence of what is produced. Finally, the MPM will need to control the general direction of the musical narrative, modulating to particular keys, for instance, and repeating or developing sections as required to ensure longer-term coherence.

Remarkably, this synthesis of fragments and features, borrowed and original, must all occur in 'real time' as an improvisation proceeds. Even more extraordinary is the fact that the brain can manage the process quite intuitively, without the need for conscious intervention on the part of the musician concerned (although this can, of course, occur). Inevitably, there will be an element of chance in the way that things turn out, depending on which ideas float to the surface in a composer's stream of musical thinking. For every idea that emerges to become audible, we can assume that there are plenty of others that remain silently unused in the depths of the subconscious.

So there is nothing inevitable about the design of any piece of music, despite what the theorists such as Rudolph Reti and Heinrich Schenker, whose understanding of musical creation is essentially teleological, would have us believe. Which motifs become juxtaposed is rather like falling in love: it may seem as though it was 'supposed to be that way', and that the happy couple (or motifs) were 'made for each other'. This simply isn't what happens, though. In either case there are so many possibilities – literally billions of them – that we couldn't possibly evaluate the suitability of more than a microcosm.

An intriguing counterview to that of the teleologists has been developed in recent years by the UK music theorist Steven Jan.[30] He builds on Richard Dawkins' notion of the 'meme' – a unit of human culture that can be replicated and evolve in a way analogous to the transfer and development of genes.[31] The theory goes that, just as genes propagate themselves in the gene pool by leaping from body to body via sperm or eggs, so memes reproduce by jumping from brain to brain, via imitation. Hence there is an obvious overlap with zygonic theory. Musical memes (or 'musemes') can comprise any element of music that is replicable. Jan's work takes the 'meme's eye' view of musical evolution, in which developments in style occur through the success (or failure) of musical memes to be selected by composers. It is a matter of 'survival of the fittest'.[32]

But there is a problem with this analogy: the development of music across the centuries cannot reasonably be equated with biological evolution for the simple reason that the stylistic changes that occur in music over time, unlike evolution in nature, are not determined by natural selection – Richard Dawkins' 'blind watchmaker'. Rather, the choice of musemes is in the hands of a multiplicity of musical deities – composers – who are entirely free to dictate which fragments and features of music will be carried forward from one piece to another and which won't: which will survive, which will thrive and which will wither. Like Gods, composers can create entirely new entities, *de novo*. Like the Neo-classicists, they can even resurrect musical dinosaurs. It is the musemes that are blind and composers who are the watchmakers.

Finally, there is one more form of musical borrowing that we should consider: quotation – that is, where a composer quite deliberately copies a feature of another piece and intends the appropriation to be recognised by listeners. The result, as in literature, can be a complex fusion of ideas, arising both from the significance of the extract in its original context, as well as from the way in which the old material casts fresh light on the new, and *vice versa*. The blended meaning can be gently amusing, knowingly ridiculous, piquantly ironic or even, occasionally, profound. But (unlike language), music rarely has symbolic meaning, so what is it that is transferred from one piece to another? In the case of melodies taken from songs, the sense of the text can be imported. Towards the end of Bach's lengthy *Goldberg Variations* for harpsichord, for example, before the return of the 'Aria' with which the work began, the composer pulls a 'quodlibet' out of the hat – a humorous Baroque mash-up of German folksongs, which the recipient of the work, the insomniac Count Keyserling, would have recognised. Although today only two of the melodies can be identified, 'Ich bin so lang nicht bei dir g'west, ruck her, ruck her' ('I have so long been away from you, come closer, come closer') and 'Kraut und Rüben haben mich vertrieben, hätt mein' Mutter Fleisch gekocht, wär ich länger blieben' ('Cabbage and turnips have driven me away, had my mother cooked meat, I'd have opted to stay') the sentiment is clear: the music pleads for the return of the theme.

There are two important points to be made here. First, the music makes perfectly good sense (although the humour is lost) to listeners who are ignorant of the allusions – as indeed, we are to an extent today, as only two of them are known. And second, aside from Bach's ingenuity in making the tunes fit together with the pre-existing harmonic structure originally set out in the Aria, is his use of the 'chameleon' effect, noted above in relation to Derek's rendition of the *Chromatic Blues*. That is to say, the folksongs can be used since the information they convey in terms of pitch and rhythm is *relative*, comprising melodic intervals and the ratios between IOIs, and capable of realisation in any key and at any tempo, at any level of loudness and using any timbre.

On other occasions, music can be imported that has no verbal association – though to be telling as a quotation, it is likely to have significance beyond its intrinsic musical qualities. For example, in his *Golliwog's Cakewalk* for piano, Debussy appears to be cocking a snook at Wagner when he introduces the composer's famous 'Tristan' chord – as much a cultural leitmotif for Wagner himself as it is a depiction of 'desire' in his opera *Tristan and Isolde*. Surprisingly, given its essentially abstract nature, music can sustain parody just as persuasively and powerfully as words (see Figure 92).

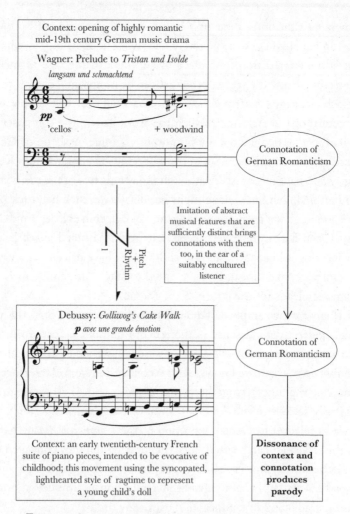

Figure 92 *Connotations can be transferred with purely musical imitation, here producing the effect of parody.*

What Constitutes a Piece of Music?

An easy question: what is the *Mona Lisa*? A straightforward answer: it's a painting by Leonardo da Vinci, which has been housed in the Louvre for over two hundred years. Although it has been imitated, parodied and reproduced countless times, there is only one *Mona Lisa*. It is a unique, physical entity. We all understand that copies are *not* the original painting but representations of it. A difficult question: what is Beethoven's 5th Symphony? This time there is no straightforward answer, but hopefully the discussion that follows will shed some light on what is a surprisingly complex issue.

We have already established that music exists only in the minds of listeners: it is not the scores purchased from a shop or downloaded from the internet, nor the mp3 files stored on a digital playback device. These are proxies for the real thing, merely comprising sets of instructions for humans or computers in visual or electronic form; and even the sounds they spawn – ultimately nothing more than waves of compression and rarefaction in the air – are just the physical correlates of series of sensations that occur in our minds. But that poses a problem when we try to define what a particular *piece* of music is.

Imagine an audience attending a recital at which Satie's *Première Gymnopédie* is performed (see Figure 50). For the pianist, playing from memory, the piece comprises a sequence of internalised sounds, which have come to be associated with sets of memorised finger patterns. As she plays, we can assume that her memories of the sounds of the piece are matched and reinforced with fresh auditory images. And we can say that her unfolding mental experience over the next three and a half minutes *is* the piece of music called *Gymnopédie*. But clearly that's not the only instance of *Gymnopédie* that will arise at the concert, since members of the audience will also hear the performance. Will their experience of the music be the same as the pianist's, though? If not, then we have an ontological difficulty, as it means that there isn't a single phenomenon that we can label as being '*Gymnopédie*'.

The problem is that we can never truly know how others perceive the world: we can't borrow their ears to hear as they do, or usurp their minds to gauge how they think and feel. But we can make some reasonable assumptions. Although everyone's ears physically differ, they almost all function in essentially the same way, converting mechanical vibration into neural impulses. And although there are variations between one auditory cortex and another, they almost all do equivalent work.[33] Beyond this, most people show comparable physiological responses to music, and describe what they have heard in broadly similar ways. The important word here, though, is 'similar'. We are not saying that one person's experience of the performance of *Gymnopédie* could ever be identical to someone else's – or, indeed, be precisely replicable on future occasions through the availability of a recording – even if we discount external factors (such as variability in acoustics) and other internal ones (such as disparities in concentration and motivation). For only a relatively small number of the myriad potential relationships between the notes of *Gymnopédie* will win through in the tussle for the limited cognitive resources that a listener has available at any one time, and, due to the complexity of the situation, these will almost inevitably vary from one occasion to another. But we can assume, nonetheless, that there will be enough connections in common for us to define a particular rendition of the *Première Gymnopédie* as giving rise to a *set* of broadly homogeneous experiences, whose areas of intersection and boundaries are somewhat fuzzy, but with enough commonality to be regarded as a single conceptual entity.

Nonetheless, we should acknowledge that, within the confines of this commonality, some people's experiences – such as those of prodigies and a proportion of children who are on the autism spectrum – may be more elaborate, more detailed, more vivid than others. For example, a member of the audience with AP – or indeed, the pianist, watching as she presses the keys – may perceive the chords as rather more than fused aggregations of notes that emanate a particular harmonic colour: in addition, every note may be heard as a distinct entity in its own right. For listeners like this, there will quite simply be more to hear in *Gymnopédie*: more notes, more relationships between them; more structure, more content. To appreciate what this means, take an artistic analogy offered by pointillism. Georges Seurat painted his masterpiece *La Parade de Cirque* around the same time that Satie was composing the *Première Gymnopédie*. Using thousands of tiny dots, the painting is of a circus scene at night, with the audience and performers clearly visible. The effect is one in which the representative nature of the image is still evident, but 'zoom in' and the individual dots become apparent – rather like the separate notes that make up the chords in *Gymnopédie*.

It seems that those with AP can appreciate both the dots *and* their place in the picture at the same time. We know this because people like

Anthony and Derek can make sense of the musical detail and the broader narrative at once. For example, they can imitate complex chords (implying that they have heard each of their constituent notes) while transforming the melody notes that sit atop them.[34] The effect is all the more magical, knowing the skill that is involved.

While there are inevitably differences in the way that an individual perceives a recording of a given performance on separate occasions, it is also fascinating to consider how different *renditions* of a piece relate to a person's perception and memory of the work in question. As a preliminary step, we need to consider why it is that different interpretations of a piece are not only possible, but inevitable and, indeed, desirable (for if every rendition of a work were to be identical, then the need for continued live performances would largely be obviated). Indeed, the notion that a piece could exist as anything other than a set of different realisations only became a reality with the advent of music notation, since before then (and long prior to the possibility that performances could be captured for posterity through recording) music was only represented as sets of memories in the minds of those belonging to a given culture. Hence any knowledge held by musicians that they failed to pass on before their demise was irretrievably lost: as Isidore of Seville, writing in the early seventh century, said, 'unless sounds are held by the memory of man, they perish, because they cannot be written down.'[35] And since recall (in any modality) is a process of creative reconstruction, there would inevitably have been some variation in a piece every time it was played or sung. One only has to look to collections of folk music to appreciate just how diverse a song could become. For example, the American musicologist and composer Charles Seeger reports on finding around 300 versions and variants to the tune of *Barbara Allen* in the US.[36]

This situation was ameliorated with the emergence of ever more precise notation, in the West starting in the ninth century with 'neumes', comprising wavy lines placed above religious texts, moving on to Guido d'Arezzo's eleventh-century creation of a four-line staff that identified particular pitches, and finally arriving at the 'modern' Western system (dating from the fifteenth and sixteenth centuries), with its stave of five lines. However, the problem of the precise transmission of musical ideas was never entirely resolved, since music notation is nothing more than a set of variously inexact instructions, some of which tend to be explicit – for example, those defining the principal qualities of pitch and rhythm – while others are implied through performance traditions, such as the use of vibrato, 'rubato' (the small changes in timing that make a performance sound expressive) and the precise shaping of dynamics. Even the instructions that musicians generally take to be precise (those pertaining to pitch and rhythm) are often only indicative, and players and singers are often startled to discover just how wayward their tuning and timing in expressive performance really are. Strangely, the departures from a metronomic beat and scales in equal temperament don't come across as errors; they merely give the impression that the music is being produced with feeling (it may or may not be, of course, since performers learn how to convey emotion in music without experiencing it themselves). In any case, without the micro-variation in time (and, where it is available, pitch), music would sound strangely wooden.

Here, for example, is my own rendition of a piece I called *Romantic Rollercoaster*, which was used in another memory experiment with Derek Paravicini (see Figure 93). Time is represented along the horizontal axis, and notes by lines, whose start and end points show where the sound began and ended.

How do such traditions work? Through imitation. Just as composers borrow ideas through copying fragments and features of extant works, so performers echo each other's ways of realising a score. Hence zygonic theory applies in this domain of activity too, and we can speak of 'styles' or conventions of performance brought about through countless instances of 'micro-imitation' of articulation, phrasing and nuances in the ways that levels of volume fluctuate. An example occurs in my rendition of *Romantic Rollercoaster*, in which the third note of a rhythmic pattern is consistently shortened. To continue the genetic analogy through which material is transferred between pieces in the process of composition (p. 248), the modifications created by performers are akin to 'epigenetic' variation, which do not alter the substance of the music (its core patterns of melodic and harmonic intervals and IOIs), although the precise ways in which these are expressed are subject to modification.

Figure 93 *Western music as performed is only approximately represented by standard notation.*

Some of the more prominent characteristics of a performance may even be captured in notation, ensuring that they will be conveyed indirectly to a large body of would-be players and singers – beyond those who have the opportunity to hear a performer's interpretation directly. Occasionally, a performer may stray into what could reasonably be considered the composer's territory. Take, for example, the nineteenth-century pianist Carl Czerny's habit of doubling the bass lines of Bach's fugues at their peroration (rather like the effect of an additional 16' stop on the organ) – a custom that was captured in the 1837 Peters edition of *The Well-Tempered Clavier*. Rather than 'musical epigenesis' this is likely to sound rather too much like 'genetic modification' for modern ears, which grew up listening to music in an era of 'historically informed' performance.

So, a performer's realisation of a piece will typically borrow some ideas from previous renditions, while other aspects are likely to be distinctive to the player or singer concerned – perhaps even unique to a particular occasion. Hence any interpretation of a piece will combine similarities and differences with previous performances. But what does this mean for listeners? How do memories of different readings of a work interact cognitively?

Remarkably, it seems that the musical mind, familiar with a given style, can distinguish between the 'genetic' and 'epigenetic' components of a piece in performance quite intuitively, without the need for formal training or some intricate music-theoretical explanation. We know that this must be the case since different renditions of a piece can be understood to be alternative manifestations of what is fundamentally the 'same thing', implying that the ear is capable of penetrating a welter of surface variation to extract the core information about a work's musical identity. Even children in the early years, having been exposed to different versions of the same nursery rhymes, can isolate these songs' invariant features and use them to produce their own renditions – typically without using the expressive devices such as vibrato and rubato that may originally have been present. As we observed (p. 200), it tends to be later, in adolescence, when these elements of 'mature' musical performance kick in (at *Sounds of Intent* Level 6).

So what are our memories of a piece likely to comprise? We certainly have far more musical data squirrelled away than we could ever access without prompting; or, to put it in more formal terms, there appears to be a huge disparity between the *reactive* capacity of our musical memory, which enables us to recognise pieces with which we are familiar and perhaps recollect certain aspects of a particular performance, and our *proactive* capabilities, whereby we can reproduce works – or at least elements of them – that we have heard before. This chasm between the reactive and the proactive (or in psycholinguistic terms, between the 'receptive' and 'expressive') is, in my view, one of the most extraordinary features of the human brain: people can understand many more words than they are able to use; they can identify hundreds of faces yet are unable to reproduce them graphically; and in music, children and adults alike can recognise thousands of pieces of music – or, at least, snippets of them – from advertising jingles and ring tones to pop songs and symphonies, yet appear to lack the capacity to re-create more than a few of them.

This remarkable imbalance was first brought home to me when, as a young teenager, I took a job as the organist at my local church on the Isle of Wight. The choir largely comprised some of the women from the village and two or three men (including my father). All of them had been used to singing the melodies of hymns and chants, and steadfastly refused to make any attempt to sing in harmony, saying it was beyond their unschooled musical abilities to manage separate parts. So in an effort to inject more variation into proceedings I enthusiastically embraced the church organists' tradition of re-harmonisation: using different chords to support the later verses of hymn tunes, which continued unchanged. The strange thing was that any changes I did make – even quite subtle ones – would be noticed and comments made after the service. Evidently, the members of the choir had mental representations of the harmonic structure of the hymns, but they were unable to externalise them.

So just what is it that people do typically remember of music? There is very little research to turn to for answers with regard to what we can generally recall in everyday situations – no doubt on account of the difficulty that most of us have in physically reproducing the music that's in our heads – although what evidence there is points to musical data being stored in 'chunks': rhythmic, melodic and harmonic motifs, which, as we have seen, are largely responsible for giving pieces of music their identity. In terms of *Sounds of Intent*, this is very much the territory of Level 4, and it seems to be here where a good deal of our musical memories reside that can be used proactively – as fragments and features that can be accessed and extracted. And the phenomenon is easy enough to demonstrate. Ask people (other than musicians who are used to working from memory) to hum through a favourite piece of music – something more substantial than a short song – and see how far they are able to get. They probably won't be able to manage more than the introduction or the main theme. Prompted, they may be able to recall some other passages, but the chances are that they won't be able to remember how these were supposed to be connected. In fact, it is in the *transitions* between chunks where our recollection of pieces appears to be least secure, where even experienced musicians know that they have to 'mind the gap'; consequently they will often devote special attention in learning and rehearsal to points in the musical narrative where a phrase or a section comes to an end, and from where different directions of travel are conceivable.[37]

This is partly, no doubt, because motifs, the fundamental elements in most musical design, recur so frequently throughout pieces, constantly reinforcing listeners' long term mental images of them, whereas the ways in which they are connected are far more varied, and therefore may potentially lay down contradictory memories. So the very variety – ambiguity, even – that lends richness to the listening experience, works against memory. Moreover, relationships between motifs are likely to be weaker than those that function within them: the musical logic connecting two groups of notes may literally hang by a single zygonic thread in contrast to the internal Gestalt forces of proximity and similarity that often work in parallel across pitch, perceived time, timbre and loudness. So it seems that the structure of musical memory matches the structure of music itself.

There is clearly more to our capacity to remember music than assortments of motifs, though, since people can detect changes in pieces that they know well. And if you were to request that they sing along with a familiar work, then they would no doubt be able to recall far more than they would unprompted. So what is going on here?

It is as though hearing the music afresh scaffolds memory, providing the framework upon which the motifs that are remembered can be located in pitch and time, and supplying salient features that can serve as *aides-memoires*. It is rather like asking for directions: people's descriptions of routes – even those that they make frequently – often lack crucial topological detail (was it the fourth right or the fifth right, the second set of traffic lights or the third?) or are downright mistaken. Usually these lacunae or errors are of no significance because of the constant stream of visual cues that serve to structure the journey. But in their absence, things can quickly fall apart.

There is another important constraint on musical memory, and that relates to the limitations of what we are able to hear in the first place through perception. The majority of us, it seems, pay most attention to the melody in any musical texture – typically the highest part that is playing at any given time. The accompaniment, variously comprising subsidiary tunes, parts with a rhythmic function, chords and a bass line seem to be encoded in more summary form. As we saw with the choir's reaction to changes to the chords of hymns I made on the organ, these may be heard in general terms – without the specificity for a listener to be able to reproduce them. There are exceptions, of course. In the 1970s, I was listening to a band in the company of a school friend, when he suddenly asked (in a less than complimentary tone) whether I could *believe* what the bass player was doing. I had to admit that the bass line hadn't been on my auditory radar, since my attention had largely been taken up with the antics of the female lead vocalist. But then, my classmate was Mark King, shortly to emerge as the great slap-bass guitarist in the pop group Level 42. Little wonder that he was particularly interested in what fellow bassists were up to. Evidently, although we were both being exposed to the same physical array of sounds, what we were hearing – and remembering – was very different.

Interestingly, a similar position seems to exist in relation to musical savants as well as some 'neurotypical' musicians with AP. My student Annamaria Mazzeschi played a series of 120 chords on the piano comprising from four to nine notes one at a time, and had six musical savants, including Anthony and Derek, attempt to imitate each of them immediately, just by listening. A group of advanced music students from the Royal Academy of Music in London who had AP also participated in the experiment.

This is an extremely challenging task – most musicians wouldn't be able to do it at all. By some margin, Derek and Anthony were the most successful, between them reproducing over 90 per cent of the pitches correctly, followed by another savant, with 82 per cent. The highest 'neurotypical' score was 79 per cent. *All* the savants, and the highest scoring 'neurotypical' musicians (with a success rate of 58 per cent or more), were best at reproducing the *lowest* notes in the chords. The participants who were least able to perform the task seemed to be attending more to the *highest* notes, as these were correctly recalled most frequently. Clearly, some approaches to hearing harmony, whether intuitive or consciously learnt, by feeding more perceptual detail into memory, will enable a fuller picture of a piece to be held in the mind.

Finally, we need to consider how memories of different *performances* work alongside each other in memory. It seems that music that is used a great deal in everyday situations (children's songs, for example) and pieces that are often heard in different renditions (for instance, by those who attend concerts regularly) are stored in consolidated form – a composite of information culled from many performances, from which certain, largely relative, data have been abstracted and other more specific (or 'absolute') details lost – or at least stored only within broad parameters. How do these memory traces interact with the experience of listening to a piece with which one is familiar through different interpretations? Take, for example, the *Hallelujah Chorus* by Handel. I have heard this performed on what must surely be hundreds of occasions, at different tempos, with different instrumental and vocal forces and even in different keys (due to the difference in tuning between modern and 'period' instruments). There is no one interpretation that is particularly important to me, which I have heard significantly more often than the others. So I assume that the *Hallelujah Chorus* as it is stored in my brain is a rather flexible affair, allowing it to accommodate (at least temporarily) the streams of new auditory information that would necessarily be mapped against it during my attendance at a new performance of *Messiah*. Of course, it may be that I encounter a new rendition that is particularly striking in some way – perhaps by being on a large scale in an outdoors venue. This interpretation may cause, in Piagetian terms, 'assimilation' to occur: a permanent change in my memory of the piece.

It is interesting to note that, when a single performance of a work is heard repeatedly (through listening to a recording on multiple occasions), some absolute values of pitch *do* seem to be stored in long-term memory, even in listeners without AP in the conventional sense. The American neuroscientist and musician Dan Levitin undertook a simple but telling experiment in the 1990s[38] in which 46 psychology students at Stanford University sang two songs that they knew very well from commercial recordings, not having heard them for a while. All told, around a quarter of their renditions were at the correct pitch. This suggests that, for music with which we are extremely familiar, it is not only intervals that are retained. However, unlike for those with AP 'proper', the aesthetic effects of recognising a general difference in pitch are likely to be modest, as the new pitches would rapidly overwhelm the relatively weak representations of the old ones held in long-term memory thanks to the 'chameleon' effect.

As we live in a fuzzy world in which similarity is encountered more often than sameness, in which approximation rules over exactitude, and in which our mental representations of things are partial and imperfect rather than complete and flawless, the way we perceive and understand music has to be forgiving too. Unlike the unambiguous (if inscrutable) *Mona Lisa*, Beethoven's 5th Symphony can never be captured as a single entity and somehow stored, pristine, in the controlled environment of a gallery or museum. Rather, the symphony is both blessed and cursed with the foibles and idiosyncrasies of an art form that only comes to life through human interaction in the 'real world'. But it is surely the richer for that.

Understanding the Listening Experience

A good deal of the psychological research devoted to how listeners perceive music has concerned itself with *expectation* – having a sense of what is coming next, and when. Perhaps this isn't so surprising, given that the ability to make judgements about the future based on memories from past and present experiences is wired deep in our neural architecture,[39] and it is obvious, in an everyday sense, that expectation is key to human understanding and survival.[40] Without it we could not foresee what the consequences of our actions might be; we could not anticipate (and therefore avoid) danger; and we could not plan ahead on the basis of reasonable assumptions.

The notion of expectation lies at the heart of a good deal of contemporary music theory too, often extending the paths pioneered by Leonard Meyer. Meyer's original thinking, set out in 1956, combined four main streams of thought: the Western tradition of music theory, the principles of Gestalt psychology (in particular, the work of Kurt Koffka), John Dewey's hypothesis of emotional arousal through inhibition, and Claude Shannon's then newly-conceived 'information theory'. In brief, Meyer's proposition was this: the patterns of notes that constitute music set up

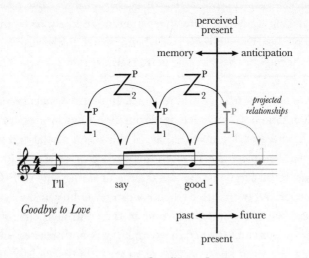

Figure 94 *The opening three notes of* Goodbye to Love *create an ascending pattern that, according to Meyer, has a perceived urge to continue.*

expectations in listeners that, at any given point, particular continuations will occur. The most important of these pertain to rhythm and pitch (in the form of melody and harmony). An emotional response to music will arise when a composer frustrates a listener's expectations – by deferring the arrival of a note that is implied by what has gone before, for example.

Was Meyer right? Perhaps – examples that seem to support his theory abound in a wide range of styles. Take, for instance, *Goodbye to Love*, made famous by Karen Carpenter as the first 'power ballad', written by her brother Richard and the lyricist John Bettis. Stop the song after the first three notes to which the words 'I'll say good-' are set. They form an ascending progression that you may well hear as wanting to rise to the next note in the scale. According to Meyer, this anticipation is triggered by the ear's natural propensity to expect patterns to continue. In terms of zygonic theory this occurs through the projection of past imitation into the future at the level of *events*: each note is separated from the one preceding by an interval of one scale-step that is copied from what has gone before (we have already shown how this process works in relation to IOIs – see Figure 50). Hence after the first three notes of *Goodbye to Love* – G, A and B – the most likely continuation is C.

Indeed, many tunes take this direct path: just listen to a melody of the same early 1970s vintage as the Carpenters' hit, *Eye Level* (the *Van der Valk* TV theme), by Simon Park, for example. There are no surprises here, and the music may well come across as easy on the ear and unchallenging emotionally – self-consciously bland, even. But this is the last thing that Richard Carpenter wanted in his ballad: to match the sentiment of the lyrics, the music needs an injection of poignancy, and this he achieves (in line with Meyer's theory) by delaying the arrival of the top note of the scale through the insertion of two extra pitches, D and D flat (to the words '-bye to') – see Figure 95. These also clash with the underlying harmony – a dissonance that listeners are likely to hear as contributing an added piquancy at this point in the music.

This line of reasoning seems straightforward enough. But there have been objections to Meyer's theory, not least since people's enjoyment of music – the strength of their emotional response – appears to increase the better they know a piece; anecdotal evidence that is supported by British-born psychologist Daniel Berlyne's pioneering work in experimental aesthetics.[41] The issue is this: how can something sound unexpected when you have heard it before? When you *know* the course that Richard Carpenter's melody is going to take, how can surprise play a part in the way it is perceived?

Part of the answer lies in the fact that the continuation of the ascending pattern is not the only form of expectation that is likely to be invoked when listeners hear the opening of the song. Their sense of anticipation will also be influenced by having heard, on countless previous occasions, series of notes in other pieces that fulfil the same sequence of functions in relation to the tonal *frameworks* to which they pertain. Put simply, in music, as in everyday life, we predict that things will happen in the future according to how often (and in what contexts) they have occurred in the past.

The impact of this intuitive, 'statistical' learning on the way we hear and understand music is comprehensively set out by Ohio-based music psychologist David Huron in his landmark book *Sweet Anticipation*.[42] What would he have to say about the initial phrase of *Goodbye to Love*? The first three pitches function as the fifth, sixth and seventh degrees of a major scale ($\hat{5}, \hat{6}$ and $\hat{7}$), and so the most likely transition from $\hat{7}$ is $\hat{1}$. That is to

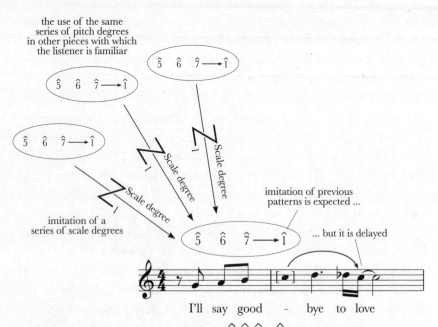

Figure 95 *Having heard the transition from $\hat{5}, \hat{6}, \hat{7}$ to $\hat{1}$ many times before, a listener will expect the same sequence to occur again, through imitation of previous appearances.*

say, just as expectation at the level of *events* suggests that C (the first degree of the scale) should follow the first three notes of the melody (G, A and B), so does statistical learning, which pertains to tonal *frameworks*. This is one explanation of why the opening of *Goodbye to Love* still has the capacity to arouse an emotional response even after many hearings, since it still sounds relatively surprising in the context of a listener's entire repertoire.

As will become apparent, however, there are more factors at work in repeated hearings than this, and to understand what is happening, we first need to tackle another issue with the two models of expectation bequeathed us by Meyer (which operate at the level of events and frameworks): namely, that they offer only a *general* impression of what is going to occur next (and when). For example, while C (the tonic) was deemed to sound like the most probable continuation of the first three notes of Carpenter's famous tune, it was by no means the only possibility, as the convoluted course of the melody shows. To examine this principle in

Figure 96 *What expectations are likely to be at work on first hearing the main theme from the third movement of Rachmaninoff's 2nd Symphony?*

more detail, we will consider the opening of another well-known theme, which opens the third movement of Rachmaninoff's 2nd Symphony. The first three notes are A, C sharp and E (scale degrees $\hat{1}$, $\hat{3}$ and $\hat{5}$, which comprise the 'tonic triad'). What are listeners who haven't heard the tune before likely to expect will occur next?

There are a number of options that follow logically from what has gone before through 'internal' patterning (the regularity inherent in the $\hat{1}, \hat{3}$ and $\hat{5}$ ascent): any one of the three initial pitches may be imitated directly, or other pitches may be derived from extrapolation from the intervals that exist between them. Through such means, analysis has shown that all *seven* of the notes that make up the scale of A major make perfect sense as continuations – indeed, all are found in pieces of Western classical music that were composed before Rachmaninoff's 2nd Symphony.[43] Hence, in terms of statistical learning, it is only safe to say that some pitches are likely to be perceived as slightly more probable continuations than others.

So neither the expectation operating on the basis of a pattern being continued nor that arising from the statistical learning pertaining to scale-steps offers the listener any reasonable certainty as to what will occur next. Yet experience suggests that specific expectations *do* arise at various points in the piece when it is heard for the first time. Clearly, then, there is a form of anticipation in play that is not captured by either of Meyer's original insights.

To consider what this may be, let us return to a fundamental premise of zygonic theory: that musical structure can occur at the level of events, groups or frameworks. Events have an immediate correspondence with the expectation that occurs through the patterns that exist between one note and the next, and frameworks seem to fit well with the statistical learning inherent in the system of Western tonality. But what of groups? Is this the missing element that enables specific expectations to be generated, even in broadly unfamiliar contexts?

A postgraduate student, Michael Thorpe, and I tested this hypothesis in the following way. I composed a frankly anodyne new melody, which was constructed from essentially two different motifs, with three instances of repetition and one example of transposition (see Figure 97).[44]

Thorpe then asked 40 students, each of whom demonstrated that they could sing in tune, to try to anticipate what would happen next following each note in the melody. They indicated their choice by singing or humming the pitch that they thought most likely to occur. They also had to rate how confident they were in their response. It was a somewhat

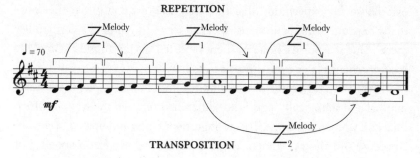

Figure 97 *The synthetic melody that was used to test expectation in music.*

laborious task, as the tune comprises 26 notes. Nonetheless, the findings give a fascinating insight into what people hear when they hear music.

We anticipated that, to begin with, when many continuations were logically possible, there would be a range of responses (based on note-to-note patterns and intuitive probabilities from having heard many other melodies), but that this would narrow sharply once it was recognised that a motif was being heard again. And this, indeed, is broadly what happened. Overall, there was a 95 per cent correspondence between the predictions of a zygonic model and the pitches that participants sang, and it was clear that, on a first hearing, by far the most important form of expectation was that arising between groups of notes that had been heard before.

However (as is ever the case with this kind of research), people's responses raised a number of other questions. For example, the range of pitches that participants sang after hearing each of the notes in the melody was astonishing. Following the first note, for instance, responses varied over a range of an octave-and-a-half (twelve scale-steps). And even at the end, when 93 per cent of the pitches that were sung correctly anticipated the final note, there was still a surprising variety (a range of five scale-steps). At no point was the range of responses less than this. So one has to ask, what were people hearing? How could the music – a very simple melody – possibly make sense to them when their predictions for what would happen next were so far from what actually occurred? Of course, it could be argued that the range of responses was an artefact of the experiment, as when people usually listen to music they don't have to externalise any expectation that they may feel (assuming that they normally have any sense of anticipation at all when listening to an unfamiliar piece). But afterwards, none of them reported having found the melody incomprehensible or even difficult to follow.

There were other unforeseen findings too. For example, there was a marked and statistically significant difference between the ways in which men and women responded: on average, the 16 men anticipated 14 pitches correctly, and the 25 women, 10. Was this somehow a consequence of gender stereotyping at some stage in the participants' lives that was now influencing how they acted? It is difficult to see how, though the men were consistently more *confident* than the women in their predictions, a gap that widened at each attempt as prognostication was made. Moreover, women were seven times more inclined to guess that a given pitch would be followed by another the same. Why should this be the case? Of course, the number of participants was relatively small, but the results could nonetheless be indicative of something more fundamental at work in the way that men and women process musical structure – a possibility that has some neuropsychological support. For example, neuroscientist Stefan Koelsch and his team found that an electrophysiological correlate of music-structural processing appears to functioning in both halves of the brain in women, and predominantly in the right hemisphere in men.[45]

* * *

Finally, we return to the question of repeated hearings. In seeking to unpack the listener's experience, we will take a step back and return to the work of Meyer. His original proposition was that an affective response will be aroused when an expectation activated by a musical stimulus, a tendency to respond, is temporarily inhibited or permanently blocked,[46] and a recurring concern has been how to reconcile the uncertainty purported to be necessary to stimulate affect with the matter of repeated hearings, since we can perform or listen to the same piece of music many times and continue to enjoy it. As the psychologist and neuroscientist Thomas Bever says, it cannot be the case for a piece that one has memorised 'that the ebb and flow of partially fulfilled expectations control one's

Figure 98 *Repetition at the level of groups means that anticipation of the second appoggiatura in the third movement of Rachmaninoff's 2nd Symphony is almost inevitable.*

enjoyment of it: every note is exactly what is expected'.[47] Meyer himself countered arguments of this type in a number of ways. One to which he returned in his last thoughts on the subject is the 'willing suspension of disbelief', through which listeners supposedly enter into an aesthetic illusion, unwittingly (or even deliberately) ignoring their knowledge of a piece, and hearing it as if for the first time.[48]

There are, however, a number of difficulties with this view. Consider, again, the opening of the third movement of Rachmaninoff's 2nd Symphony. Based on listeners' retrospective accounts, John Sloboda found this to be prototypical of passages that provoke tears, in that it utilises melodic appoggiaturas, and forms a melodic and harmonic sequence whose underlying chords descend through the 'circle of fifths'[49] to the tonic.[50] Sloboda believes that this finding and others similar offer some confirmation of Meyer's theory that affect stems from the creation and potential violation of expectancy within musical structures. But is this actually what the passage shows? Let us move on from the opening three notes of the main melody shown in Figure 96, and hear what happens in the following two bars.

Take, for example, the appoggiaturas, which Meyer considers to cause 'affective expressive experience' since 'they delay (inhibit) the arrival of the expected and anticipated structural tone'.[51] One can test this out by mentally replaying the first bar of the Rachmaninoff movement, feigning ignorance of what should follow, in accordance with Meyer's proposition. There are two sources of predictive information upon which we can draw: the patterning inherent in the opening material itself and the similarity of its sequence of tonal functions to melodies found in other pieces (see Figure 98). But, as we discovered, these provide listeners with only a general sense of what may come next, since all the degrees of the scale potentially provide logical continuations and all are used by Western classical composers. Accordingly, there is no reason to believe that the note that Rachmaninoff chooses – a G sharp in the fifth octave – will be anticipated to the exclusion of any other.

The dissonant G sharp has a perceived urge to resolve by step to the nearest consonance (the A), but this effect (and any corresponding affect) will occur *as the discord is heard*. Hence, while expectation may well play a part in our aesthetic response at this (slightly later) point in the melody, it will derive from the stylistic tendency of appoggiaturas to resolve to neighbouring notes, not from the preceding melodic context – the 'anticipation before the event' mentioned by Meyer. Before this (as the third note of the melody is heard) there appears to be *too great* a level of uncertainty to enable the theory of inhibited response to function. Conversely, once the resolution has been heard – in retrospect – the position is rather different: listeners may well appreciate (typically at a subconscious level) that the G sharp did indeed delay the arrival of the A, taking the melody on a circuitous route; but at this stage, clearly, there could be *no uncertainty*, since the events have passed.

Hence Meyer's proposition that emotion and meaning in music stem through expectation from events around which there is an element of doubt appears to be in difficulty, even for a first-time listener. Moreover, this thesis becomes even harder to sustain as the passage proceeds, since projections *between groups* kick in: subsequent appoggiaturas *and their resolutions* are strongly implied through the sequential patterns that occur in what follows. A similar sense of inevitability, a teleological drive, characterises the inner parts too and, crucially, the bass line, since it bears the harmonic burden of the musical fabric as a whole.

In summary, then, it seems inconceivable that one could listen to these opening bars without *anticipating* the appoggiaturas with which they begin (after the first). To stylistically competent listeners, even if they are listening to the passage for the first time, there is little or no uncertainty as to the course of the melody once the sequence gets underway. Moreover, the first-time listener is the exception rather than the rule. So what is one to make of Meyer's theory? As Ray Jackendoff puts it: 'Everyone has the experience of thinking "Here comes that beautiful place!" – enjoying it in the full knowledge of exactly what it is going to sound like, with both memory and affect fully engaged.' The problem with Meyer's argument is that it attempts to 'conflate enjoying a piece with not remembering how it goes.'[52] However, Jackendoff does offer the possibility of 'rescuing' Meyer's expectation theory, suggesting that violations of what is expected may occur on a subconscious level, involving a 'closed module' for music-processing that exists in the brain – a 'parser' – which in effect always hears a piece as if for the first time, thereby ensuring that affect remains intact.[53] Cognitive psychologist Jamshed Bharucha describes the position thus: 'Even when a piece has been heard often enough to be familiar, it cannot completely override the generic, automatic expectations. Surprises in a new piece thus continue to have a surprising quality because they are heard as surprises relative to these irrepressible expectations.'[54] Perhaps, then, Meyer's original assertion would be better couched in terms of expectation in music working through the *nonconscious* (rather than the willing) suspension of disbelief.

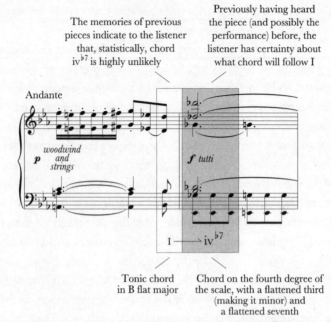

The memories of previous pieces indicate to the listener that, statistically, chord $iv^{\flat 7}$ is highly unlikely

Previously having heard the piece (and possibly the performance) before, the listener has certainty about what chord will follow I

Tonic chord in B flat major

Chord on the fourth degree of the scale, with a flattened third (making it minor) and a flattened seventh

Figure 99 *Anticipation of the relatively unexpected in the slow movement of Mozart's Symphony No. 40, K. 550, is liable to evoke a powerful affective response, before, during and after the event.*

For me, an enduring example occurs in the slow movement of Mozart's late symphony K. 550, where, in the context of a major key, a minor chord with a flattened seventh on the fourth degree of the scale occurs, effecting a harmonic transition that is highly unusual in the classical style. Mozart emphasises the sense of surprise by having the whole orchestra play the chord with a sudden 'forte'. When listening to the piece I always look forward to the moment when this exotic harmony occurs and often get the physical tingling sensation associated with a heightened emotional response. However, I can imagine that if I listened to nothing but the passage repeatedly at the expense of all other music, the effect would gradually wear off – not because I was any more certain that the chord would occur than before, but because it would (temporarily) skew my statistical learning, and what was previously surprising in the context of all other harmonic transitions would become the norm.

To sum up: whatever the neurocognitive processes involved, reflection on the listening experience suggests that *being able to anticipate what is in stylistic terms the relatively unexpected enables us to relish it all the more.* This accords with David Huron's hypothesis that a key component in the pleasurable experience that music affords – its 'sweet anticipation' – is the succession of unconscious cognitive rewards that our ability to make correct prognostications offers. These are all ultimately enabled by imitation of one form or another, whether 'general' or 'specific', whose universal presence and function in music lies at the heart of zygonic theory.

The Problem of 'Atonal' Music

In the twentieth century, the world of Western classical music had to confront a new, entirely self-imposed, challenge. A number of composers consciously chose to eschew certain of the structural and expressive principles that had previously, more or less unthinkingly, been adopted: in particular, the notion of 'tonality', based on the frameworks of intervals and the idiosyncratic patterns of usage that lie in the background of almost all music. Arnold Schoenberg and his students Alban Berg and Anton Webern led the way in producing music of this type, which was subsequently labelled 'atonal'. To this day, the works they created in this 'style' (if one can call it such) remain the preserve of a minority of enthusiasts. However, the view among aficionados is that, in time, audiences of 'mainstream' classical music will 'catch up', and that sufficient exposure is all that is required for a reasonable level of understanding and appreciation of atonal music to be acquired. But is this true? Has atonal music the capacity *ever* to succeed in attracting wider, 'non-specialist' audiences, or will much of it ultimately represent little more than a stylistic cul-de-sac in the broad span of Western music's evolution? Conversely, are there strategies that the composers of atonal music could consider adopting to make their pieces more readily approachable by the majority of listeners, each of whom has a natural propensity to understand and enjoy the music to which he or she is exposed?

To better understand the issue, we will call upon Fred Lerdahl's notion of 'musical grammars': limited sets of rules to which the structures of pieces conform. Lerdahl identifies two main kinds of grammar: one related to listening and the other pertaining to composition. In the majority of cultures, most of the time, listening and compositional grammars largely overlap: composers and improvisers and their audiences intuitively tapping into the same set of rules that they have learnt implicitly through exposure to a similar corpus of music. Here, communication is not a problem: there is enough intuitively recognisable repetition and regularity for the burden of the musical message to be conveyed, even if, as we should expect, there are subtle shades of difference in the aesthetic response to the auditory information as it is created and received.

However, for hundreds of years – at least since the fourteenth century when composers such as Guillaume de Machaut constructed highly intricate 'isorhythmic motets' – composers of Western 'art' music have quite deliberately introduced additional, 'conceptual' constraints. These 'artificial' grammars worked alongside, or fused with, the 'natural' grammars prevalent at the time.[55] Again, effective musical communication was not compromised provided that sufficient of the natural grammars was audible for the music to 'make sense' in the ears of listeners. Take, for example, much of the music of Bach – for instance, the opening *Kyrie* of his great B Minor Mass. It is perfectly possible for listeners to be deeply moved by this long, contrapuntal chorus without ever being aware of the ingenuity with which the five-part fugue unfolds (compare with Scenario E in Figure 85).

This belt and braces approach to composition, of ensuring that compositional grammars are supported by the safety net of listening grammars, was characteristic of all Western composers, from Dufay, Palestrina and Bach, to Mozart, Schumann and Brahms, for example; that is, from the Middle Ages right up until the end of the nineteenth century. Indeed, there is evidence that composers themselves were aware of the relationship between the two forms of structure, and knew how to engineer it, so that both their artistic instincts as a composer and the practical need to produce music with sufficient immediacy to please patrons and audiences could be satisfied. For example, in a letter to his father of December 28, 1782, Mozart wrote that he still had two more piano concertos to complete of the three that he was working on for his 1783 subscription concerts (K. 413–415):

These concertos are a happy medium between what's too difficult and too easy – they are Brilliant – pleasing to the ear – Natural without becoming vacuous; – there are passages here and there that only connoisseurs can fully appreciate – yet the common listener will find them satisfying as well, although without knowing why.[56]

However in the early 1900s, Schoenberg promoted a line of thinking that persisted throughout the twentieth century, in which the principle of music having a natural grammar – a cognitive space that was tacitly shared between composers and listeners – was consciously abrogated. Indeed, the notion of general accessibility to art music began to be seen, in some circles, as demeaning to its creators. As Schoenberg put it, 'if it is art, it is not for all, and if it is for all, it is not art',[57] a sentiment echoed in Milton Babbitt's notorious article of 1958, in which he contended that composers no longer live 'in a unitary musical universe of "common practice"', and so, at best, 'music would appear to be for, of, and by specialists'.[58]

Schoenberg's new, atonal, approach is something of an oddity, since it is the negation of a system of rules rather than their implementation: it stipulates the kinds of pitch relationships that are *not* admissible, but does not indicate which *are*. Hence, one could reasonably argue that atonality does not, on its own, constitute an artificial grammar. However, its immediate consequences for listeners can be somewhat the same, and musical communication is likely to be impaired, as audiences seek to make sense of the streams of notes that assail them.

Working with colleagues over the last decade, I have undertaken a range of research that seeks to ascertain what listeners hear in atonal music. One project, as we have seen (p. 249), involved Derek Paravicini, and explored how his capacity to learn and remember the opening bars of Schoenberg's Klavierstück, Op. 11, No. 1 shed light on the way he deals with atonality. Audiences at Derek's concerts are often intrigued by his capacity to learn, reproduce and improvise on music in a wide range of styles, working entirely by ear. Occasionally I get asked 'But what about *atonal* music? Can he learn pieces by Schoenberg, for example?' With this in mind, a musically self-contained section of a piece of atonal music was selected, the opening eleven bars of Schoenberg's Op. 11, No. 1, dubbed the *Magical Kaleidoscope*, which I was confident that Derek had never heard before. A further, tonal, passage was required for the purposes of comparison, with the same musical 'DNA', which was termed the *Kooky Minuet* – see Figure 88.

Learning and attempting to reproduce the two pieces were tasks undertaken by Derek as part of a day's other musical activities, including recording familiar repertoire and performing with a singer (a broadly typical schedule for him). Derek's first attempt to recall the first part of the *Magical Kaleidoscope* was one of the most extraordinary things that I have ever witnessed. Here is someone who can consistently disembed complex nine-note chords with a striking immediacy and over 93 per cent accuracy, and whose public piano performances are characterised by precision. Yet here, in an excerpt of textural and technical simplicity, Derek played the very first note incorrectly, substituting a C for the original B. I was listening to Derek's efforts at the time (rather than watching him play), and what I heard seemed so unlikely that I felt obliged to check that the keyboard had not somehow slipped into transposing mode. But he really had made a mistake, and the errors continued, with only 34 per cent of the short segment (just the opening three bars) being reproduced correctly. This low figure suggests that the lack of a tonal framework had engendered a high level of confusion in Derek's mind, sufficient to overwhelm his acute sense of AP: neither the individual pitches nor the relationships between them were spared. Admittedly, Derek's response does afford a sense of 'atonality', though it is rather different from the one that Schoenberg originally intended. Derek's confusion was confirmed as, in the course of the next three attempts, each time having heard the opening of the *Magical Kaleidoscope* again, he tried different pitch combinations, apparently seeking to square the circle of satisfying both the need for accurate reproduction of individual notes and seeking to make them conform to a familiar tonal structure. His indecision is reflected in uncharacteristic hesitations and slips (see Figure 100).

What happened with the *Kooky Minuet*? My immediate impression was that Derek's first attempt was far more successful and, indeed, he reproduced 68 per cent of the notes correctly. The errors that he did make, which, surprisingly, grew in number as the experiment proceeded, were largely due to the increasing *addition* of material, whereby Derek 'filled in' the implied harmonic gaps left by the open texture. Given that errors could be made at the level of events, groups or frameworks, it is of interest

Schoenberg, Klavierstück, Op. 11, No. 1, bars 1–3

Derek's first attempt

Figure 100 *Derek's first four attempts to play the opening bars of Schoenberg's Klavierstück, Op. 11, No. 1.*

to note that, if something had to 'give' in Derek's mind, it was invariably the former rather than the latter – the tonal system constituting an accurately remembered backdrop upon which surface detail was reproduced with greater or less fidelity. Given the structural equivalence of the two pieces in all respects apart from the presence or absence of a pitch framework deployed according to the 'common practice' conventions of Western major tonality, it is reasonable to assume that it was Derek's recognition of this feature that accounted for his greater success in recalling the material from the faux-Mozart. In order to ascertain what the long-term effects of the presence or absence of that framework may have on his memory, Derek agreed to take part in two further tests, respectively one week and a year after the learning phase.

Derek's version of the *Magical Kaleidoscope* after the seven-day break is startling. There is very little of the original material left. It appears that he constructed a tonal version of the opening motif and improvised on it. In his version, the first phrase is cast as a series of 'dominant seventh' chords,[59] which resolve onto one another in various ways in a manner reminiscent of western late-Romantic harmonic sequences – the style from which Schoenberg's atonality evolved. It is as though Derek put the history of Western classical music in reverse, and took a stylistic step back to regain his tonal footing (see Figure 101).

Figure 101 *Derek's attempt to play the opening bars of the*
Magical Kaleidoscope *one week after having heard it.*

In contrast, his version of the *Kooky Minuet* one week on strongly resembles the original, though his recollection of the global structure is eccentric. He played his versions of the first two segments four times followed by a period of silence, at which point he was prompted verbally with 'anything else, Derek?', whereupon he played his rendition of the final segment twice. When put alongside the *Magical Kaleidoscope* data, these findings reinforce the idea that the recognition of frameworks of pitch, together with their probabilistic patterns of utilisation, greatly facilitate the operation of Derek's long-term musical memory.

Finally, Derek was asked, one year later, to play whatever he could remember of the two pieces. The results were as follows (see Figure 102). In relation to the *Magical Kaleidoscope*, it is interesting to note that Derek paused and asked to hear the recording first – an unusually explicit indication from him that he did not feel he could recall the piece. Indeed, he articulated his uncertainty again during the course of the attempt, saying 'Can't remember' after the first two phrases (although he did subsequently add two more). The transcription shows that, at this stage, the trace of the *Magical Kaleidoscope* has almost entirely decayed. The *Kooky Minuet* produced a very different result, however, with 67 per cent of the original material recalled (and 80 per cent from his last attempt twelve months earlier). That is to say, Derek's memory of the piece hardly seemed to have shifted in the course in the intervening period. Again, given the equivalence of the *Magical Kaleidoscope* and the *Kooky Minuet* in terms of their musical 'DNA', this provides further evidence that the presence of a recognisable tonal framework is important to the successful functioning of Derek's musical memory.

Of course, while these results are of potential value – not least to those

Magical Kaleidoscope

Kooky Minuet

Figure 102 *Derek's complete attempts to play the* Magical Kaleidoscope *and* Kooky Minuet, *one year after having heard them last.*

such as me who seek to support Derek in learning new repertoire – of more general interest is the extent to which they may be more broadly applicable. That is: what do the results suggest, if anything, about how 'neurotypical' listeners process atonal pieces? It could be argued that to seek to generalise from Derek's data would be inappropriate, since, as a savant, he is by definition an 'atypical' musician; his acute sense of absolute pitch alone, for example, sets him apart from the great majority of other listeners. There is, however, evidence that militates against this view, one source of which is to be found in the precedents of other researchers having previously used savant data to consider the nature of 'neurotypical' human abilities – to test issues of 'modularity' in intelligence, for instance.[60]

A second reason for seeking to generalise from Derek's efforts lies in the fact that other musicians frequently learn and practise pieces alongside him, and engage with him in sophisticated improvisations, implying a commonality in the way that they and he are processing music. Arguably, then, Derek functions like most other people as a *listener* (a 'super listener', perhaps, given his ability to recognise pitches and disaggregate chords) in that his musical understanding is implicit rather than explicit, perceptual rather than conceptual, intuitive rather than intellectual. However, where he differs from the vast majority is in his capacity to reproduce what he hears on the keyboard – entire, complex musical textures that amount to far more than the short vocal fragments that are all most people can manage to replicate. Inevitably, then, most empirical research in music relies on indirect evidence obtained through verbal or other responses, whereas Derek offers us a privileged window direct into his musical mind and, perhaps, into 'the musical mind' more generally.

Let us consider how the findings pertaining to Derek's efforts at recall potentially illuminate the cognitive processing that may occur in most people in relation to atonal music. For many listeners, atonal pieces sound 'discordant' or simply 'wrong', and are hard to memorise and recall.[61] Both these observations accord with Derek's attempts to reproduce the *Magical Kaleidoscope*, in that he 'corrected' notes that were outside a traditional diatonic framework and found it difficult to remember the music in the short term – and impossible over extended periods of time. Hence it may be the case that 'typical' listeners attempt to make sense of the music by imposing familiar frameworks (and hearing notes outside these as 'errors'). And it may be that, by failing to encode musical material in an efficient way, they are unable to store or retrieve it.

Finally, to return to our original question: is atonal music ever likely to succeed in attracting broadly-based, non-specialist audiences, who are not prepared or able to listen to music in other than in a non-conceptual (non-musicological) way? The answer must surely lie in composers providing alternative or supplementary structures that can be grasped quickly and intuitively: in Lerdahl's terms, to provide listeners with an accessible listening grammar. As Béla Bartók says:

> atonal music does not exclude certain exterior means of arrangement, certain repetitions (in a different position, with changes, and so forth),

… refrain-like appearances of certain ideas, or the return to the starting point at the end.[62]

That is to say, if structure pertaining to tonal frameworks is absent, then other forms of organisation will be required to make the music generally comprehensible, memorable and, ultimately, enjoyable.

Coda

This chapter used zygonic theory to interrogate the three roles commonly associated with Western popular and classical music: composing, performing and listening. Although these functions can be fulfilled by a single person (when musicians improvise for their own amusement, for example), the process of engaging with music usually involves at least three people. Hence the interpersonal transmission of musical ideas – sometimes through sound, sometimes through other means (such as scores) – is inevitable. And it is in this process of transmission that ontological challenges arise: just what is it that we are talking about when we refer to 'a piece of music'?

Works do not exist in isolation, but borrow ideas from hundreds, even thousands of other pieces, through indirect and sometimes direct imitation. So compositions only exist and fully make sense as part of something bigger: a *set* of stylistically congeneric works. Then, each piece is not a single entity, but a *set* of potential cognitive representations, whose variety stems from the expectation that performers will bring their own interpretation to a composer's score – which only amounts to a series of rather imprecise instructions. And, as we noted in relation to the folksong *Barbara Allen*, a comparable principle applies in aural traditions, in which pieces are learnt by ear: here performers are *expected* to add their own voice to proceedings. Finally, every listener will process and understand the musical message that is sent in a slightly different way. Hence, during a performance, a piece of music exists as a *set* of mental phenomena in each audience-member's mind.

So, we can say that a piece of music is not an absolute thing, but a somewhat fuzzy set of experiences. This is possible because music is, quite literally, super-structured, with a degree of repetition far beyond that required for any message to make sense. In terms of information

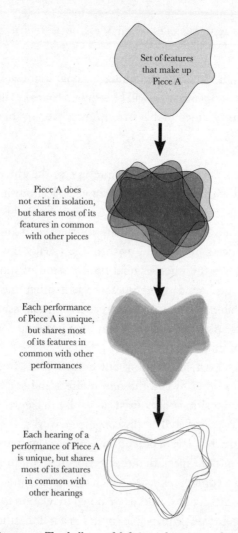

Set of features
that make up
Piece A

Piece A does
not exist in isolation,
but shares most of its
features in common
with other pieces

Each performance
of Piece A is unique,
but shares most
of its features in
common with other
performances

Each hearing of a
performance of Piece A
is unique, but shares
most of its features
in common with
other hearings

Figure 103 *The challenge of defining what a piece of music is.*

theory, a high level of redundancy permits the successful transmission of
ideas, even when there is a lot of noise in the system. But more than this,
it is in music's fuzziness that its charm lies; it is the very imprecision of
its message that ultimately makes a piece of music, as an object of human
interpretation, interesting, sustainable and enjoyable.

Notes Compared

It had seemed a simple enough request: the man in the control room was asked to bring the stage lights back up 10 seconds after the start of the piece. What could go wrong? The musicians of the Orchestra of St John's had memorised the first few bars of their parts and practised playing them as an ensemble without being able to see the conductor, John Lubbock. And for the piano soloist – Derek Paravicini – performing in the dark was of no concern, since he was totally blind. Derek, then aged 32, was a musician at the height of his powers, whose extraordinary talents were internationally celebrated.

The occasion was the first performance of a piano concerto written especially for Derek by the composer Matthew King, at London's Queen Elizabeth Hall in 2011. Matthew had worked on the piece for over a year, improvising with Derek, and drawing inspiration from one of the savant's favourite composers, George Gershwin. The opening bars of the concerto were intended to represent some of the confusion that Derek's family and friends believed that he must have experienced early in his life, when the world whirled around him as a succession of fleeting and apparently unconnected auditory, tactile and olfactory sensations; and when the language that well-meaning adults used to try to explain what was going on amounted to little more than bursts of sound that hung in the air, unattached to visual images that would have given them meaning. But amidst the perceptual chaos, there was one thing that Derek *did* come to comprehend, and to an extraordinary degree: the endlessly repeated patterns of sound that constitute music.

It was with fragments of music – isolated notes, which subsequently coalesced into motifs, disparate at first – with which the piano concerto began. These dabs and blotches of sound were intended to continue for 20 seconds or so, until the first hint of a complete theme emerged. But the failure of the lights to fade in at the appointed moment meant that, on the night of the concerto's première, the musical disarray rapidly changed from verisimilitude to reality. As the musicians reached the end of the lines they had memorised, parts started to be missed. Others were misremembered and appeared at the wrong time. Sitting next to Derek at the piano, I heard John curse under his breath. 'Lights!' he hissed. And again, more urgently, *'Lights!'* In the darkness, the tension was palpable and rising fast. Surely we'd have to halt proceedings and begin the concerto again. What an embarrassment! And worst of all, the team around Derek would have let him down in front of 900 people.

And then something uncanny happened. The music seemed to be getting itself back on track. The missing jabs of sound and fragments of melody started to reappear. They were not emanating from the orchestra, though, but from the piano. Then I understood. In addition to playing his own, sustained notes low down on the keyboard, Derek had followed his musical instincts and somehow started to fill in the blanks. Given this scaffolding in sound, the members of the orchestra were able to relocate their parts in the musical narrative as it led towards the emergence of the main theme. As it began, the lights finally went up. The effect – though quite unintended – was magical. And beyond the first few rows of the auditorium, where those seated had (we later discovered) assumed that John's less than *sotto voce* requests for light was a feature of the piece, other members of the audience had apparently been unaware that anything untoward had happened.

Looking back today, I still marvel at the brilliance of Derek's musicianship that shone through the challenges of that night. Having previously observed him learning the concerto, a feat that he accomplished just by listening to a somewhat jarring rendition of the score on a computer, I was aware that all 11,000 or so of the notes that made up the technically demanding piano part were secure in his mind and in his fingers. By any standards, this was a remarkable achievement. But when, in the darkness, I heard Derek play the instrumental parts that were missing, it became evident that these, too, had been committed to memory. And although he had never tried to play this material before – to *practise*, as neurotypical musicians are wont to do – Derek had been able to add the extra notes to his existing contribution without a second thought. Talking to him afterwards, it was clear that he had no notion of his own musical ingenuity. Here was the 'copy game' from his childhood writ large.

And just as the 'copy game', some thirty years ago, first offered a new insight into how music makes sense, so the mature Derek's performance on the South Bank brought home to me more powerfully than ever before the paradox that, as a music teacher-cum-psychologist, I had a fair idea of *how* Derek did what he did, although I couldn't have begun to attempt to do it myself; while Derek, lacking the necessary capacity for introspection, had no idea how he managed to achieve his astonishing musical exploits. And it struck me that, in some respects, Derek's relationship with music had more in common with the intuitive responses of the members of the public who attended his concert than with the carefully considered contributions of his fellow musicians on stage. But that didn't mean the performers had enjoyed hearing the concerto any more – or any less – than the audience; knowing in a conceptual way how music works doesn't automatically equate to a more pleasurable listening experience. And even I have to admit, when listening to music for my own amusement, I tend to turn off what Leonard Meyer would call the absolutist part of my listening faculty and become an unalloyed referentialist.

So, why this book? Why music theory? Why should we worry about zygonic relationships?

There are a number of reasons. Turning again to Derek and the many other young people with learning difficulties whom I have tutored over the years, understanding how music functions has enabled me to appreciate more fully how they are likely to engage with music – how they listen, how they learn, how they interact with others through sound. This means that I am more likely to be effective as a teacher, able to direct strategies and resources with greater precision, having gauged the level of a child's musical development using the *Sounds of Intent* framework, which, as we have seen, derives from zygonic theory. More recently, this capacity has been extended to 'neurotypical' early childhood too, as the research set out in Chapter 4 shows: the findings of the *Sounds of Intent in the Early Years* project offer parents and practitioners a detailed account of what it is their young children are likely to be experiencing when they listen to music, and the kinds of activities that will have the greatest chances of success in promoting musical engagement and development. Most exciting of all, knowing how musicality develops within us adds another piece in the multidimensional jigsaw that comprises our evolving understanding of ourselves, both as a species and as individual human beings.

Beyond this, zygonic theory has provided a way of thinking about music that has facilitated reasoned discussion about a host of issues that are often regarded as being just too difficult to pin down, that traditionally occupy the conceptual space somewhere between music philosophy and psychology. And if the theory (to the frustration of some) does not always generate definitions and data that are precise enough to build algorithms that machines could use, since it is not just about repetition (that would be easy for a computer to deal with) but repetition *with intentionality*, then I would say that *fuzzy* boundaries around a concept to do with human beings can be a good thing – perhaps an inevitable thing (in contrast to the postmodern notion of having no boundaries at all, which is distinctly unhelpful). Above all, the zygonic conjecture sets out one way of enabling us to distinguish between what can and what can't reasonably be regarded as music. Because music exists only in the mind of listeners, inevitably some human interpretation will creep in wherever patterned sources of sound exist. Birds may not hear their songs as music, but humans can; autistic children may hear music in the hum of the microwave (in contrast to their parents); and the sound qualities of Morse code – not in itself music – may nonetheless be grist to the composer's mill. The way that each of us compares notes is a personal thing, but there are enough similarities in the comparisons that we all draw for music truly to be regarded as a universal language.

Finally, zygonic theory enables us to cast our ears forward in time, and to indulge in a little musical futurology. What will music be like in 10, 100, 1,000 years? Will it be completely different or just consist of more variations on the same well-established themes? Will future generations want to listen to the pieces that are being written and performed today, or will the music that we currently cherish be consigned to oblivion? Will people still sing along to songs by the Beatles in the year 3000, just as they currently enjoy performing the 800-year-old medieval English round *Sumer Is Icumen In*?

The answer can perhaps be found in our relationship to the past; in the twenty-first century, we seem to have a greater appetite than ever to hear music from previous eras – to have direct contact with the way our ancestors thought and, above all, felt. The only thing that prevents us from delving further and further back into musical history is the lack of scores. But the music that we *can* reconstruct from what was written down appears to be as appealing to contemporary ears as historical accounts suggest that it was in the past. This is the case, because, although music has developed enormously over the last millennium, and the dialects have undoubtedly changed, the underlying language is still the same. The principle of imitation has remained constant. Hence there is no reason to think that the next 1,000 years should not see a comparable musical evolution (rather than revolution): more material growing from the same root-stock and shaped by the same principles of musical understanding and appreciation, which zygonic theory seeks to explain. There may be creative culs-de-sac en route, as there have been in the past (in the 2060s, people will surely look back on the fires that were lit and the butterflies that were released in the name of art with a wry smile), but there is no reason to be anything other than optimistic. The musical echoes from the future appear to be as resonant as those from the past.

Notes

Prelude: Insights from the Blind

1. See J. Sloboda, S. O'Neill and A. Ivaldi (2001) 'Functions of music in everyday life: an exploratory study using the experience sampling method', *Musicae Scientiae*, 5(1), 9–32.
2. E. Husserl (1905–1910/1964) *The Phenomenology of Internal Time-Consciousness*, The Hague: Martinus Nijhoff.

1. How does Music Work?

1. L. Meyer (1956) *Emotion and Meaning in Music*, Chicago, IL: University of Chicago Press.
2. See D. Kahneman (2011) *Thinking, Fast and Slow*, London: Penguin Books Ltd.
3. *Der Freie Satz* was first published (posthumously) in 1935 by Universal Edition in Vienna. The English translation by E. Oster – *Free Composition* – was published by Longman in 1979. The quotation and related material are to be found on p. xxiii.
4. For example, H. Schenker (1969) *Five Graphic Music Analyses*, New York, NY: Dover Publications.
5. Ibid., pp. 32 and 33.
6. From *Der Freie Satz*, pp. 4–10.
7. See J. Levinson (1997) *Music in the Moment*, New York, NY: Cornell University Press.
8. A notable exception being E. Narmour (1997) *Beyond Schenkerism: The Need for Alternatives in Music Analysis*, Chicago, IL: University of Chicago Press.
9. *Der Freie Satz*, p. 3.

10. C. Ballantine (1984) *Music and its Social Meanings*, Johannesburg: Ravan Press.
11. Ibid., p. 5.
12. Although the tendentious title was apparently added editorially.
13. See A. Forte (1973) *The Structure of Atonal Music*, New Haven, CT: Yale University Press.
14. *Music and its Social Meanings*, pp. 32 and 33.
15. Ibid., p. 33.
16. D. Tovey (1935) *Essays in Musical Analysis*, Volume 1, Oxford: Oxford University Press, p. 121.
17. For example, R. Solie (1995) *Musicology and Difference: Gender and Sexuality in Music Scholarship*, Berkeley and Los Angeles, CA: University of California Press.
18. For example, P. Brett, E. Wood and G. Thomas (eds) (1994) *Queering the Pitch: The New Gay and Lesbian Musicology*, New York, NY: Routledge.
19. See, in particular, J. Straus (2011) *Extraordinary Measures: Disability in Music*, New York, NY: Oxford University Press.
20. S. McClary (1991) *Feminine Endings: Music, Gender and Sexuality*, Minneapolis, MN: University of Minnesota.
21. For more recent studies on gender and music, undertaken from the perspective of cognitive psychology, see, for example, D. Sergeant and E. Himonides (2014) 'Gender and the performance of music', *Frontiers in Psychology*, 5, 276; D. Sergeant and E. Himonides (2016) 'Gender and music composition: a study of music, and the gendering of meanings', *Frontiers in Psychology*, 7, 411.
22. L. Bernstein (1973) *The Unanswered Question*, Cambridge, MA: Harvard University Press, p. 153.
23. See, for example, J.-J. Nattiez (1982) 'Varèse's "Density 21.5": a study in semiological analysis' (trans. A. Barry), *Music Analysis*, 1(3), 243–340; (1998) 'Le solo de cor anglais de Tristan und Isolde: essai d'analyse sémiologique tripartite', *Musicæ Scientiæ*, 2(1) (supplement), 43–61; N. Ruwet and M. Everist (1987) 'Methods of analysis in musicology', *Music Analysis*, 6(1/2), 3–9 and 11–36.
24. R. Brown (1957) 'Linguistic determinism and the part of speech', *The Journal of Abnormal and Social Psychology*, 55(1), 1–5.
25. 'Methods of analysis in musicology', p. 16
26. Adapted from J. Dunsby and A. Whitall (1988) *Music Analysis in Theory and Practice*, New Haven, CT: Yale University Press, p. 224.
27. 'Methods of analysis in musicology', p. 32.
28. F. Lerdahl and R. Jackendoff (1983) *A Generative Theory of Tonal Music*, Cambridge, MA: MIT Press.
29. Ibid., p. 113.
30. Ibid., p. 106.

31. A. Schoenberg (1967) *Fundamentals of Musical Composition*, London: Faber and Faber.

32. See *The Phenomenology of Internal Time-Consciousness*.

33. R. West, I. Cross and P. Howell (1987) 'Modelling music as input-output and as process', *Psychology of Music*, 15(1), 7–29.

34. *Fundamentals of Musical Composition*, p. 20.

35. D. Huron (2008) *Sweet Anticipation: Music and the Psychology of Expectation*, Cambridge, MA: MIT Press.

36. *Fundamentals of Musical Composition*, p. 9.

37. P. Boulez (1963/1971) *Boulez on Music Today* (trans. S. Bradshaw and R.R. Bennett), London: Faber and Faber.

38. J. Sloboda (1985) *The Musical Mind: The Cognitive Psychology of Music*, Oxford: Clarendon Press, p. 259.

39. See M. Schneider (1957) 'Primitive music', in E. Wellesz (ed) *The New Oxford History of Music*, Vol. 1, *Ancient and Oriental Music*, London: Oxford University Press, pp. 1–82 (p. 11).

40. A. Bregman (1990) *Auditory Scene Analysis: The Perceptual Organization of Sound*, Cambridge, MA: MIT Press.

41. I. Pollack and L. Ficks (1954) 'Information of elementary multidimensional auditory displays', *Journal of the Acoustical Society of America*, 26, 155–158.

42. G. Miller (1956) 'The magical number seven, plus or minus two: some limits on our capacity for processing information', *Psychological Review*, 63(2), 81–97.

43. Summarised in M. Epstein (2011) 'Correlates of loudness', in M. Florentine, A. Popper and R. Fay (eds), *Springer Handbook of Auditory Research*, Vol. 37, pp. 89–107.

44. *The Unanswered Question*, p. 162.

45. A. Roskies (1999) 'The binding problem', *Neuron*, 24(1), 7–9.

46. H.-W. Chang and S. Trehub (1977) 'Auditory processing of relational information by young infants', *Journal of Experimental Child Psychology*, 24, 324–331.

47. D. Fabian, R. Timmers and E. Schubert (eds) (2014) *Expressiveness in Music Performance: Empirical Approaches across Styles and Cultures*, Oxford: Oxford University Press.

48. Z. Kaminska and J. Woolf (2000) 'Melodic line and emotion: Cooke's theory revisited', *Psychology of Music*, 28(2), 133–153.

49. *Fundamentals of Musical Composition*, p. 8.

2. The Zygonic Conjecture

1. B. de Sélincourt (1920) 'Music and duration', *Music and Letters*, 1(4), 286–293.

2. Ibid., p. 290.

3. V. Zuckerkandl (1956) *Sound and Symbol: Music and the External World* (trans. W. Trask), Princeton, NJ: Princeton University Press.

4. Ibid., p. 213.
5. S. Macpherson (1915) *Form in Music*, London: Joseph Williams Ltd; W. Berry (1966/1986) *Form in Music* (2nd Edition), Englewood Cliffs, NJ: Prentice Hall Inc.; C. Chávez (1961) *Musical Thought*, Cambridge, MA: Harvard University Press; I. Stravinsky (1942) *Poetics of Music*, Cambridge, MA: Harvard University Press.
6. *Sound and Symbol*, p. 42.
7. E. Cone (1987) 'On derivation: syntax and rhetoric', *Music Analysis*, 6(3), 237–256.
8. For a full account of Derek's early life, see A. Ockelford (2007) *In the Key of Genius: The Extraordinary Life of Derek Paravicini*, London: Random House.
9. See http://www.huffingtonpost.com/adam-ockelford/autism-genius_b_4118805.html
10. For example, the round *Sumer Is Icumen In* dates to the mid-thirteenth century.
11. H. Maturana and F. Varela (1980) *Autopoiesis and Cognition: The Realization of the Living*, Dordrecht: D. Reidel Publishing Company.
12. For more information on zygonic theory see, for example, A. Ockelford (1999) *The Cognition of Order in Music: A Metacognitive Study*, London: Roehampton Institute; (2005) *Repetition in Music: Theoretical and Metatheoretical Perspectives*, Aldershot: Ashgate Publishing, Ltd; (2009) 'Zygonic theory: introduction, scope, prospects', *Zeitschrift der Gesellschaft für Musiktheorie*, 6(1), 91–172; (2012) *Applied Musicology: Using Zygonic Theory to Inform Music, Education, Therapy and Research*, Oxford: Oxford University Press.
13. In earlier explications of the theory, the 'I' stood for 'Interperspective': that is, 'between *per*ceived a*spect*s' of sound.
14. See, for example, J. Clendinning and E. Marvin (2011) *The Musician's Guide to Theory and Analysis* (2nd Edition), New York, NY: W.W. Norton and Company, pp. 113–121.
15. W.J. Dowling (1972) 'Recognition of melodic transformations: inversion, retrograde, and retrograde inversion', *Perception and Psychophysics*, 12(5), 417–421; D. Temperley (1995) 'Motivic perception and modularity', *Music Perception*, 13(2), 141–169.
16. See https://insights.spotify.com/uk/2015/05/06/most-popular-keys-on-spotify/ – of the 30,000,000 tracks on Spotify in 2015, around two thirds were in major keys, and one third in minor.
17. See, for example, R. Parncutt (2012) 'Major-minor tonality, Schenkerian prolongation, and emotion: a commentary on Huron and Davis (2012)', *Empirical Musicology Review*, 7(3/4), 118–137.
18. Richard Wagner conceived of melody as being the 'surface of harmony'; see A. Anbari (2007) *Richard Wagner's Concepts of History*, PhD thesis, University of Texas at Austin, p. 66.

19. See, for example, R. Crowder (1984) 'Perception of the major/minor distinction: I. Historical and theoretical foundations', *Psychomusicology*, 4(1/2), 3–12.

20. H. Riemann (1896) *Harmony Simplified, or The Theory of the Tonal Function of Chords*, London: Augener Ltd, reprinted by Cornell University, Library, 2009, p. 6.

21. See, for example, E. Schubert (2004) 'Modeling perceived emotion with continuous musical features', *Music Perception*, 21(4), 561–585.

22. In the West, studies of the distribution of melodic intervals range from folksongs and classical music to popular songs of the twentieth century – see, for example, W. Fucks (1962) 'Mathematical analysis of the formal structure of music', *Institute of Radio Engineers Transactions on Information Theory*, 8, 225–228; T. Jeffries (1974) 'Relationship of interval frequency count to ratings of melodic intervals', *Journal of Experimental Psychology*, 102(5), 903–905; W.J. Dowling (1978) 'Scale and contour: two components of a theory of memory for melodies', *Psychological Review*, 85(4), 341–354; D. Huron (2006) *Sweet Anticipation: Music and the Psychology of Expectation*, Cambridge, MA: MIT Press, pp. 74 and 158–161.

23. See *The Cognition of Order in Music*.

24. See A. Ockelford (2009) 'Similarity relations between groups of notes: music-theoretical and music-psychological perspectives', *Musicæ Scientiæ*, 13(1) (supplement), 47–98.

25. Observe that some relationships use filled arrowheads and some open. In zygonic theory, the filled arrowheads indicate a *set* of relationships that are the same (that connect individual phenomena that have a duration in time, such as pitch), while the open arrowheads show a *single* relationship (linking onsets, for example). For further information see A. Ockelford (1991) 'The role of repetition in perceived musical structures', in P. Howell, R. West and I. Cross (eds), *Representing Musical Structure*, London: Academic Press, pp. 129–160.

26. See J. Pressing (1983) 'Cognitive isomorphisms in pitch and rhythm in world music: West Africa, the Balkans, and Western tonality', *Studies in Music*, 17, 38–61.

27. P. Fraisse (1978) 'Time and rhythm perception', in E. Carterette and M. Friedman (eds), *Handbook of Perception*, Vol. 8, *Perceptual Coding*, New York, NY: Academic Press, pp. 203–54.

28. Terms introduced into the musicological lexicon by Curt Sachs in the middle of the twentieth century – see C. Sachs (1953) *Rhythm and Tempo: A Study in Music History*, New York, NY: W.W. Norton and Company.

29. K. Agawu (2003) *Representing African Music: Postcolonial Notes, Queries, Positions*, New York, NY: Routledge, pp. 93–95.

30. A. Winold (1975) 'Rhythm in twentieth-century music', in G. Wittlich (ed.), *Aspects of Twentieth-Century Music*, Englewood Cliffs, NJ: Prentice Hall Inc., pp. 208–269.

31. J. London (2001) 'Rhythm', in S. Sadie and J. Tyrrell (eds), *The New Grove Dictionary of Music and Musicians*, Volume 21, London: Macmillan Publishers, pp. 277–309.

32. See *The Musical Mind: The Cognitive Psychology of Music*.

33. D. Levitin and P. Cook (1996) 'Memory for musical tempo: additional evidence that auditory memory is absolute', *Perception & Psychophysics*, 58(6), 927–935.

34. See *Fundamentals of Musical Composition*, p. 58.

35. This feature is explored in A. Ockelford (2004) 'On similarity, derivation and the cognition of musical structure', *Psychology of Music*, 32(1), 23–74.

36. A. Schoenberg (1983) *Theory of Harmony* (trans. R. Carter), Berkeley and Los Angeles, CA: University of California Press.

37. T. Elliott, L. Hamilton, and F. Theunissen (2013) 'Acoustic structure of the five perceptual dimensions of timbre in orchestral instrument tones', *Journal of the Acoustical Society of America*, 133(1), 389–404.

38. B. Nettl (1965/1973) *Folk and Traditional Music of the Western Continents*, Upper Saddle River, NJ: Prentice Hall Inc., p. 140.

39. 'The magical number seven, plus or minus two: some limits on our capacity for processing information'.

40. E. Narmour (2000) 'Music expectation by cognitive rule-mapping', *Music Perception*, 17(3), 329–398.

41. 'The role of repetition in perceived musical structures'; (1993) 'A theory concerning the cognition of order in music', unpublished PhD thesis, University of London; *The Cognition of Order in Music: A Metacognitive Study*.

42. Summarised in *Auditory Scene Analysis: The Perceptual Organization of Sound*, pp. 344ff.

43. M. Schmuckler (1989) 'Expectation in music: investigation of melodic and harmonic processes', *Music Perception*, 7(2), 109–150.

44. See, for example, A. Ockelford (2002) 'The magical number two, plus or minus one: some limits on our capacity for processing musical information', *Musicæ Scientiæ*, 6(2), 177–215; (2005) 'Relating musical structure and content to aesthetic response: a model and analysis of Beethoven's Piano Sonata Op. 110', *Journal of the Royal Musical Association*, 130(1), 74–118; (2006) 'Implication and expectation in music: a zygonic model', *Psychology of Music*, 34(1), 81–142; (2007) 'A music module in working memory? Evidence from the performance of a prodigious musical savant', *Musicæ Scientiæ* (Special Edition: 'Performance Matters'), 5–36; (2008) 'D. Huron's *Sweet Anticipation*: music and the psychology of expectation', *Psychology of Music*, 36(3), 367–382; (2010) 'Exploring the structural principles underlying the capacity of groups of

notes to function concurrently in music', *Musicæ Scientiæ*, 14(2) (supplement), 149–185; (2011) 'Another exceptional musical memory: evidence from a savant of how atonal music is processed in cognition', in I. Deliège and J. Davidson (eds), *Music and the Mind: Essays in Honour of John Sloboda*, Oxford: Oxford University Press, pp. 237–288; (2013) 'What makes music "music"? Theoretical explanations using zygonic theory', in J.-L. Leroy (ed.), *Actualités des Universaux en Musique/Topics in Universals in Music*, Paris, France: Edition des Archives Contemporaines, pp. 123–147; A. Ockelford and D. Sergeant (2013) 'Musical expectancy in atonal contexts: musicians' perception of "antistructure"', *Psychology of Music*, 41(2), 139–174; R. Grundy and A. Ockelford (2014) 'Expectations evoked on hearing a piece of music for the first time: evidence from a musical savant', *Empirical Musicology Review*, 9(2), 47–97; A. Ockelford (2016) 'Shape in music notation: exploring the cross-modal representation of sound in the visual domain using zygonic theory', in Daniel Leech-Wilkinson and Helen Prior (eds), *Music and Shape* (Studies in Music Performance as Creative Practice, Volume 3), Oxford: Oxford University Press.

45. A. Ockelford (2008) 'Beyond music psychology', in S. Hallam, I. Cross and M. Thaut (eds), *Oxford Handbook of Music Psychology*, New York, NY: Oxford University Press, pp. 539–551.

46. See, for example, A. Ockelford (2006) 'Using a music-theoretical approach to interrogate musical development and social interaction', in N. Lerner and J. Straus (eds), *Sounding Off: Theorizing Disability in Music*, New York, NY: Routledge, pp. 137–155; (2007) 'Exploring musical interaction between a teacher and pupil, and her evolving musicality, using a music-theoretical approach', *Research Studies in Music Education*, 28(1), 3–23; (2012) 'Imagination feeds memory: exploring evidence from a musical savant using zygonic theory', in D. Hargreaves, D. Miell and R. MacDonald (eds), *Musical Imaginations: Multidisciplinary Perspectives on Creativity, Performance, and Perception*, New York, NY: Oxford University Press, pp. 31–61; (2012) 'Songs without words: exploring how music can serve as a proxy language in social interaction with autistic children', in R. MacDonald, A. Kreutz and L. Mitchell (eds), *Music, Health and Well-being*, New York, NY: Oxford University Press, pp. 289–323; K. Shibazaki, A. Ockelford and N. Marshall (2013), 'Extending zygonic theory to analyse patterns of musical influence in children's group composition', *Musicæ Scientiæ*, 17(4), 429–471; A. Ockelford and J. Vorhaus (2017) 'Identity and musical development in people with severe or profound and multiple learning difficulties', in R. Macdonald, D. Hargreaves and D. Miell (eds), *The Oxford Handbook of Musical Identities*, New York, NY: Oxford University Press, pp. 642–667.

47. For example, in his book *Sweet Anticipation*.

48. See, for example, L. Trainor (2006) 'Innateness, learning and the difficulty of determining whether music is an evolutonary adaptation: A commentary

on Justus and Hutsler (2005) and Mc Dermott and Hauer (2005)', *Music Perception*, 24(1), 105–110.

3. How We Construct Musical Meaning

1. Thelonius Monk, Frank Zappa and Elvis Costello are other contenders.
2. E. Bigand, S. Filipic and P. Lalitte (2005) 'The time course of emotional responses to music', *Annals of the New York Academy of Sciences*, 1,060, The Neurosciences and Music II: From Perception to Performance, 429–437.
3. Since, as psychologists Philip Johnson-Laird and Keith Oatley observe, survival often requires that, as sentient creatures interacting with highly complex environments that are ultimately irreducible to logical analysis, we gauge sensory input intuitively – see P. Johnson-Laird and K. Oatley (1992) 'Basic emotions, rationality, and folk theory', *Cognition and Emotion*, 6(1), 201–223.
4. A. Gabrielsson and E. Lindström (2001) 'The influence of musical structure on emotional expression', in P. Juslin and J. Sloboda (eds), *Music and Emotion: Theory and Research*, New York, NY: University Press, pp. 223–248.
5. K. Watson (1942) 'The nature and measurement of musical meanings', *Psychological Monographs*, 54(2), 1–43.
6. K. Scherer and J. Oshinsky (1977) 'Cue utilization in emotion attribution from auditory stimuli', *Motivation and Emotion*, 1(4), 336–346.
7. 'The nature and measurement of musical meanings'; L. Wedin (1972) 'Multidimensional study of perceptual-emotional qualities in music', *Scandinavian Journal of Psychology*, 13(1), 241–257.
8. W. Thompson and B. Robitaille (1992) 'Can composers express emotions through music?', *Empirical Studies of the Arts*, 10(1), 79–89.
9. R. Gundlach (1935) 'Factors determining the characterization of musical phrases', *American Journal of Psychology*, 47(4), 624–644.
10. L.-L. Balkwill and W. Thompson (1999) 'A cross-cultural investigation of the perception of emotion in music: psychophysical and cultural cues', *Music Perception*, 17(1), 43–64.
11. See 'The nature and measurement of musical meanings'.
12. See 'Factors determining the characterization of musical phrases'.
13. S. Nielzén and Z. Cesarec (1982) 'Emotional experience of music as a function of musical structure', *Psychology of Music*, 10(1), 7–17.
14. P. Juslin (1997) 'Perceived emotional expression in synthesized performances of a short melody: capturing the listener's judgement policy', *Musicæ Scientiæ*, 1(1), 225–256.
15. L. Meyer (2001) 'Music and emotion: distinctions and uncertainties', in P. Juslin and J. Sloboda (eds), *Music and Emotion Theory and Research*, New York, NY: Oxford University Press, pp. 341–360, (p. 342).

16. P.N. Juslin, A. Friberg and R. Bresin (2001/2002) 'Toward a computational model of expression in music performance: the GERM model'. *Musicæ Scientiæ* (Special Issue 2001–2002), 63–122 (p. 71).

17. K. Scherer, R. Banse and H. Wallbott (2001) 'Emotion inferences from vocal expression correlate across languages and cultures', *Journal of Cross-Cultural Psychology*, 32(1), 76–92.

18. S. Malloch (1999/2000) 'Mothers and infants and communicative musicality', *Musiæ Scientiæ* (Special Issue: Rhythm, Musical Narrative and Origins of Human Communication), 29–57; S. Trehub and T. Nakata (2001/2002) 'Emotion and music in infancy', *Musicæ Scientiæ* (Special Issue: Current Trends in the Study of Music and Emotion), 37–61.

19. Recent research suggests that there may be some crossover in terms of listeners' emotional response to musical sounds and the prosodic features of speech; see M. Curtis and J. Bharucha (2010) 'The minor third communicates sadness in speech, mirroring its use in music', *Emotion*, 10(3), 335.

20. This equates with a necessary condition of what Tim Horton terms 'compositionality', whereby when 'constituents are combined to produce a specific type of complex construction, the syntactic relation itself is independent of the particular constituents involved' – see T. Horton (2001) 'The compositionality of tonal structures: a generative approach to the notion of musical meaning', *Musicæ Scientiæ*, 5(2) 131–156.

21. See A. Ockelford (2013) *Music, Language and Autism: Exceptional Strategies for Exceptional Minds*, London: Jessica Kingsley.

22. R. Goulden, P. Nation and J. Read (1990) 'How large can a receptive vocabulary be?', *Applied Linguistics*, 11(4), 341–363.

23. For accounts of philosophical approaches, see, for example, A. Clark (1982) 'Is music a language?', *The Journal of Aesthetics and Art Criticism*, 41(2), 195–204; C. Philpott (2001) 'Is music a language?', in C. Plummeridge and C. Philpott (eds), *Issues in Music Teaching*, New York, NY: Routledge, pp. 32–46. For neuroscientific perspectives, see, for instance, A. Patel (2008) *Music, Language, and the Brain*, New York, NY: Oxford University Press; P. Rebuschat, M. Rohrmeier, J. Hawkins and I. Cross (2012) (eds), *Music and Language as Cognitive Systems*, New York, NY: Oxford University Press.

24. For more information, see, for example, B. Mitchell and F. Robinson (eds), *Beowulf: An Edition with Relevant Shorter Texts*, Oxford: Blackwell.

25. R. Thompson (2009) 'Habituation: a history', *Neurobiology of Learning and Memory*, 92(2), 127–134

26. See H. Barlow and S. Morgenstern (1948) *A Dictionary of Musical Themes*, London: Faber and Faber.

27. See, for example, D. Huron (1996) 'The melodic arch in Western folksongs', *Computing in Musicology*, 10, 3–23.

28. *The Unanswered Question*, p. 169.

29. See, for example, A. North and D. Hargreaves (2002) 'Age variations in judgements of "great" art works', *British Journal of Psychology*, 93(3), 397–405.

30. L. Meyer (1967) *Music, the Arts, and Ideas: Patterns and Predictions in Twentieth-Century Culture*, Chicago, IL: University of Chicago Press, p. 23.

31. Ibid., p. 24.

32. Ibid.

33. For an explanation of chords and their inversions, the reader should consult a textbook on Western harmony, such as W. Piston and M. Devoto (1988) *Harmony* (5th Edition), New York, NY: W.W. Norton and Company.

34. See, for example, B.F. Skinner (1974) *About Behaviorism*, New York, NY: Knopf.

35. J.B. Davies (1978) *The Psychology of Music*, Stanford, CA: Stanford University Press, pp. 69–70.

36. See *Plato's Republic: The Theater of the Mind*, Volume 10 (trans. B. Jowett, rev. A. Anderson), 2001, Millis, MA: Agora Publications, Inc., p. 101.

37. The *Council of Trent* (1545–63) was a meeting of Catholic Church officials to address perceived abuses within the church. As far as music was concerned, reforms were urged that were intended to ensure that the words of the liturgy were clear and the music was reverent in tone.

38. See, for example, http://www.jesus-is-savior.com/Evils%20in%20America/devils_music_no_effect.htm

39. A. North, D. Hargreaves and J. McKendrick (1999) 'The influence of in-store music on wine selections', *Journal of Applied Psychology*, 84(2), 271–276.

40. See, for example, D. Lewkowicz and G. Turkewitz (1980) 'Cross-modal equivalence in early infancy: auditory-visual intensity matching', *Developmental Psychology*, 16(6), 597–607; L. Marks (1989) 'On cross-modal similarity: the perceptual structure of pitch, loudness, and brightness', *Journal of Experimental Psychology: Human Perception and Performance*, 15(3), 586–602.

41. M. Thorpe (2016) 'The perception of transformed auditory and visual pattern structure: an exploration of supramodal pattern space', unpublished PhD thesis, London: University of Roehampton.

42. See for example, S. Baron-Cohen, L. Burt, F. Smith-Laittan, J. Harrison and P. Bolton (1996) 'Synaesthesia: prevalence and familiarity', *Perception*, 25(9), 1073–1079; J. Harrison (2001) *Synaesthesia: The Strangest Thing*, New York, NY: Oxford University Press; J. Ward (2013) 'Synesthesia', *Annual Review of Psychology*, 64, 49–75.

43. A. Ockelford and C. Matawa (2009) *Focus on Music 2: Exploring the Musical Interests and Abilities of Blind and Partially-Sighted Children with Retinopathy of Prematurity*, London: Institute of Education, p. 52.

44. For an explanation, see *Harmony* (5th Edition).

45. J. Molino (1975) 'Fait musical et sémiologue de la musique', *Musique en Jeu*, 17, 37–62.

46. J.-J. Nattiez (1990) *Music and Discourse: Toward a Semiology of Music* (trans. C. Abbate), Princeton, NJ: Princeton University Press, p. 55.

47. E. Varèse and C. Wen-Chung (1966) 'The liberation of sound', *Perspectives of New Music*, 5(1), 11–19 (p. 18).

48. W. Gaver (1993) 'What in the world do we hear? An ecological approach to auditory event perception', *Ecological Psychology*, 5(1), 1–29.

49. R. Scruton (2009) *Understanding Music: Philosophy and Interpretation*, London and New York: Continuum, p. 4.

50. F. Lerdahl (1988) 'Cognitive constraints on compositional systems' in J. Sloboda (ed.), *Generative Processes in Music: The Psychology of Performance, Improvisation and Composition*, Oxford: Clarendon Press, pp. 231–59.

51. See, for example, M. Ulvaeus and D. Rothenberg (eds) (2009) *The Book of Music and Nature*, Middletown, CT: Wesleyan University Press.

52. From his poem *Home-Thoughts, from Abroad*.

53. R. Payne and M. Sorensen (2005) *The Cuckoos: Cuculidae*, New York, NY: Oxford University Press, p. 97. Observe that, in some other species, learning (and, therefore, imitation) does occur: for example it appears that male zebra finches *do* learn songs from their fathers (S. Yanugiharo and Y. Yazaki-Sugiyama (2016) 'Auditory experience-dependent cortical circuit shaping for memory formation in bird song learning', *Nature Communications*, 7, article number: 11946).

54. See *Music, Language, and the Brain*.

55. M.L. Serafine, R. Crowder and B. Repp (1984) 'Integration of melody and text in memory for songs', *Cognition*, 16(3), 285–303; B. Morrongiello and C. Roes (1990) 'Children's memory for new songs: integration or independent storage of words and tunes?', *Journal of Experimental Child Psychology*, 50(1), 25–38; D. Schön, R. Gordon, A. Campagne, C. Magne, C. Astésano, J. Anton and M. Besson (2010) 'Similar cerebral networks in language, music and song perception', *Neuroimage*, 51(1), 450–461.

56. S. Wilson, D. Abbott, D. Lusher, E. Gentle and G. Jackson (2011) 'Finding your voice: a singing lesson from functional imaging', *Human Brain Mapping*, 32(12), 2,115–2,130.

57. W. Wallace (1994) 'Memory for music: effect of melody on recall of text', *Journal of Experimental Psychology: Learning, Memory, and Cognition*, 20(6), 1,471.

58. D. Rubin (1995) *Memory in Oral Traditions: The Cognitive Psychology of Epic, Ballads, and Counting-Out Rhymes*, New York, NY: Oxford University Press.

59. R. Lea, D. Rapp, A. Elfenbein, A. Mitchel and R. Romine (2008) 'Sweet silent thought: alliteration and resonance in poetry comprehension', *Psychological Science*, 19(7), 709–716.

60. S. Kita, K. Kantartzis and M. Imai (2010) 'Children learn symbolic words better: evolutionary vestige of sound symbolic protolanguage', in A. Smith,

M. Schouwstra, B. de Boer and K. Smith (eds), *The Evolution of Language*, Proceedings of the 8th International Conference (EVOLANG8), Singapore: World Scientific Publishing Co. Pte Ltd, pp. 206–213.

61. I. Cross (2005) 'Music and meaning, ambiguity and evolution', in *Musical Communication*, D. Miell, R. MacDonald and D. Hargreaves (eds), New York, NY: Oxford University Press, pp. 27–43.

62. S. Malloch and C. Trevarthen (eds) (2009) *Communicative Musicality: Exploring the Basis of Human Companionship*, New York, NY: Oxford University Press; S. Kirschner and M. Tomasello (2010) 'Joint music making promotes prosocial behavior in 4-year-old children', *Evolution and Human Behavior*, 31(5), 354–364; D. Gerry, A. Unrau and L. Trainor (2012) 'Active music classes in infancy enhance musical, communicative and social development', *Developmental Science*, 15(3), 398–407; G. Kreutz (2014) 'Does singing facilitate social bonding?', *Music and Medicine*, 6(2), 51–60; E. Pearce, J. Launay and R. Dunbar (2015) 'The ice-breaker effect: singing mediates fast social bonding', *Open Science*, 2(10), 150–221.

63. See, for example, A. Ockelford (2017) 'Towards a developmental model of musical empathy using insights from children who are on the autism spectrum or who have learning difficulties', in E. King and C. Waddington (eds) *Music and Empathy*, New York, NY: Routledge, pp. 39–88; T. Eerola, J. Vuoskoski and H. Kautiainen (2016) 'Being moved by unfamiliar sad music is associated with high empathy', *Frontiers in Psychology*, 7, 1,176.

64. The notion that through imitating the sound that something makes one can understand it – even become it – is a very ancient one. See M. Schneider (1957) 'Primitive music', pp. 9 and 10: 'If a man is capable of reproducing exactly the croaking of the frog or the hissing of the snake, it is because his mystic ancestor was the totem-god of the frog or the snake. When he imitates the voice of his totem with the greatest realism, he imagines he is obliterating the boundary between subject and object and identifying himself with the totem. Whoever croaks like a frog, is a frog … He becomes in fact a sound-symbol … Vocal imitation is the strongest form of mystic participation in the surrounding world.'

4. We Are All Musical

1. J. Blacking (1974) *How Musical is Man?*, Seattle, WA: University of Washington Press, p. 116.

2. For an overview, see D. Hargreaves and A. Lamont (2017) *The Psychology of Musical Development*, Cambridge: Cambridge University Press.

3. R. Parncutt (2016) 'Prenatal development', in G. MacPherson (ed.), *The Child as Musician: A Handbook of Musical Development* (2nd Edition), Oxford: Oxford University Press, pp. 3–30.

4. M. Saxton (2010) *Child Language: Acquisition and Development*, London: Sage Publications Ltd.

5. See *The Phenomenology of Internal Time-Consciousness*.

6. A. Meltzoff, and W. Prinz (2002) *The Imitative Mind: Development, Evolution and Brain Bases*, Cambridge: Cambridge University Press.

7. M. Papoušek (1996) 'Intuitive parenting: a hidden source of musical stimulation in infancy', in I. Deliège and J. Sloboda (eds) *Musical Beginnings*, Oxford: Oxford University Press, pp. 88–112 (p. 97).

8. W. Kessen, J. Levine and K. Wendrich (1979) 'The imitation of pitch in infants', *Infant Behavior and Development*, 2, 93–99.

9. P. Kuhl and A. Meltzoff (1982) 'The bimodal perception of speech in infancy', *Science*, 218(4,577), 1,138–1,141.

10. M. Legerstee (1990) 'Infants use multimodal information to imitate speech sounds', *Infant Behavior and Development*, 13(3), 343–354.

11. From 'Intuitive parenting: a hidden source of musical stimulation in infancy', p. 106.

12. G. Welch (2006) 'The musical development and education of young children', in B. Spodek and O. Saracho (eds), *Handbook of Research on the Education of Young Children*, Mahwah, NJ: Lawrence Erlbaum Associates, pp. 251–267 and 318.

13. J. Dowling (1982) 'Melodic information processing and its development', in D. Deutsch (ed.), *The Psychology of Music*, New York, NY: Academic Press, pp. 413–429 (pp. 416 and 417).

14. H. Moog (1976) *The Musical Experiences of the Pre-School Child* (trans. C. Clarke), London: Schott, p. 115.

15. D. Hargreaves (1986) *The Developmental Psychology of Music*, Cambridge: Cambridge University Press, p. 73.

16. E. Mang (2005) 'The referent of early children's songs', *Music Education Research*, 7(1), 3–20.

17. *The Developmental Psychology of Music*, pp. 76 and 77.

18. It seems as though the words were treated as an additional feature of the music.

19. https://www.evelyn.co.uk/

20. J. O'Kelly, L. James, R. Palaniappan, J. Fachner, J. Taborin and W. Magee (2013) 'Neurophysiological and behavioral responses to music therapy in vegetative and minimally conscious states', *Frontiers in Human Neuroscience*, 7, 884.

21. E. Götell, S. Brown, and S. Ekman (2009) 'The influence of caregiver singing and background music on vocally expressed emotions and moods in dementia care', *International Journal of Nursing Studies*, 46(4), 422–430.

22. B. Mampe, A. Friederici, A. Christophe and K. Wermke (2009) 'Newborns' cry melody is shaped by their native language', *Current Biology*, 19(23), 1,994–1,997.

23. See *Communicative Musicality: Exploring the Basis of Human Companionship*.

24. See, for example, G. Dehaene-Lambertz, A. Montavont, A. Jobert, L. Allirol, J. Dubois, L. Hertz-Pannier and S. Dehaene (2010) 'Language or music, mother or Mozart? Structural and environmental influences on infants' language networks', *Brain and Language*, 114(2), 53–65.

25. E. McMullen and J. Saffran (2004) 'Music and language: a developmental comparison', *Music Perception*, 21(3), 289–311; A. Brandt, R. Slevc and M. Gebrian (2012) 'Music and early language acquisition', *Frontiers in Psychology*, 3, 327. It is interesting to consider too the extent to which this *ontogenetic* model may reflect ancient, *phylogenetic* development (see p. 228).

26. See 'Intuitive parenting: a hidden source of musical stimulation in infancy'.

27. See *The Musical Experiences of the Pre-School Child* and *The Developmental Psychology of Music*. See also M. Barrett (2003) 'Meme Engineers: children as producers of musical culture', *International Journal of Early Years Education*, 11(3), 195–212.

28. See, for example, K. Hendricks (2011) 'The philosophy of Shinichi Suzuki: "Music Education as Love Education"', *Philosophy of Music Education Review*, 19(2), 136–154.

29. See *Music in the Moment*.

30. M. Howe, J. Davidson and J. Sloboda (1998) 'Innate talents: reality or myth?', *Behavioral and Brain Sciences*, 21(3), 399–407.

31. M. Gladwell (2008) *Outliers*, Boston, MA: Little, Brown and Company; though see B. Macnamara, D. Hambrick and F. Oswald (2014) 'Deliberate practice and performance in music, games, sports, education, and professions: a meta-analysis', *Psychological Science*, 25(8), 1,608–1,618.

32. https://www.musicalfutures.org/

33. L. Green (2002) *How Popular Musicians Learn: A Way Ahead for Music Education*, Aldershot: Ashgate Publishing, Ltd.

34. G. McPherson (2016) (ed.) *Musical Prodigies: Interpretations from Psychology, Education, Musicology, and Ethnomusicology*, New York, NY: Oxford University Press.

35. AP is a very rare phenomenon within the general population with some reports suggesting a prevalence level of less than 1:10,000. See A. Takeuchi and S. Hulse (1993) 'Absolute pitch', *Psychological Bulletin*, 113(2), 345–361; D. Sergeant and M. Vraka 'Pitch perception and absolute pitch in advanced performers' (2014), in I. Papageorgi and G. Welch (eds), *Advanced Musical Performance: Investigations in Higher Education Learning*, Aldershot: Ashgate Publishing Ltd, pp. 201–229.

36. L. Miller (1989) *Musical Savants: Exceptional Skill in the Mentally Retarded*, Hillsdale, NJ: Lawrence Erlbaum; D. Treffert (2006) *Extraordinary People: Understanding Savant Syndrome* (Updated Version), Lincoln, NE: iUniverse, Inc.

37. A. Ockelford, L. Pring, G. Welch and D. Treffert (2006) *Focus on Music: Exploring the Musical Interests and Abilities of Blind and Partially-Sighted Children with Septo-Optic Dysplasia*, London: Institute of Education, p. 17.

38. *Focus on Music 2*, p. 16.

39. W. Gaver (1993) 'What in the world do we hear? An ecological approach to auditory event perception', *Ecological Psychology*, 5(1), 1–29 (pp. 1 and 2).

40. The potential of music to promote health and wellbeing among those on the autism spectrum as well as more generally is not a topic covered in *Comparing Notes*. For a summary, see D. Fancourt (2017) *Arts in Health: Designing and Researching Intervention*, Oxford: Oxford University Press.

41. S. Baron-Cohen (1997) *Mindblindness: An Essay on Autism and Theory of Mind*, Cambridge, MA: MIT Press.

42. For introductory texts, see, for example, P. Hobson (1995) *Autism and the Development of Mind*, Hove: Psychology Press; F. Happé (1998) *Autism: An Introduction to Psychological Theory*, Cambridge, MA: Harvard University Press; U. Frith (2003) *Autism: Explaining the Enigma* (2nd Edition), Oxford: Blackwell Publishing; L. Wing (2002) *The Autistic Spectrum: A Guide for Parents and Professionals*, London: Constable and Robinson Ltd; J. Boucher (2008) *The Autistic Spectrum: Characteristics, Causes and Practical Issues*, London: Sage Publications Ltd.

43. See www.who.int/classifications/icd/en/

44. See https://www.psychiatry.org/psychiatrists/practice/dsm

45. See, for example, S. Baron-Cohen (2009) 'Autism: the empathizing–systemizing (E-S) theory', *Annals of the New York Academy of Sciences*, 1,156(1), 68–80.

46. See, for example, F. Happé and R. Booth (2008) 'The power of the positive: revisiting weak coherence in autism spectrum disorders', *The Quarterly Journal of Experimental Psychology*, 61(1), 50–63.

47. See, for example, M. South, S. Ozonoff and W. McMahon (2007) 'The relationship between executive functioning, central coherence, and repetitive behaviors in the high-functioning autism spectrum', *Autism*, 11(5), 437–451.

48. G. Iarocci and J. McDonald (2006) 'Sensory integration and the perceptual experience of persons with autism', *Journal of Autism and Developmental Disorders*, 36(1), 77–90.

49. A. Lamont (2008) 'Young children's musical worlds: musical engagement in 3.5-year-olds', *Journal of Early Childhood Research*, 6(3), 247–261.

50. A. Mills (1993) 'Visual handicap', in D. Bishop and K. Mogford (eds), *Language Development in Exceptional Circumstances*, Hove: Psychology Press, pp. 150–64; L. Sterponi and J. Shankey (2014) 'Rethinking echolalia: repetition as interactional resource in the communication of a child with autism', *Journal of Child Language*, 41(2), 275–304.

51. W. Fay (1973) 'On the echolalia of the blind and of the autistic child', *Journal of Speech and Hearing Disorders*, 38(4), 478–489.

52. B. Prizant and J. Duchan (1981) 'The functions of immediate echolalia in autistic children', *Journal of Speech and Hearing Disorders*, 46(3), 241–249; R. McEvoy, K. Loveland and S. Landry (1988) 'The functions of immediate echolalia in autistic children: a developmental perspective', *Journal of Autism and Developmental Disorders*, 18(4), 657–668.

53. S. Falk, T. Rathcke and S. Dalla Bella (2014) 'When speech sounds like music', *Journal of Experimental Psychology: Human Perception and Performance*, 40(4), 1,491.

54. D. Mcglone-Dorrian and R. Potter (1984) 'The occurrence of echolalia in three year olds' responses to various question types', *Communication Disorders Quarterly*, 7(2), 38–47.

55. See *Repetition in Music: Theoretical and Metatheoretical Perspectives*.

56. J. Saffran and G. Griepentrog (2001) 'Absolute pitch in infant auditory learning: evidence for developmental reorganization', *Developmental Psychology*, 37(1), 74.

57. Graham Welch found that 22 out of 34 (65%) of educationally blind pupils in special schools for the visually impaired in the UK had AP – see G. Welch (1988) 'Observations on the incidence of absolute pitch (AP) ability in the early blind', *Psychology of Music*, 16(1), 77–80. Consolidating the findings of four of my own research projects variously involving observation, parental questionnaires and case studies, indicates an incidence of AP among blind children of 66 out of 148, or 45% – see A. Ockelford (1988) 'Some observations concerning the musical education of blind children and those with additional handicaps', paper presented at the 32nd Conference of the Society for Research in Psychology of Music and Music Education at the University of Reading; *Focus on Music*; *Focus on Music 2*; A. Ockelford, S. Gott, J. Risdon and S. Zimmermann (2017) *Focus on Music 3: Exploring the Musical Interests and Abilities of Blind and Partially-Sighted Children with Leber Congenital Amaurosis*, London: UCL Institute of Education. For comparison, Roy Hamilton and colleagues found that 12 out of 21 blind musicians (57%) had AP – see R. Hamilton, A. Pascual-Leone and G. Schlaug (2004) 'Absolute pitch in blind musicians', *Neuroreport*, 15(5), 803–806.

58. Among children with partial sight, little information is available, but combining the data from the three *Focus on Music* studies yields 4 out of 37 with AP (11%).

59. With regard to those on the autism spectrum, recent estimates of the prevalence of AP, with data derived from parental questionnaires, vary between 8%, N = 118 and 21%, N = 305 – see, respectively, T. Vamvakari (2013) 'My child and music: a survey exploration of the musical abilities and interests of children and young people diagnosed with autism spectrum conditions',

unpublished MSc thesis, London: University of Roehampton; A. Reece (2014) 'The effect of exposure to structured musical activities on communication skills and speech for children and young adults on the autism spectrum', unpublished PhD thesis, London: University of Roehampton.

In a study of 27 high-functioning adolescents with autism spectrum condition, Anne-Marie DePape and colleagues found that three of them (11%) had AP – see A. DePape, G. Hall, B. Tillmann and L. Trainor (2012) 'Auditory processing in high-functioning adolescents with autism spectrum disorder', *PLOS ONE*, 7(9), e44084. See also P. Heaton, K. Williams, O. Cummins and F. Happé (2008) 'Autism and pitch processing splinter skills', *Autism*, 12(2), 203–219, who found that children on the autism spectrum with noteworthy pitch processing skills had significant language impairment.

60. A. Ockelford (2008) *Music for Children and Young People with Complex Needs*, Oxford: Oxford University Press.

61. See 'Absolute pitch' (Takeuchi and Hulse, 1993).

62. There is evidence that even AP may have different neural correlates in blind and sighted musicians – see N. Gaab, K. Schulze, E. Ozdemir and G. Schlaug (2006) 'Neural correlates of absolute pitch differ between blind and sighted musicians', *Neuroreport*, 17(18), 1,853–1,857.

63. In *Musical Savants: Exceptional Skill in the Mentally Retarded*.

64. See www.2enewsletter.com

65. In this connection, see S. Stalinski and E. Schellenberg (2010) 'Shifting perceptions: developmental changes in judgments of melodic similarity', *Developmental Psychology*, 46(6), 1,799.

66. *In the Key of Genius*.

67. Taken from http://blog.oup.com/2012/12/music-proxy-language-autisic-children/

68. Taken from http://www.huffingtonpost.com/adam-ockelford/autism-genius_b_4118805.html

69. P. Kuhl (2004) 'Early language acquisition: cracking the speech code', *Nature Reviews Neuroscience*, 5(11), 831–843.

70. See W. Apel (1969) (ed.) *The Harvard Dictionary of Music* (2nd Edition), Cambridge, MA: Harvard University Press.

71. N. Jairazbhoy (1971/1995) *The Rāgs of North Indian Music: Their Structure and Evolution*, Bombay: Popular Prakashan, p. 28.

72. G. Balzano (1982) 'The pitch set as a level of description for studying musical pitch perception', in M. Clynes (ed.) *Music, Mind, and Brain: The Neuropsychology of Music*, New York, NY: Plenum Press, pp. 321–351 (p. 348).

5. Composing, Performing and Listening

1. C. Small (1998) *Musicking: The Meanings of Performing and Listening*, Middletown, CT: Wesleyan University Press, p. 1.

2. Building on the ideas of the Austrian-born musicologist Hans Keller – see H. Keller (1955) 'Strict serial technique in classical music', *Tempo*, 37, 12–24 (p. 21).

3. This analysis is taken from *Repetition in Music: Theoretical and Metatheoretical Perspectives*.

4. See, for example, J. Feldman (2003), 'The simplicity principle in human concept learning', *Current Directions in Psychological Science*, 12(6), 227–232; T. Lombrozo (2007) 'Simplicity and probability in causal explanation', *Cognitive Psychology*, 55(3), 232–257; S. Gershman and Y. Niv (2013) 'Perceptual estimation obeys Occam's razor', *Frontiers in Psychology*, 4, 623.

5. A. Schweitzer (1911) *J.S. Bach*, Volume 2 (trans. E. Newman), London: Breitkopf and Härtel, p. 59.

6. P. Kivy (1984) *Sound and Semblance: Reflections on Musical Representation*, Princeton, NJ: Princeton University Press, pp. 12 and 13.

7. *The Cognition of Order in Music: A Metacognitive Study*, pp. 338 and 339; *Repetition in Music: Theoretical and Metatheoretical Perspectives*, p. 133.

8. D. Tovey (1935) *Essays in Musical Analysis*, Volume 1: *Symphonies*, London: Oxford University Press, pp. 18 and 19.

9. G. Ligeti (1958/1960) 'Pierre Boulez: decision and automatism in Structure Ia', *Die Reihe* (English Edn), 4, 36–62, Bryn Mawr, PA: Theodore Presser Co.

10. P. Boulez (1986) 'Necessité d'une orientation esthétique (II)', *Canadian University Music Review / Revue de Musique des Universités Canadiennes*, 7, 46–79 (p. 61).

11. 'Pierre Boulez: Decision and automatism in Structure Ia', p. 61.

12. B. Rosner and E. Narmour (1992) 'Harmonic closure: music theory and perception', *Music Perception*, 9(4), 383–411 (p. 409).

13. N. Cook (1989) 'Music theory and "good comparison": a Viennese perspective', *Journal of Music Theory*, 33(1), 117–141 (p. 117).

14. Ibid., p. 136.

15. A. Schoenberg and L. Stein (1975) *Style and Idea: Selected Writings of Arnold Schoenberg*, Berkeley and Los Angeles, CA: University of California Press pp. 405–408.

16. From *The Clown* by Heinrich Böll and *The Curious Incident of the Dog in the Night-Time* by Mark Haddon.

17. From *Paul Clifford* by Edward Bulwer-Lytton and *Nineteen Eighty-Four* by George Orwell.

18. See note 118.

19. F. Mathy and J. Feldman (2012) 'What's magic about magic numbers? Chunking and data compression in short-term memory', *Cognition*, 122(3), 346–362.

20. Published in *The Cognition of Order in Music: A Metacognitive Study* and *Repetition in Music: Theoretical and Metatheoretical Perspectives*.

21. A. Ockelford (2011) 'Another exceptional musical memory: evidence from a savant of how atonal music is processed in cognition', in I. Deliège and J. Davidson (eds), *Music and the Mind: Essays in Honour of John Sloboda*, Oxford: Oxford University Press, pp. 237–288.

22. See *The Unanswered Question*, p. 273; G. Rochberg (2004) *The Aesthetics of Survival: A Composer's View of Twentieth-Century Music*, Ann Arbor, MI: University of Michigan Press, p. 95.

23. M. Csikszentmihalyi (1997) *Finding Flow: The Psychology of Engagement with Everyday Life*, New York, NY: Basic Books.

24. See 'The "My Sweet Lord" / "He's So Fine" plagiarism suit' by J. Self, first published in *The 910 Magazine* in 1993.

25. See 'A music module in working memory?'

26. F. Bartlett (1932) *Remembering: A Study in Experimental and Social Psychology*, Cambridge: Cambridge University Press, p. 65.

27. See 'Relating musical structure and content to aesthetic response'.

28. A. Baddeley and G. Hitch (1974) 'Working memory', *Psychology of Learning and Motivation*, 8, 47–89.

29. A. Baddeley (2000) 'The episodic buffer: a new component of working memory?', *Trends in Cognitive Sciences*, 4(11), 417–423.

30. S. Jan (2007) *The Memetics of Music: A Neo-Darwinian View of Musical Structure and Culture*, Aldershot: Ashgate Publishing, Ltd.

31. R. Dawkins (1976) *The Selfish Gene*, Oxford: Oxford University Press.

32. The arguments for and against the creative process being seen as Darwinian are eloquently set out in D.K. Simonton (1999) 'Creativity as blind variation and selective retention: is the creative process Darwinian?', *Psychological Inquiry*, 10(4), 309–328.

33. J. Beament (2003) *How we Hear Music: The Relationship between Music and the Hearing Mechanism*, Woodbridge, Suffolk: The Boydell Press.

34. A. Mazzeschi (2015) 'Music savants: perception and cognition', unpublished PhD thesis, London: UCL Institute of Education.

35. S. Barney, W. Lewis, J. Beach and O. Berghof (2006) *The Etymologies of Isidore of Seville*, Cambridge: Cambridge University Press, p. 95.

36. C. Seeger (1966) 'Versions and variants of the tune of "Barbara Allen"', *Selected Reports of the Institute of Ethnomusicology*, 1(1), available online at https://www.loc.gov/folklife/LP/BarbaraAllenAFS_L54_sm.pdf

37. R. Chaffin and G. Imreh (1997) 'Pulling teeth and torture: musical memory and problem solving', *Thinking and Reasoning*, 3(4), 315–336.

38. D. Levitin (1994) 'Absolute memory for musical pitch: evidence from the production of learned memories', *Perception & Psychophysics*, 56(4), 414–423.

39. K. Kveraga, A. Ghuman and M. Bar (2007) 'Top-down predictions in the cognitive brain', *Brain and Cognition*, 65(2), 145–168.

40. *Sweet Anticipation: Music and the Psychology of Expectation*, p. 3.

41. D. Berlyne (1971) *Aesthetics and Psychobiology*, New York, NY: Appleton-Century-Crofts.
42. See note 35, Chapter 1.
43. See 'Implication and expectation in music: a zygonic model'.
44. M. Thorpe, A. Ockelford and A. Aksentijevic (2012) 'An empirical exploration of the zygonic model of expectation in music', *Psychology of Music*, 40(4), 429–470.
45. S. Koelsch, B. Maess, T. Grossmann and A. Friederici (2003) 'Electric brain responses reveal gender differences in music processing', *Neuroreport*, 14(5), 709–713.
46. *Emotion and Meaning in Music*, p. 31.
47. T. Bever (1988) 'A cognitive theory of emotion and aesthetics in music', *Psychomusicology*, 7(2), 165–175 (p. 166).
48. 'Music and emotion: distinctions and uncertainties'.
49. A sequence in which the roots of chords are five descending scale-steps apart.
50. J. Sloboda (1991) 'Music structure and emotional response: some empirical findings', *Psychology of Music*, 19(2), 110–120 (p. 115).
51. *Emotion and Meaning in Music*, p. 207.
52. R. Jackendoff (1991) 'Musical parsing and musical affect', *Music Perception*, 9(2), 199–230 (pp. 224 and 225).
53. Ibid., p. 228. See also J. Fodor (1983) *The Modularity of Mind*, Cambridge, MA: MIT Press; E. Margulis (2005) 'A model of melodic expectation', *Music Perception*, 22(4), 663–714.
54. J. Bharucha (1994) 'Tonality and expectation', in R. Aiello and J. Sloboda (eds) *Musical Perceptions*, New York, NY: Oxford University Press, pp. 213–239 (pp. 215 and 216).
55. 'Cognitive constraints on compositional systems', p. 235.
56. R. Spaethling (2000) *Mozart's Letters, Mozart's Life*, New York, NY: Norton, p. 336.
57. *Style and Idea: Selected Writings of Arnold Schoenberg*, p. 124.
58. M. Babbitt (1958) 'Who cares if you listen?', *High Fidelity*, 8(2), 38–40 (p. 38).
59. See footnote 30, Chapter 2.
60. See, for example, N. Smith and I.-M. Tsimpli (1995) *The Mind of a Savant: Language, Learning and Modularity*, Oxford: Blackwell.
61. See footnote 12, Chapter 5.
62. B. Bartók (1920/1976) 'The problem of new music', in B. Suchoff (ed.), *Béla Bartók Essays*, London: Faber and Faber, pp. 455–459 (p. 458).

Further Reading

Comparing Notes draws principally on research and thinking in the fields of music psychology and music theory, which is largely published in academic journals, including *Psychology of Music, Music Perception* and *Musicae Scientiae*, and *Music Analysis*, the *Journal of Music Theory* and *Music Theory Spectrum*.

Comprehensive footnotes throughout the text point readers to these and other specialist sources of information. *The Oxford Handbook of Music Psychology* edited by Susan Hallam, Ian Cross and Michael Taut and published by Oxford University Press (OUP) in 2016, provides a wide-ranging introduction to the subject. However, the main academic text from which the ideas set out in *Comparing Notes* are derived is my book *Applied Musicology: Using Zygonic Theory to Inform Music Education, Therapy, and Psychology Research*, which was published by OUP in 2012.

Prelude: Insights from the Blind

The first book that I encountered about visually impaired children, and one which left a lasting impression, was Selma Fraiberg's *Insights from the Blind*, published by Souvenir Press in 1977 – just two years before I first visited Linden Lodge. Sketched within a psychoanalytical frame, Fraiberg's vivid accounts of young blind children with autism are as fresh today as they were four decades ago. However, the failure to mention music, which plays such an important part in the lives of many blind and autistic children, means that important details in the picture the Fraiberg paints are missing. My *Focus on Music* studies (Ockelford, Pring, Welch and Treffert, 2006; and Ockelford and Matawa, 2009), which examine the impact of different forms and degrees of visual impairment on children's developing musicality, seek to redress that imbalance.

Chapter 1: How Does Music Work?

The book that frames this chapter is Leonard Meyer's classic *Emotion and Meaning in Music* (University of Chicago Press, 1956) – a volume that I encountered by chance in the 1980s, and started to read without any preconceptions. I was still engrossed several hours later. Having been temporarily intoxicated with the 100° proof logic of analysts such as George Perle (*Serial Composition and Atonality: An Introduction to the Music of Schoenberg, Berg and Webern*, University of California Press, 1962) and Allen Forte (*The Structure of Atonal Music*, Yale University Press, 1973), and then intellectually hung over when I realised their theories bore little if any relationship to the lived musical experience, Meyer's ideas leapt off the page with a vivid authenticity: here was someone speaking to my head and my heart at the same time.

Meyer came to influence musicological thinking more and more as the second half of the twentieth century progressed, perhaps because his was the first systematic attempt to bridge the gap between music psychology and music theory – a challenge subsequently taken up by writers such as Fred Lerdahl and Ray Jackendoff in *A Generative Theory of Tonal Music* (The MIT Press, 1985), Robert Gjerdingen in *A Classic Turn of Phrase: Music and the Psychology of Convention* (University of Pennsylvania Press, 1988), Eugene Narmour in, for example, *The Analysis and Cognition of Melodic Complexity: The Implication-Realization Model* (University of Chicago Press, 1992) and Lawrence Zbikowski in *Conceptualizing Music: Cognitive Structure, Theory, and Analysis* (OUP, 2002). These theorists were mapping out new interdisciplinary spaces that share a good deal in common with what became known as 'empirical musicology' (a term brought to prominence by Eric Clarke and Nicholas Cook in their pioneering volume *Empirical Musicology: Aims, Methods, Prospects*, OUP, 2004). It was in accordance with this line of thinking that David Huron wrote his magnum opus *Sweet Anticipation: Music and the Psychology of Expectation* (The MIT Press, 2008), which is second only to Meyer's *Emotion and Meaning in Music* as a text to which I repeatedly return as a model of how to describe complex musicological concepts in an engaging and accessible way.

Chapter 2: The Zygonic Conjecture

There is a good deal of information about Derek Paravicini and my early efforts to teach him on the internet, in the form of a number of television documentaries that have been put online, and the TED talk we gave together, which can be found at https://www.ted.com/talks/derek_paravicini_and_adam_ockelford_in_the_key_of_genius. The main source of information, though, is my biography of Derek, *In the Key of Genius: The Extraordinary Life of Derek Paravicini*, which was published in 2008 by Random House.

The relationship between repetition and imitation – between musical structure and intentionality – is one that I first explore in depth in *The Cognition of Order in Music: Theoretical and Metatheoretical Perspectives* (The University of Roehampton, 1999) and *Repetition in Music: Theoretical and Metatheoretical Perspectives* (Routledge,

2005). The latter was intended partly as a response to David Lewin's celebrated *Generalized Musical Intervals and Transformations*, first published in 1987 by Yale University Press, which focuses on the way in which a quality of one musical event (such as the pitch or length of a note) can theoretically be transformed to create another. Zygonic theory argues that only a small subset of such relationships are *musical* in the sense of being likely to be perceived (or, indeed, being perceptible). Nonetheless, *Generalized Musical Intervals and Transformations* and zygonic theory share an important similarity in that both build on the observation that the relationships we formulate when we 'compare notes' – comparisons that enable us to make sense of music – in the realms of pitch, time, loudness and timbre, are the same in logical terms. Precedents of this approach are to be found in earlier work that I admire: David Epstein's *Beyond Orpheus* (The MIT Press, 1979), for example, and Jay Rahn's *Theory for All Music: Problems and Solutions in the Analysis of Non-Western Forms* (University of Toronto Press, 1983).

Chapter 3: How We Construct Musical Meaning

The nature of the relationship between music and language is fascinating, and has engaged those working in a range of disciplines, from musicians (Leonard Bernstein, *The Unanswered Question: Six Talks at Harvard*, Harvard University Press, 1973), semioticians (David Lidov, *Is Language a Music? Writings on Form and Signification*, Indiana University Press, 2004), archaeologists (Steven Mithen, *The Singing Neanderthals: The Origins of Music, Language, Mind and Body*, Weidenfeld and Nicholson, 2005), philosophers (Peter Kivy, *Music, Language, and Cognition: And Other Essays in the Aesthetics of Music*, Clarendon Press, 2007), neuroscientists (Aniruddh Patel, *Music, Language, and the Brain*, OUP, 2007) and cognitive scientists (Patrick Rebuschat, Martin Rohmeier, John Hawkins and Ian Cross, *Language and Music as Cognitive Systems*, OUP, 2012). The nature of music's being – its ontology – has attracted philosophers with a range of views. *The Routledge Companion to Philosophy and Music*, edited by Theodore Gracyk and Andrew Kania (Routledge, 2011), offers a comprehensive introduction. Monographs range from Malcolm Budd's *Music and the Emotions: The Philosophical Theories* (first published by Routledge in 1985) to Peter Kivy's *Music Alone: Philosophical Reflections on the Purely Musical Experience* (Cornell University Press, 1990) and *The Fine Art of Repetition: Essays in the Philosophy of Music* (Cambridge University Press, 1993); from Stephen Davies's *Musical Meaning and Expression* (Cornell University Press, 1994) and *Themes in the Philosophy of Music* (OUP, 2002) to Roger Scruton's *Understanding Music: Philosophy and Interpretation* (Continuum, 2009).

Chapter 4: We Are All Musical

The first book I ever encountered on children's musical development is now regarded as a classic: Helmut Moog's *The Musical Experience of the Pre-School Child* (Schott, 1968). Moog put children's early efforts at singing on the psychological map, and he coined the delightful term 'potpourri song' for toddlers' attempts to sing whole songs, which exist as a fusion of motifs from different pieces they encounter in the environment. However, it was another two decades passed before my colleague David Hargreaves sketched out how children evolve musically from the very beginning, by bringing together the most important research that was available at the time in *The Developmental Psychology of Music* (Cambridge University Press, 1986). Hargreaves believed his interdisciplinary endeavour offered a way of bridging the gulf between music education and music psychology research that had opened up in the 1980s. Since the publication of Hargreaves' seminal text, investigations into children's musical development have proliferated, and a new swathe of work was captured a decade after *The Developmental Psychology of Music* in *Musical Beginnings: Origins and Development of Musical Competence*, edited by Iréne Deliége and John Sloboda (OUP, 1996). The turn of the century saw a step-change in thinking about babies' engagement with music, which placed them in a reciprocal, interactive dyad with their caregivers, in which vocal sounds are a key strand – an idea encapsulated in the notion of 'communicative musicality'. Here, the key text, edited by Stephen Malloch and Colwyn Trevarthen, is *Communicative Musicality: Exploring the Basis of Human Companionship*, published by OUP in 2010. Helpful summaries of our understanding of children's musical engagement as it exists in the second decade of the twenty-first century are provided by Gary McPherson's edited volume *The Child as Musician: A Handbook of Musical Development* (OUP, 2016) and David Hargreaves and Alex Lamont's *The Psychology of Musical Development* (Cambridge University Press, 2017).

The first comprehensive view of exceptional musical development in children is offered by another book edited by Gary McPherson, *Musical Prodigies: Interpretations from Psychology, Education, Musicology, and Ethnomusicology* (OUP, 2016). The subject of musical (and other) savants was popularised by the psychiatrist Darold Treffert's book *Extraordinary People: An Exploration of the Savant Syndrome*, first published by Bantam Press in 1989. In the same year, Leon Miller's *Musical Savants: Exceptional Skill in the Mentally Retarded* appeared, published by Lawrence Erlbaum – a masterful account of Miller's psychological research in the area. Biographies of savants include the account of the Japanese composer Hikari Ōe by his father and Nobel-prize-winning author Kenzaburo Ōe, first published in English by Kodansha Ltd in 1995; *Some Kind of Genius: The Extraordinary Journey of Musical Savant Tony Deblois* by Janice Deblois and Antonia Felix (Rodale Press, 2005); *Rex: A Mother, her Autistic Child and the Music that Transformed their Lives*, by Cathleen Lewis (Thomas Nelson, 2008); and my own biography of Derek Paravicini (*In the Key of Genius*, mentioned above).

Chapter 5: **Composing, Performing and Listening**

A strand of thought that weaves its way through this chapter is *creativity* – what it is and how it works in different musical contexts. Classic texts in this field include *The Creative Mind: Myths and Mechanisms* by Margaret Boden, first published by

Weidenfeld and Nicolson in 1990, and *Creativity: The Psychology of Discovery and Invention* by Mihaly Csikszentmihalyi, first published by HarperCollins in 1996. Composers' own accounts of the thinking that lies behind the creative process are often compelling too, and among those that lodge in my mind are Igor Stravinsky's *Poetics of Music*, (Harvard University Press, 1942), Roger Sessions' *The Musical Experience of Composer, Performer and Listener* (Princeton University Press, 1950), Aaron Copland's *Music and Imagination* (Harvard University Press in 1952), and Carlos Chávez's *Musical Thought* (Harvard University Press, 1961). There are a number of books devoted to the act of performing music, which has proved – to say the least – challenging to pin down in music-psychological terms, including Jonathon Dunsby's *Performing Music: Shared Concerns* (OUP, 1995), John Rink's edited volume *Musical Performance: A Guide to Understanding* (Cambridge University Press, 2002), Aaron Williamon's *Musical Excellence: Strategies and Techniques to Enhance Performance* (OUP, 2004), and Nicholas Cook's *Beyond the Score: Music as Performance* (OUP, 2013). Among the texts on listening to music that repay close attention are Martyn Evans' *Listening to Music* (MacMillan, 1990), Eric Clarke's *Ways of Listening: An Ecological Approach to the Perception of Musical Meaning* (OUP, 2005), and Erik Wallrup's *Being Musically Attuned: The Act of Listening to Music* (Ashgate, 2015).

Postlude: Notes Compared

Comparing Notes ends as it began, with a story of exceptional musicality, a potential stepping-off point to one volume in particular: Oliver Sacks's *Musicophilia: Tales of Music and the* Brain, first published by Knopf in 2007. As it happens, Derek was involved in the television programme made by Alan Yentob to complement the book. A meeting between savant and sage was arranged in London, following a public lecture by Sacks to promote *Musicophilia* in the UK. Unfortunately, the traffic was particularly bad in the capital that night, and Derek and I arrived late. With a BBC film crew in tow, we surreptitiously joined the end of queue of people waiting to have books signed. After a seemingly endless wait, the encounter finally took place. I was on tenterhooks, wondering how the great man would interact with my protégé of so many years. This would surely be one of the highlights of my life.

> Oliver: 'Hi Derek'
> Derek: 'Very well, thank you.'
> Oliver: 'Did you enjoy my talk?'
> Derek: 'What talk?
> Oliver: 'I hear you play the piano.'
> Derek: 'You *do* hear me play, Oliver.'

Sadly, one of my favourite moments with Derek didn't make the final cut!

List of Figures

1. The opening bars of Liszt's Sonata in B Minor. 5
2. Anthony playing *Summertime*. 6
3. Schenker's 'chord of nature' can be reproduced on the piano. 13
4. Fragment of Schenker's analysis of Bach's chorale *Ich Bin's, Ich Sollte Büssen*, 1969 © Dover Publications, Inc. 14
5. The opening bars from the Air and Variations of Handel's *Harmonious Blacksmith*. 15
6. Schenker's 'fundamental structure' transforms the harmonic series, extending it in time. 16
7. The opening theme of Beethoven's *Eroica* Symphony. 21
8. The opening melody of Bach's *Brandenburg Concerto No. 3* uses a musical form of anaphora. 26
9. Examples of chiasmus in music. Schubert: *Unfinished* Symphony (first movement, second theme). Benny Andersson and Björn Ulvaes: 'Super Trouper', © 1980 Union Songs AB. 27
10. The opening of the British national anthem. 30
11. Grouping by similarity and proximity in visual patterns and music. 33
12. Motifs of four, three and two notes from music in a range of styles. Rodgers and Hammerstein: *Climb Ev'ry Mountain*, © 1959 Richard Rodgers and Oscar Hammerstein II. Sacha Skarbek, James Blunt and Amanda Ghost: *You're Beautiful*, © 2004 EMI Music Publishing Ltd and Bucks Music Ltd. Scott Joplin: *The Entertainer*. Stevie Wonder: *Sir Duke*, © 1976 Jobete Music Co., Inc. and Black Bull Music. Bach: *Toccata and Fugue in D Minor*. Richard Strauss, *Also Sprach Zarathustra*, © 1932 C.F. Peters. 35
13. *Frère Jacques* comprises four motifs, each repeated immediately. 37

14. Dynamics become the main focus of attention with repeated motifs in the first movement of Beethoven's *Pastoral* Symphony.   42

15. The repetition of motifs in the second movement of Schubert's *Unfinished* Symphony gives a sense of suspended animation.   43

16. Examples of the transposition of motifs in Western music. Beethoven: 5th Symphony (first movement, opening theme). Paul Simon: *The Sound of Silence*, © 1964 Paul Simon. *Hickory, Dickory Dock*.   45

17. Examples of melodic intervals. Puccini, *Nessun Dorma*. Rodgers and Hammerstein: *Do-Re-Me*, © 1959 Richard Rodgers and Oscar Hammerstein II. *When the Saints*. Danny Elfman: *The Simpsons Theme*, © 1990 Fox Film Corporation. Rice and Lloyd Webber: *Close Every Door*, © 1969 Novello & Co., Ltd. Bernstein and Sondheim: *Somewhere*, © 1957 Amberson Holdings LLC and Stephen Sondheim. Arlen and Harburg: *Over the Rainbow*, © 1938 Metro-Goldwyn-Mayer Inc. Irving Berlin: *White Christmas*, © 1940 Irving Berlin. *Greensleeves*. *Auld Lang Syne*. Weiss, Peretti and Creatore: *Can't Help Falling in Love*, © 1961 Gladys Music, Inc. *My Bonnie Lies over the Ocean*. Waaktaar, Furuholmen and Harket: *Take on Me*, © 1984 Sony/ ATV Songs LLC.   46

18. Helping Derek, aged eight, with his fingering (image © 1987 Robert Maidment-Evans).   59

19. Step 1 was my decision to play a particular note – the lowest C on the keyboard, with aim of Derek copying what I produced.   62

20. Step 2 was the perception by Derek and me of the C sharp that I'd played.   62

21. Step 3 was the decision by Derek to copy the C sharp.   62

22. Step 4 was for Derek and me to hear the low C sharp being played.   63

23. Imagined relationships between the two C sharps.   63

24. A sense of derivation produced through voices imitating each other in *Row, Row, Row Your Boat*.   65

25. Consciously repeating a note produces a sense of derivation through imitation.   66

26. Hearing a sense of derivation through imitation in familiar melodies. *Sur le Pont d'Avignon*. Handel: *Lascia ch'io Pianga*. Haydn: *Surprise Symphony* (second movement). Lennon and McCartney: *Help!*, © 1965 Northern Songs Limited.   67

27. Illustration of a zygonic relationship of pitch: a mental connection between two pitches that are the same, and through which one is felt to derive from the other.   72

28. Examples of zygonic relationships of pitch assumed to function reactively in pieces that use repeated pitches. *God Save the Queen*. Handel: *Lascia ch'io Pianga*. Haydn: *Surprise Symphony* (second movement). Lennon and McCartney: *Help!*, © 1965 Northern Songs Limited.   72

29. *When the Saints* beginning on C.   73

30. Derek's version of *When the Saints* beginning on F.   73

31. Illustration of an 'interval': the perceived connection between two pitches that are different. 74
32. Derek's imitation of the *difference* between pitches (rather than the notes themselves) results from a 'connection between connections': a *secondary* zygonic relationship of pitch between intervals that are the same. 75
33. *Non Nobis Domine*: a canon in three parts, which relies on the imitation of intervals through secondary zygonic relationships of pitch – 'connections between connections'. 77
34. Transposition in a melody functions through 'connections between connections'. 78
35. Melodic intervals of the same size but opposite polarity. 80
36. Melodic inversion. *Nellie the Elephant* by Ralph Butler and Peter Hart, © 1956 Dash Music Company Limited. 81
37. Melodic inversion heralds the opening of Brahms' 4th Symphony. 81
38. The major scale is based on an asymmetrical pattern of two different intervals. 83
39. The ascending and descending forms of the melodic minor scale (beginning on C). 84
40. Examples of perfect cadences. Beethoven: Piano Sonata No. 11, Op. 22. *Sloop John B.* 86
41. The subtle combination of similarity and change in the opening of Bach's Prelude, BWV 846 produces a sense of yearning at once simple yet complex, immediate yet profound. 87
42. Schubert uses a change of mode (from major to minor), combined with repetition, to produce a sense of sadness *supplanting* happiness in *Der Lindenbaum*. 89
43. The change to major in *Gute Nacht* is poignant given the broader context of the minor mode. 90
44. Each melodic interval in the opening of K.333 is heard to exist in imitation of the one that precedes through connections between connections – secondary zygonic relationships of pitch. 92
45. Potential networks of imitative relationships exist between intervals that are the same. 93
46. Intervals from a single melody that are the same, between which direct imitation seems unlikely to be perceived. 94
47. The tiles of the mosaic function to create 'foreground' and 'background' patterns in the mind. 96
48. Rhythmic imitation created and recognised through secondary zygonic relationships of onset during a rendition of the first line of *O Come, All Ye Faithful*. 98
49. A chain of identical IOIs that opens Mozart's Piano Sonata, K.333, deemed to exist through imitation. 99

50. The sense of a regular beat emerges through the projection of imitation into the future in Erik Satie's *Première Gymnopédie*. 100

51. *Rockin' All Over the World* expresses a hierarchy of four pulses in the ratio 2:1. John Foggerty: *Rockin' All Over the World*, © 1975 Wenaha Music Company, USA. 101

52. The imaginary two-dimensional framework of pitch and time that lies in the background of music. Arlen and Harburg; *Over the Rainbow*, © 1938 Metro-Goldwyn-Mayer Inc. 102

53. Rhythms are stored in long-term memory as ratios at secondary level. Arlen and Harbur: *Over the Rainbow*, © 1938 Metro-Goldwyn-Mayer Inc. 103

54. Hearing the regularity of the accelerando in *Pacific 231* implies cognitive processing at the tertiary level. *Pacific 231*, © 1924 Editions Maurice Senart, Paris. 104

55. Uniform change in intervals in a common walking bass pattern is likely to be heard harmonically rather than through tertiary-level imitation of pitch. 105

56. The first six phrases of *You Are My Sunshine* all use the same rhythm with varying patterns of pitch. *You Are My Sunshine*, © 1940 Jimmie David and Charles Mitchell. 107

57. Patterns of intervals are repeated in combination with rhythmic transformation in Richard Strauss's Oboe Concerto, ensuring the movements are integrated thematically. Richard Strauss: *Oboe Concerto*, © 1948 Hawkes & Son Ltd. 108

58. Direct imitative relationships of timbre that occur at the end of the second movement of Bach's *Brandenburg Concerto No. 1*, BWV 1046. 110

59. The imitation of pitch, rhythm, timbre and texture working together in the first movement of Schubert's *Unfinished* Symphony. 111

60. The multidimensional nature of sound enables contrast to function within a framework of musical coherence. 127

61. To the suitably encultured listener, the second interval of *Twinkle, Twinkle* brings to mind a major chord and, from that, the pitch framework of the major scale. 135

62. Repetition of repetition binds changes of pitch coherently into the unfolding melodic narrative. 137

63. Structural connections ensure aesthetic unity in the first two lines of *Twinkle, Twinkle*. 139

64. The development of musical ideas through the simplest of means characterises lines 2 and 3 of *Twinkle, Twinkle*. 141

65. The end of the second section of *Twinkle, Twinkle*, and the beginning of the third, overlap. 141

66. Similarities between J.C. Bach, Sonata Op. 5, No. 3 and Mozart, Sonata K.333, and probable elements of derivation. 152

67. A third of the appoggiaturas in J.C. Bach's Sonata, Op. 5, No. 3 are not structurally embedded. 154

68. The integration of structure and content in K.333 means that the appoggiaturas function expressively both 'in the moment' and to articulate the emotional undulations of the broader musical narrative. 155

69. Different melodic and harmonic forms of symmetry are integrated in the classical style. 156

70. The three stages through which birdsong becomes perceived as music in Beethoven's *Pastoral* Symphony. 170

71. In the right context, Morse code can be heard as music but still retain something of its musical identity. 173

72. The simple structure comprising four zygonic relationships that underlies the opening motif of Beethoven's 5th Symphony. 186

73. Relationships between *groups* of notes are cognitively more demanding, as they involve greater numbers of musical events occurring over longer periods of time. 187

74. Relationships between *frameworks* of pitch are more cognitively demanding still, involving the consolidation of large quantities of data over longer periods of time to produce highly abstract mental representations. 188

75. The emerging streams of music and language processing in auditory development. 196

76. A transcription of Róża's 'pot pourri' song. 198

77. Some everyday sounds may be processed as music by blind children and those on the autism spectrum. 213

78. Speech may also be processed in musical terms by some blind children and some of those on the autism spectrum. 214

79. A typical taunting playground chant. 218

80. Apparent melodic disintegration in the development section of the last movement of Mozart's Symphony No. 40, K. 550. 233

81. Lewin's analysis of the melody as a series of overlapping motifs. 234

82. Series of equally spaced melodic leaps are commonplace in music. 236

83. Model of the universe of relationships that theoretically exist between the musical events that make up a piece, and their likely significance in human terms. 238

84. Listeners' grasp of the relationships that potentially exist between musical events will vary according to their level of musical development and their degree of familiarity with a piece and its style. 240

85. Different approaches to composition and analysis utilise relationships between musical events of differing perceptual and conceptual status. 243

86. Example of conceptualised imitation that has become embedded in the day-to-day listening experience. 244

87. A series of three identical notes in music is insufficient to define a piece. *The Mulberry Bush*. Bach: Fugue, BWV 874. Lennon and McCartney: *Help!*, © 1965 Northern Songs Limited. — 247

88. The opening of the *Magical Kaleidoscope* and the *Kooky Minuet*, with a high level of 'genotypical' overlap, but 'phenotypically' contrasting. — 250

89. Sigmund Spaeth's whimsical analysis of *Yes! We Have No Bananas* purporting to show its derivation from pieces such as the *Hallelujah Chorus* from Handel's *Messiah* and *My Bonnie Lies Over the Ocean*. *Yes! We Have No Bananas*, © 1923 Skidmore Music Co. Inc. — 253

90. Derek's process of creative remembering is evident in the first four bars of his rendition of *Chromatic Blues*. — 257

91. Derek's use of new material deriving from the presumed fusion of memories of fragments and features of other pieces, stimulated by similarities with *Chromatic Blues*. *The Dirty Dozens*, 1929. *It's Only a Paper Moon*, © 1933 Chappell & Co., Glocca Morra Music and S.A. Music Co. — 258

92. Connotations can be transferred with purely musical imitation, here producing the effect of parody. — 264

93. Western music as performed is only approximately represented by standard notation. — 269

94. The opening three notes of *Goodbye to Love* create an ascending pattern that, according to Meyer, has a perceived urge to continue. *Goodbye to Love*, © 1972 Almo Music Corp. and Hammer and Nails Music. — 276

95. Having heard the transition from $\hat{5}$, $\hat{6}$, $\hat{7}$ to $\hat{1}$ many times before, a listener will expect the same sequence to occur again, through imitation of previous appearances. *Goodbye to Love*, © 1972 Almo Music Corp. and Hammer and Nails Music. — 278

96. What expectations are likely to be at work on first hearing the main theme from the third movement of Rachmaninoff's 2nd Symphony? — 279

97. The synthetic melody that was used to test expectations in music. — 281

98. Repetition at the level of groups means that anticipation of the second appoggiatura in the third movement of Rachmaninoff's 2nd Symphony is almost inevitable. — 283

99. Anticipation of the relatively unexpected in the slow movement of Mozart's Symphony No. 40, K. 550, is liable to evoke a powerful affective cognitive response, before, during and after the event. — 286

100. Derek's first four attempts to play the opening bars of Schoenberg's Klavierstück, Op. 11, No. 1. — 291

101. Derek's attempt to play the opening bars of the *Magical Kaleidoscope* one week after having heard it. — 292

102. Derek's complete attempts to play the *Magical Kaleidoscope* and *Kooky Minuet* one year after having heard them last. — 293

103. The challenge of defining what a piece of music is. — 29

Index

'Mc' and numbers in headings are filed as spelt out in full, with exception of entries for levels of musical development, which are filed in chronological order. Page locators in bold denote information in a figure or table.

A

Aboriginal music 36, 112
absolute expressionist approach 11
absolute formalist approach 11
absolute pitch (AP) 17, 79, 163, 204–205, 266–67; in savants 57, 58, 216–19, 223–25, 227, 273
absolute pitch data capture 219
absolutist approach 10, 11, 19, 25–38, 49, 51, 158, 299
abstract art 176
additions 255–56
additive metre 100
adolescents 183, 194, 200, 202, 270
agency 34, 53, 54–55, 61, 64, 65, 66–67, 156
Ah! Vous dirai-je, Maman 129, 148, 149
Akio 192
alliteration 172
Also Sprach Zarathustra (Strauss) 35, 123
American Debate (Brant) 113
anadiplosis 142
anaphora 26
Anna 210
Anthony 3–7, 9, 55, 205, 226, 267, 273

anticipation 37, 37–38, 276, 277, 280–87 *see also* expectation
Anushka 192–93
AP *see* absolute pitch (AP)
appoggiaturas 34, 148, 151, 152–55, 284, 285
Arezzo, Guido d' 267
art 176–77
artificial grammar 288, 289
ascending intervals 47, 83–84, 134, 233, 277
assimilation 274–75
asymmetry 5, 73, 82–83, 85–86, 153, 219, 226
atonal music 35, 242, 248–49, 287–95
auditory development 195–97, 206–207, 212–15, 223
auditory perception 37, 50, 197, 207, 216 *see also* binding
Auld Lang Syne 46
autism spectrum 1–2, 9, 183, 205, 207–29 *see also* Anthony; Paravicini, Derek (Derek)
autopoiesis 69
Ave Maria (Gounod) 86–88

B

B Minor Mass (Bach) 48, 288
Babbitt, Milton 20, 25, 32, 289
baby vocal sounds 190, 191–92, 195, 196
Bach, J C, Sonata for Piano (or
 Harpsichord), Op 5, No 3 149–57,
 245, 252
Bach, Johann Sebastian (J S) 204, 252;
 B Minor Mass 48; B Minor Mass
 Kyrie 288; *Brandenburg Concerto
 No 1* (BWV 1046) 110; *Brandenburg
 Concerto (No 3)* 26; *Dies Sind Die
 Heiligen Zehn Gebot* (BWV 635)
 240–41, 243; 1st Prelude, Book 1,
 Well-Tempered Clavier (BWV 846)
 86–88; Fugue in D Major, *Well-
 Tempered Clavier* (BWV 874) 246,
 247; *Goldberg Variations*, Aria 263; *Ich
 Bin's, Ich Sollte Büssen* 14; *Toccata and
 Fugue in D Minor* (BWV 565) 35
background 94, 95, 96, 149–51, 157,
 246
Baddeley, Alan 259–60
Ballantine, Christopher 19, 20–23, 24
Ballet Mécanique (Antheil) 70
Barbara Allen 267, 295
Bartlett, Sir Frederic 255
Bartók, Béla 294; 4th String Quartet
 2; *Music for Strings, Percussion and
 Celesta* 111–12; 3rd Piano Concerto
 126, 199
Becky 193
Beethoven, Ludwig van 231; 5th
 Symphony 10–11, 45, 108, 174,
 186–88, 201, 247; 9th Symphony
 11, 24; *Pastoral* Symphony 41–42,
 170, 174; *Pathétique* Sonata 221, 223;
 2nd Symphony 26; 3rd Symphony
 (*Eroica*) 21–23; Violin Concerto 126
Bell Jar, The (Plath) 246–47
Ben 210, 216
Berg, Alban 248–49, 287
Berlyne, Daniel 277

Berne Convention (1886) 252
Bernstein, Leonard 11, 25–28, 34, 143–44
Berz, William 260
Bever, Thomas 282–83
binding 43–44, 50, 211–12
birdsong 169–71
blended meaning (music and words)
 90, 135–36, 262–63
blind children 183, 205–208, 211–14,
 216–29 *see also* Anthony; Derek
Blue Rondo à la Turk (Brubeck) 101
Boulez, Pierre 39, 41, 242, 243, 245
Brahms, Johannes; 4th Symphony 23,
 80–81, 244–45; *Haydn Variations*
 221, 222
Brandenburg Concerto No 1 (Bach) 110
Brandenburg Concerto No 3 (Bach) 26
Bregman, Al 40

C

Callum 210
Canon and Gigue (Pachelbel) 236
canons 76, 77, 146, 235–36
Can't Help Falling in Love (Weiss,
 Peretti, Creatore) 46
capabilities; proactive 71, 104, 120,
 133; reactive 65, 270
Carpenter, Karen 276
Carpenter, Richard 276, 277
censorship 160
central coherence 210
central executive 259
chameleon effect 259, 263, 275
Chang, Hsing-Wu 45
chiasmus 27–28, 106
child development 180–81, 182–85,
 189–229, 299–300 *see also* Anthony;
 Derek; Joshua; prodigies; savants
Chomsky, Noam (Chomskyan
 linguistics) 11, 25, 28, 31
chord of nature (harmonic series)
 12–14, 16, 18, 49 *see also* major
 harmonies

Chromatic Blues 254, 256–59, 260, 263
church, the 160
Cindy 192
classic autism 56, 208
classical performers 203
Climb Evr'y Mountain (Rodgers &
    Hammerstein) 35
clock chimes (ticks) 68, 69–70
Close Every Door (Rice & Lloyd
    Webber) 46
cognitive capacity (development) 115,
    119, 120, 178–79, 185–89
cognitive environment 164 *see
    also* exceptional early cognitive
    environment (EECE)
coherence 53, 126–27, 142, 210
colour 163–64
communicative musicality 195
composing 231–63
Composition #5 (Young) 175–76
Compositions 1960 (Young) 175–76
computers 9, 114–15, 213, 231, 265, 300
concealed structural components 242
conceptual art 177
conceptual blending 174
conceptual relationships 238–39,
    240–41, 243, 244–45
conditioning theory 158
Cone, Edward 53–54, 55
connections between connections *see*
    secondary zygonic relationships
connections between connections
    between connections *see* tertiary
    zygonic relationships
connections between things *see*
    primary zygonic relationships
consistency of style 147
content 124–27, 144, 153–58
continuity illusion 119
contrast 126–28
Cook, Nicholas 17–18, 244
'copy game' 59–60, 61–64, 66, 94,
    97–98, 299

copyright 251, 252
coro spezzato 113
creative reconstruction 254–59, 267
crescendos 41
Cross, Ian 177
Cubism 176–77
cuckoos 169–71
cumulative musical development
    200–201
Czerny, Carl 58, 269

D
Davies, John Booth 159
'Darling they're playing our tune'
    (DTPOT) 159, 161
Dawkins, Richard 31, 245, 262
Declan 193
deductive research 184
defective theory of mind 210
Derek 55–64, 72–75, 211, 220, 249–51,
    268, 273, 289–94, 297–99; *Chromatic
    Blues* 254, 256–60
derivation 54–55, 60, 65, 67, 76, 92,
    110, 133, 163, 166–68
descending intervals 47
development sections 154
Dies Sind die Heiligen Zehn Gebot
    (Bach) 240–41, **243**
difference (and sameness) 30, 31–35,
    38, 44–45, 48, 50, 82, 87
diminished harmonies 88
direct imitation 248
Dirty Dozens, The (Basie) 258–59
divisive metre 100
Do-Re-Mi (Rodgers & Hammerstein)
    46
DTPOT 159, 161
dynamics 41–43, 126, 149, 241, 242,
    268

E
Eastwood Nursery School 191–93
echo effect 42

echoi 229

echolalia 1, 58, 210, 214–15, 260

ecological model of auditory
   development 195–97, 206–207,
   212–15, 223

EECE (exceptional early cognitive
   environment) 212, 214–17, 226

Eine Kleine Nachtmusik (Mozart) 47

elaboration 13–14, 33–34, 49, 154, 156

Ellen 191, 192

Emotion and Meaning in Music
   (Meyer) 10, 53

emotional response 8, 83–85, 86,
   87–90, 123–24, 133–34, 135,
   158–59, 276–78, 285–86

Ennals, Sir Paul 2–3

Entertainer, The (Joplin) 35

environment 158–61, 162, 193, 204,
   213–14; cognitive 164; exceptional
   early cognitive environment 212,
   214–17, 226

epigenetics 268, 269, 270

episodic buffer 260

Eroica (Beethoven) 21–23

Essays in Musical Analysis (Tovey) 242,
   243

Études des Bruits (Schaeffer) 70

events 189, 190, 195, 201, 202, 207,
   238, 276, 278, 280

everyday listening 165, 195, 207

everyday sounds 168–70, 196, 197, 205,
   206–207, 210, 212–14 *see also* clock
   chimes (ticks)

exact repetition 38–39, 44

executive dysfunction 210

expectation 38, 99, 119, 140, 147, 149,
   158, 275–87 *see also* anticipation

expressionist approach 10–11

expressive vocabulary 181

external repetition 32

extrinsic factors 164

Eye Level (Park) 277

F

fast brain responses 10–11

Fauconnier, Gilles 174

Feminine Endings (McClary) 24

Ficks, Lawrence 40

figurative speech 130, 131

flow 231, 251

Focus on Music 206

folk music 149, 252, 255, 263, 267, 295

foreground 94, 95, 96, 151, 246

formalist approach 10, 11, 16–17, 160

Forte, Allen 20, 25, 32, 232, 242, **243**,
   249

4'33" (Cage) 174–75

frameworks 190–91, 192, 277, 278,
   280; of pitch 81–96, 137, 187–89;
   pitch-time 101–102, 186, 199–200;
   two-dimensional 101–102, 136

Freddie 211, 213, 225–26, 227

Freie Satz, Der (Schenker) 12, 18

Frère Jacques 36–37, 39, 64

Fugue in D Major, *Well-Tempered
   Clavier*, BWV 874 (Bach) 246, **247**

functions, scale degrees 85

fundamental structure (Ursatz) 16,
   17–18, 23, 49

Fundamentals of Musical Composition
   (Schoenberg) 35–38, 48

G

Gabrieli, Giovanni 42

Gaver, William 165, 195, 206–207

gender, and musical structure 282

generation 54, 60, 65, 66, 133

Generative Theory of Tonal Music, A
   (Lerdahl & Jackendoff) 11, 31–35

genetic factors 69, 204, 206, 248, 269, 270

Gestalt effect (psychology) 32, 53, 78,
   272, 275

Glennie, Evelyn 194

God 11, 12, 19, 69

God Save the Queen 29–31, 72

Goldberg Variations (Bach) 263

Golliwog's Cakewalk (Debussy) 263–64
Goodbye to Love (Carpenter & Bettis) 276–77, 277–78
Goodnight Ladies 80
Gould, Glenn 204, 241
Gounod, Charles 86, 87
Grande Messe des Morts (Berlioz) 113
'greatness' in music 146–58
Greensleeves 46, 47
groups: of notes 32–33, 187, 192, 280–82 *see also* motifs; of sounds 189, 190, 193, 197–99
Grünewald, Matthias 177
Gruppen (Stockhausen) 113, 241, 243
Gute Nacht (Schubert) 89–90, 95

H
Handel: Air and Variations, 5th Suite for Harpsichord (*Harmonious Blacksmith*) 13–14, 15, 16–17, 107–108; *Hallelujah Chorus* 252, 253, 274; *Hornpipe* 159; *Lascia ch'io Pianga* 67, 72
Hargreaves, David 75, 161, 190
harmonic series (chord of nature) 12–14, 16, 18, 49
Harmonielehre (Schoenberg) 112
Harmonious Blacksmith, The (Handel) 13–14, 15, 16–17, 107–108
Harrison, George 251
Haydn Variations (Brahms) 221, 222
Help! (Lennon & McCartney) 67, 72, 247
Here We Go Round The Mulberry Bush 246, 247
Hickory, Dickory, Dock 44, 45, 77–78
hierarchies 31–33, 100–102, 119, 167, 185–86, 189–90, 249
L'homme à la Guitare (Braque) 176–77
hooks 35
Hornpipe (Handel) 159
Huron, David 120, 277–78, 287
Husserl, Edmund 8, 53

I
I Got Rhythm (Gershwin) 258
Ich Bin's, Ich Sollte Büssen (Bach) 14
imagination 178
Imagine (Lennon) 126
Imani 192
imitation 60–71, 119–20, 134–43, 162, 166–68, 248, 268, 301; and children 189–90, 197; of intervals 74, 76–78, 91–96, 186; and repetition 74
imperceptible conceptualised relationships 238, 241
In and Out of Love (Hirst) 177
Indian music 229
indirect imitation 248
indirect zygonic relationships 94–96, 99, 109
inductive research 184
inference 256
influence 55
information extraction 50
information theory 40–41
inhibition 181, 275
Inspector Morse (Pheloung) 172–74
instruments 200, 219, 227 *see also* keyboards (keyboard music)
integral serialism 41, 242
intellectual property rights 252
intent (intentionality) 61, 62, 64, 65, 66–67, 68, 71, 197
inter-onset intervals (IOIs) 97–100, 103, 136, 150, 186, 235
internal patterning 32, 37, 280
intervals 45–49, 72, 79–81, 105 *see also* inter-onset intervals (IOIs); pitch frameworks; ascending 83–84, 134, 233, 277; imitation of 74, 76–78, 91–96, 186
intrinsic factors 164
inverse zygonic relationship 80
inversion 79–81, 233–36
Ionisation (Varèse) 70
Isenheim Altarpiece 177

isorhythmic motets 288
It's Only a Paper Moon (Arlen) 258, 259

J

Jackendoff, Ray 11, 31–35, 285
James 192–93
Jan, Steven 262
jazz music 35, 56, 104, 110
Joshua 163

K

Kai 192
Kennedy, John F 27
keyboards (keyboard music) 73, 150,
157, 218, 219, 224, 227
Keyserling, Count 263
King, Mark 273
King, Matthew 297
Kivy, Peter 241
Klavierstück, Op 11, No 1 (*Magical
Kaleidoscope*) (Schoenberg) 249–51,
289–94
Klavierstück V (Stockhausen) 241
Koelsch, Stefan 282
Koffka, Kurt 32, 275
Kooky Minuet 249, 250, 251, 289–93

L

Lady Macbeth of Mtsensk
(Shostakovich) 160
language 128–32, 144–46, 161,
171–74, 177, 181, 185, 195–97, 215,
246 *see also* anadiplosis; anaphora;
figurative speech; syntax; words
Lascia ch'io Pianga (Handel) 67, 72
leitmotifs 161–62, 263
Lerdahl, Fred 11, 31–35, 166, 287–88,
294
Level 1 musical development 193, 194
Level 2 musical development 194, 195,
228, 239, 240
Level 3 musical development 194,
195–97, 228, 239, 240

Level 4 musical development 194,
197–99, 228, 229, 239, 240, 252–53,
271–72
Level 5 musical development 199–200,
228, 229
Level 6 musical development 200,
270
Levitin, Dan 274–75
Lewin, David 32, 232–37, 242
Liam 206
Ligeti, György 242, 243
Linden Lodge 1, 2–6, 7, 55, 69, 205
Lindenbaum, Der (Schubert) 88–89
linguistic listening 195
linguistic models 25–35
liquidation 108
listening (listeners) 66–68, 195,
237–39, 242–45, 247–48, 265–66,
275–87, 295 *see also* repeated
hearings; everyday 165, 207; musical
165, 207; neurotypical 167, 183, 195,
205, 208, 216–17, 218, 273, 293, 299
Liszt, Sonata in B minor 5
location of sound source 40, 42, 113
London's Burning 64, 246
long-term memory 103, 187, 188, 218,
253, 260–61, 274, 275, 292–94 *see
also* absolute pitch (AP)
loudness 39–44, 108–13, 116, 117, 124,
149–50, 162
Lubbock, John 297, 298

M

McClary, Susan 11, 24–25, 69
Machaut, Guillaume de 288
Magic Flute (Mozart) 126
Magical Kaleidoscope (*Klavierstück*,
Op. 11, No. 1) (Schoenberg) 249–51,
289–94
'magical number 2+1 115–18
'magical number seven, plus or minus
two' 40
Mahler, 5th Symphony 26

major harmonies 12, 15, 86, 88–90, 124
  see also chord of nature (harmonic
  series)
major scale 82–84, 85, 86
major 3rd 74, 79, 94, 219, 247
Mang, Esther 190
Marcus 192
Mathis de Maler (Hindemith) 177
Maturana, Humberto 69
May the God of Wit Inspire (Purcell) 42
Mazzeschi, Annamaria 273
mechanical sounds 70, 237
*Méditation sur le Premier Prélude de
  Piano de S Bach* (Gounod) 86–88
melodic formulae 228, 229
melodic intervals 46–47
melody types 228–29
Meltzoff, Andrew 189
memes 245, 262
memory: long-term 103, 187, 188,
  218, 253, 260–61, 274, 275, 292–94
  see also absolute pitch; musical 245,
  260, 270–75, 292; short-term 260;
  working 49, 187, 247, 256, 259–61
memory tests 254–56
Mendelssohn, *Wedding March* 126
Menuhin, Yehudi 200
Messiaen, Olivier 41, 163, 204
metre 100–103, 150, 171
Meyer, Leonard 10–11, 32, 124, 147,
  157–58, 275–76, 277, 278, 282–85;
  Emotion and Meaning in Music 53
middle sections 139–40
Miller, Leon 217
Minnesota Composers Forum Newsletter
  (1987) 24
minor harmonies 88–90, 124, 148, 153
minor scale 84–85
minor 3rd 47, 84–85, 88, 219
Miserere (Goodman) 123
modes 229
modified repetition 38
Morse code 172–74, 300

motifs 18–19, 35, 95, 186–87, 197–99,
  247, 251, 252–54, 259, 272 *see also*
  leitmotifs; *God Save the Queen* 29,
  30; repetition of 26, 28, 36–38,
  41–43; transposition of 44–45;
  Vltava (Smetana) 41
Mozart, Leopold 203–204
Mozart, Wolfgang Amadeus 203–204,
  248, 288–89; *Eine Kleine Nachtmusik*
  47; G minor symphony, No 40
  (K. 550) 232–36, 286; *Magic Flute*
  126; Piano Sonata (K. 333) 91–93, 95,
  99, 147–58, 245, 252; Variations for
  Piano (K. 265) 24–25, 128, 147–49
MPM (music processing module)
  260–61
'Muddle instead of Music' 160
musemes 262
music (defined) 8, 144–46, 165–68,
  177–79; content 124–27, 144,
  153–58; 'greatness' in 146–58; jazz
  35, 56, 104, 110; keyboard 73, 150,
  157, 218, 219, 224, 227; music-
  making activities 51, 200, 202,
  224–26; piece of 264–75, 295–96;
  pop 35; in school 203; shop 161
Music and its Social Meanings
  (Ballantine) 19, 20–21, 24
Music and Letters 52–53
Music for Strings, Percussion and Celesta
  (Bartók) 111–12
music processing module (MPM) 260–61
music psychology 8, 44–45, 51, 119,
  123–24, 212, 229, 277–78
musical development 146, 180–203,
  215, 228, 239, 240, 252–53, 270,
  271–72, 299–300
musical epigenesis 268, 269, 270
musical expression 181–82
Musical Futures 203
musical genetical similarity (DNA)
  248–50
musical grammars 287–89

tonality 85–86, 287 *see also* atonal
music; *Generative Theory of Tonal
Music, A* (Lerdahl & Jackendoff)
tonic triad 16, 279
Tovey, Donald 23–24, 242, **243**
transformational generative grammars
25
transposition 44–49, 73–74, 76–77,
85–86, 98, 140
Treffert, Darold 205
Trehub, Sandra 44–45
Tristan and Isolde (Wagner) 263–64
Tune Detective, The 252
Twinkle, Twinkle, Little Star 24–25, 33,
128–31, 133–43, 147–49, 199
two-dimensional framework of pitch
and time 101–102, 136
two-part texture 150

U
Unanswered Question, The (Bernstein)
11, 25–28, 41–42
uncertainty 147–48
Unfinished Symphony (Schubert)
27–28, 43, 110–11
units (of notes) 29, 32
Ursatz (fundamental structure) 16,
17–18, 23, 49

V
Varela, Francisco 69
Varèse, Edgar 70, 112, 165–66
variation 38, 51 *see also* repetition and
change
Variations for Piano K. 265 (Mozart)
24–25, 128, 147–49
Violin Concerto (Beethoven) 126
visual images 162–64
visuo-spatial sketch pad 259
Vltava (Smetana) 41
vocabulary 181
Voyajolu, Angela 191–93

W
walking bass pattern 105
Waller, Fats 56
War of the Ghosts, The 255
weak central coherence 210
Webern, Anton 112, 248–49, 287
Wedding March (Mendelssohn) 126
Welch, Graham 190
Well-Tempered Clavier BWV 846–893
(Bach) 86–88, 246, 247
Western musical culture 83–84,
111–13, 144, 168, 181–82, 251
When the Saints 46, 73, 74, 80
White Christmas (Berlin) 46
'Who cares if you listen?' (Babbitt) 20
William Tell Overture (Rossini) 33
Winterreise, Die (Schubert) 88–90
words (development of) 138, 185–86
see also blended meaning
working memory 49, 187, 247, 256,
259–61

Y
Yes! We Have No Bananas (Silver &
Cohn) 252, **253**
Yesterday (McCartney) 34, 47
You Are My Sunshine 106, 107
Young, La Monte 175–76, 177
You're Beautiful (Skarbek, Blunt &
Ghost) 35

Z
Zuckerkandl, Viktor 53, 54, 55, 64
zygonic relationships 71–80, 91–96,
120, 133; indirect 99, 109; of pitch
116–18; primary 111, 112, 115,
116; proactive 104; reactive 104;
secondary 97–98, 100, 103, 111–13,
115, 117, 135–37; tertiary 103–105,
115, 118, 163, 187
zygonic theory 118–20, 124–26,
166–68, 184, 230–31, 280–81,
300–301